# Life
# is a
# Mirror:

Defense Mechanisms and their Spiritual Consequences

## CATHERINE RICCHETTI, CSW

AmErica House
Baltimore

© 2001 by Catherine Ricchetti.

First printing

ISBN: 1-58851-789-6
PUBLISHED BY AMERICA HOUSE BOOK PUBLISHERS
www.publishamerica.com
Baltimore

Printed in the United States of America

This book is dedicated to my husband Matthew and our daughter Amelia... with love.

# Acknowledgements

A warm and sincere thank you goes to Kenneth Wapnick. As a teacher you are invaluable to me. Thank you for freely giving of your time, your suggestions, ideas and support for this book. I have great respect and love for you Ken.

Thank you to Sandee Piculell for editing my 'creative grammar' and to Lucinda Taylor for reading the Galleys to catch typos!

A special thank you to my husband, Matthew, for encouraging my passion for *A Course In Miracles* and for never complaining about my spending weeks at the *Foundation*. I appreciated your 'high-tec' help too Buddy!

Thank you to the teachers and staff at the Foundation for *A Course In Miracles*. I am very grateful for your teaching and your example. I have benefited from your role modeling and your lectures.

I would like to acknowledge my parents, Dorann and Gene Ricchetti. You have shown me through your example that God is loyal, forgiving and endlessly patient. I love you both very very much.

Amelia, I adore you girly-girl! Thank you for being born the day after I sent this manuscript off to my literary agent. Your timing is impeccable!

To my nieces and nephews who light up my life with silliness, Michael Storz, Matthew Bourguignon, Megan Wilson, Jessica Ricchetti, Tory Storz, Amanda Bourguignon, Vanessa Ricchetti, Elizabeth Ricchetti and Bernadette Sharkey. Isn't it fun to see your name in print!

I would like to acknowledge my siblings for all the lessons and all the love, Denise & Steve, Eugene, Jeanine & Phillip, Robert & Joann, Karen Ann and Nancy. I love you guys!

Acknowledgements to my extended family, Donna & George Brown, Terry Wilson, Kip Wilson, Barbara and Bob Schultz, Kathleen Pellagrino, Liz and John Keary, Regina and John DeStefano, Ronald Pellegrino, Marvin and Georgia Wilson, Don and Judy Sulesky, Lawrence and Anita Ricchetti, Marie and Phil Leone, Pat Carro, all of my many cousins. I would not be the woman I am without my grandmothers' love. You both live in my memory: Catherine Schulz and Henrietta Ricchetti. To the family members who I love and will always remember; Ronald Pellegrino Sr., Joseph Carro Sr., Helen

Ricchetti, (Babbu) Eugene Ricchetti Sr., Francis Farrell and the grandfather who I never met Robert Schulz.

Thanks for the legal advice to my friend dear and attorney, Jill Polk.

Thank you Layla VanHall for Shenteng and for you too.

Thank you to Finesse Literary Agency for seeing the value of *Life Is A Mirror* and pursuing its publication.

To the wonderful friends and teachers in my life. To all the people I have learned from and wrote about in this book. Some of you read through my manuscript and gave me suggestions, some of you influenced my life, for others I changed your names and rearranged your stories but you are in here! I would like to acknowledge Trisha Barry, Cathy Ilich, Jayson Ilich, Lori Hansel, Dave Eilers, Dave Valo, Joann Grover, Tim Gray, Ilene Miller, Deb Rudlotz, Susan Peerless, Jennye Cooke, Rod Smith, Bernard Groom, Gernot Kettler, Paul Adelman & Kate Giard (love & miss you two), Fergie Ferguson, Susanne LaFevre, Liz & Keith Longdon and Sean Thompson. Dawn Rosati, Lisa Schectel, Susan Gerringer, Kim Carlin, Leigh and CarolynWalrath, Pattie Canova, Kevin Pratt, Colleen Horan. Also my Tuesday evening '*Course*' group friends Anna, Gary and Jonathan. All of you have touched my writing in some way. For giggles and grins and with warm regards Mary Sise, Ann Waldorf and John Chupka

And last but certainly not least I would like to thank The Big 'G' (a.k.a. Jesus)- my forever Friend, my Self, my endless Love.

# Table of Contents

Please note: *A Course In Miracles* is three books in one. All quotes that start with *Text, Workbook, Manuel for teachers* and *Clarification of terms* are quotes from *A Course In Miracles*. The Clarification of terms is a section at the end of the Manuel for teachers.

# Chapter 1:

### Permanent Peace

In his book *Ethics for the New Millennium* his Holiness the Dalai Lama speaks of a wanting to begin a spiritual revolution to help heal the unhappiness in which we human beings seem to be stuck. He emphasizes ethics of compassion, kindness, and forgiveness. Living our ethics from the inside out involves being responsible as individuals for how we impact upon others and ourselves. We have lost our connection to a deep internal peace. This peace is the key to happiness and it directly reflects how we choose to think. In the desire to find peace we have searched outside of our self in the world, and in things. We have forgotten that peace begins and remains an inside-out process. We strive for happiness, a feeling of safety and peace, but these ideals slip like water through our fingers. Perhaps this is because we are looking in the wrong places. I want the peace of which His Holiness the Dalai Lama speaks. I have the desire to attain a peace that cannot be shattered by people and events outside of myself. I want to learn how to decide for peace in every instant of my life. What we nurture within our selves can help us to reach the goal of happiness. I view happiness as a state of internal calm, and a spiritual connection to God. It is a connection that is not easily disturbed by forces outside of the self. Happiness is a state of being that is genuinely owned by the mind that chooses it.

Happiness must be nurtured for it to be a lasting state of mind. We are responsible to consciously decide what qualities will foster peace within us and to nurture these qualities. The process of fostering happiness is two-fold. As we nurture the ideals that will help us maintain a lasting happiness, we also need to have a deep understanding and respect for what brings us internal discord so that we are not negatively affected by these thoughts, feelings and beliefs. Looking at what 'steals our peace' with honesty, combined with recognizing the consequences of nurturing the discord within, frees our minds to choose what we want to nurture within.

Spiritual peace comes from knowing who you are in the eyes of God. God sees us on the level of Spirit or Soul. We have concepts of ourselves that begin and often end in the world. We see ourselves as bodies and personalities. Our view of who we are varies greatly from God's. God knows us as extensions of Himself; as abstract, limitless thoughts that contain only Love (Workbook page 421 W-252.1-5). I believe that true peace comes from knowing one's self as God knows you... your True Self as God created you. There are thousands of ways to discover your True Self. In this book I will discuss some of the fundamental concepts from *A Course In Miracles*, which is one way to get to know your True Self. When you experience your Self from God's perspective, peace and happiness are easier to keep. Compassion, kindness and forgiveness are the natural consequences of seeing yourself through the eyes of God.

The Foundation for *A Course In Miracles* is a teaching organization that has had a strong influence on my study of the *Course*. Dr. Kenneth Wapnick is a psychologist who founded this organization together with his wife Gloria. I consider Ken my *Course* teacher. I will refer to his ideas throughout this book. I am a strong auditory learner, which will make it difficult for me to quote Ken. Many times when I refer to Ken's influence on my understanding and practicing *A Course In Miracles* I will be referring to a lecture from which I have taken notes, or a tape series which I have listened to a number of times. It is safe to say that my inspiration for writing this manuscript came from two classes I attended at the Foundation in the summer of 1999 and two taped series of Dr. Wapnick teaching which I have listened to many times. The tape series are *"Climbing the Ladder Home"* and *"Separation and Forgiveness The Four Splits and Their Undoing"*. In an effort to avoid constant reference to "Ken says…" I will often quote from the tape series, which addresses the idea I am explaining. These references, although not precise, will keep this writing honest. Much of how I learn the *Course* is through my incorporating Ken's ideas into my thought process. So in many places I am teaching myself by processing his lessons. The classes I attended that summer were each two weeks long. One was focused on death and how the *Course* views and interprets death and the second was about international relations and the Middle East Arab and Israeli conflict from a *Course* perspective. At the back of this book is information for contacting the Foundation for *A Course In Miracles.*

### Personal Identity

Within the world we have an identity that is limited. We see our self as limited to this body and its senses. We feel a combination of emotions that include joy, love, peace, happiness, fear, hate, anger, pain and suffering. Concepts of our self that limit our awareness of Truth have to be corrected. Ideas that expand our self-concept to include God's knowledge of who we are have to be introduced (Text page 656 T-31.V.1) (Text page 656 T-31.V.2.1-4). The changing of our self-concepts from who we believe we are to seeing our self as extensions of God can awaken great resistance within us. These changes in beliefs about us can be a bit unnerving. Yet, uncovering the truth behind the mistaken identity is an experience that is full of hope. As you recognize your mistaken self-concepts you slowly remove the blocks in your thoughts that keep the experience of God from your awareness (Text introduction T-in.1). This awareness nurtures the qualities that maintain internal happiness and peace. It is in knowing who you truly are, that peace, compassion and forgiveness are easily maintained. Peace, love and compassion will be owned by you because they are You.

A miracle in *A Course in Miracles* is a correction. It is a reminder that what you believe about your self and what you believe about the world around you is open to reinterpretation by God. A miracle is not an event in the world; it is an event in your thoughts. It is a change of mind from the world's perception to a perception of holiness (Text page 11 T-1.IV.2.3-7). The *Course* speaks of God providing us with teachers to help us exchange our view of the world for His. In the *Course* those Teachers are Jesus and the Holy Spirit. Any spiritual guidance that helps you is appropriate. The *Course* comes in a Christian framework. The text clearly states that a universal theology is not possible, but a universal experience of God is not only possible, it is essential (Clarification of Terms, page 77C-in.2.5). The manner in which you find internal peace is irrelevant - the result is what is important.

Defense mechanisms create the blocks that keep us from an awareness of who we are in Truth. Blocks are mistaken beliefs and self-concepts that limit us (Text page 153. T-8.VII.10). To correct the mistakes of our limited self-concept, we need to understand defense mechanisms. Defensive thinking is the cause of unhappiness within. In discussing defensive thinking I will use *Course* language and refer to ego-based thinking or thinking with your ego. The ego and defensive thinking are the same thing. In the next chapter I will spend some time discussing defense mechanisms to give you an understanding of what is required to look at your ego to have it's perception reinterpreted by the Holy Spirit.

**Spiritual and psychological self-awareness and responsibility**
When I was in the first few weeks of tenth grade I had a remarkable insight that has led me down a path of self- discovery. Years later, in graduate school during a class on ego-psychology, I realized that I was witnessing the defense mechanism of projection during High School. As a tenth grader I had no name for the phenomenon… I simply referred to it as my "life is a mirror theory". Projection is the psychological process of taking thoughts that you do not like about yourself and seeing them in someone else. Psychologically you deny that you have the qualities that you find

unbecoming and you 'give them away' to another person. Let me tell you what the experience was.

I was talking with a girl named Sue who I had just met. Sue was cut from the kick-line team and she was upset. She began gossiping about my best friend Colleen. She did not know the closeness of my relationship with the girl about whom she was complaining. She referred to Colleen as "stuck-up and mean." She added that, "Colleen talks about everyone behind their backs." She went on to say that Colleen was "back- stabbing and selfish." She was full of venom and hatred for a girl who she had only met 2-3 times during tryouts for the team. I stood there listening to her talk, wondering about whom she was really talking. I knew that the qualities that she was describing had nothing at all to do with my friend. Sue had not known Colleen long enough to draw such conclusions. So, the question I asked myself was *"Then whom is she talking about?"* In that moment it became clear to me that Sue was talking about herself. She projected qualities that she rejected in herself and gave them to Colleen.

How did I draw this conclusion? It was simple deduction. Sue only met Colleen at the tryouts for the team. They did not have a relationship outside of a possible hello, good luck and maybe glares of competition. They attended different Junior High Schools, so they had no history of each other. Sue was surmising a great deal of information concerning a girl about whom she had very little information. She could not have known if Colleen was selfish, backstabbing, or a gossip. What she did know was that Colleen made the team. She had seen Colleen perform under the pressure of coaches and judges. She assumed things that had no basis in an experience of Colleen as a peer.

The only person about whom Sue gave me information that day was Sue. You see "thoughts begin in the mind of the thinker" (Text page 97 T-6.II.9)… and I clearly understood that, in that instant, as a tenth grader. The power of listening to your own thoughts will give you great insight into yourself. Sue, it turned out, was a jealous competitive teen. She talked about people behind their backs a lot… I was not at all surprised.

Many of us today have lost faith in the world in which we live. We are searching for answers in a world where the media has emphasized human mistakes. We struggle to help. We worry about the violent nature of our culture on a large and small scale; we question the motivation of most companies, the impact of violent TV and video games on our children. We expect governments to lie to us. We have lost our faith in the system under which we live.

I have not met many Americans who aren't asking themselves how they can insure their physical, emotional and spiritual safety in such a violent world. We question when to stand up for what we believe in when the problems appear so insurmountable. We hesitate, as a world we have become rude, judgmental and intolerant. We are frightened people. We see how people 'snap' and shoot up a day care, or kill each other over petty events. We have lost hope in many respects and I believe that more and more of us are turning to spiritual support to make sense out of senselessness. Americans are asking how can we help each other and how can we help ourselves not be so afraid. I believe it is our fear that keeps us stuck, and our lack of deeper meaning in life, which leaves us feeling so hopeless. The world keeps rolling and many of us feel like mice on a treadmill... going nowhere. If we could change our mind about how we see the world we might find the key to stepping off the treadmill. Looking into my mirror has helped me to believe that there is another way to see the world that is peaceful. I want to teach that other way. To give people the basic tools to begin the journey off the treadmill, through the process of looking into their personal mirror with spiritual help.

Understanding defense mechanisms like projection has helped me change my perspective of the world. I have begun to realize that it is my own thoughts I fear. This shift of perspective has brought hope back into my life (Workbook page 375 W-196.7.3). By looking at life as a mirror I have deepened my relationship first with myself and then with God. It is difficult to continue to blame others for things when you recognize that life is a mirror of how you choose to see it. Everyone who knew me well in High School can tell you that I would often look at what I was doing and smile to myself saying... "Life is a mirror after all". My spiritual growth as a student of *A Course in Miracles* has accelerated this process for me in a profound sense. I am writing this book for some personal reasons; I want to learn the *Course* by devoting myself to its study. There is no better way to learn a curriculum than to teach it (if only to yourself). If the information in this book is helpful to you and makes your life somewhat more insightful then that is great. If you find the information does not 'speak to you,' perhaps this is not a path of insight that you would find helpful. My prayer is to be truly helpful in my life--to help teach happiness and a path to peace in an attempt to attain it.

What does my insight as a tenth grader and the emotional, psychological and spiritual decay of the world have in common? A lot, as a matter of fact. I hope to explain a way that we can help ourselves (and perhaps in the process others will benefit) from the intra-psychic process of looking at our own projections. Projection was defined as a defense mechanism to me in graduate school. I believe that projection is much more than a defense mechanism; it is a way of thinking. It is the basis of every thought that every human being has. I would say that projection, as a thought process is a psychological law (Text page 97-98 T-6.II.9). Repression, denial, rationalization, justification and reaction formation are other defensive ways of thinking that I will review to help explain how we project.

Ken has taught me to recognize the great cost to my personal happiness, which results from not looking at how I project. I have heard him teach this lesson about how we do not look inside. He has explained that observing how you prevent yourself from looking into your own mirror can help you to begin to look. Then you cannot justify your projections as easily. Projection is a thought process. The purpose of observing a projection is not to stop projecting, but to stop projecting in a fashion that keeps you justifying and rationalizing what you are doing. This only keeps you stuck on the treadmill of unhappiness. As you recognize how you project and accept responsibility for your projections you will be amazed at how liberated you feel. Your thinking is the one thing that you have complete power over... No one can take this power from you. Thought is the place where the power of change lies. Within the power of your thinking lies true hope. Still you cannot change what you do not recognize as a problem. Thinking can be a major obstacle to inner peace. The bad habits of thoughts can and do keep us unhappy. Focusing on these bad habits so that you can ask for guidance in changing the thoughts that keep you stuck is the goal. The reinterpretation of damaging thoughts can result it a greater sense of peace and happiness. One important thing to keep in mind as you practice this is that focusing on damaging thoughts does not mean indulging them. As you focus on what limits your happiness and peace it is essential that you are aware of the fact that you could have peace instead of pain (Text page 68 T-4.VI.3). That damaging thoughts damage the thinker and bring unhappiness. Unhappiness and internal discord is the cost of destructive ego based thinking. Looking at your defensive mirror without keeping the cost of unhappiness in the forefront of your mind can encourage indulging your ego. Staff at the Foundation have helped me to see this trap. It is an easy one in which to fall.

A defense mechanism in western culture has a negative connotation. We connect using a defense mechanism with having a mental health problem. Each and every one of us uses defense mechanisms. People who suffer with mental illness use defense mechanisms in pathological ways. All of us project. Many of us use projection in a way that takes the power of our thinking and leaves it outside of us. Many of us have some dysfunctional habits of projection. This does not make us mentally ill; it does leave us unaware of our power to choose how we think.

# Chapter 2:

## Defense Mechanisms

Any behavior that goes to an extreme is likely to harm an individual in one way or another. Having a glass of wine at a meal can benefit your health according to some medical research but drinking a bottle or two of wine a day will have an adverse affect on a person's health. The same behavior done in a maladaptive way can be harmful. Repression, denial and projection are ways that humans make sense of and sort out a complicated world. More often than not, a defense mechanism is unconscious. Once you can see how you have used the defense and it is exposed, it is less effective. You will see yourself using the defense mechanism and that will lead to self-insight and reflection. Bringing a defense from unconscious to conscious does not eliminate it from your 'bag of tricks' and defenses... but it will help you to stop justifying the defense (Text page 479 T.22.V.2.1-5). In this chapter I will explain how defenses operate and how they can give you great insight into yourself and into your relationship to God. The exposing of the defense mechanism from unconscious to conscious brings the power of the mind back to the thinker.

Looking inward at defense mechanisms can bring up fear in many of us. I have found that I must ask for spiritual help when I attempt to look at how I defend myself from my thoughts. Yes my own thoughts. Projection is defending you from your thoughts. Many defenses keep us from looking at how we think. When I attempt to look at my own thinking without defenses it is essential that I ask for the help of the Holy Spirit to see my thinking from His perspective. Without this spiritual support, my thoughts (which I must fear if I am keeping myself so cut off from them) will frighten me and I will not feel safe looking within. As you attempt to look at how you think defensively request that a spiritual Teacher accompany you in your thoughts.

## Projection

In non-clinical terms projection is simple. You have a thought that you do not want to accept as part of your thinking. So you see the reflection of that thought in someone or something else. I want to take that example one step further. I said before that projection is how all of us think. "Thoughts begin in the mind of the thinker, from which they reach outward" (Text pages 97-98 T-6.II.9). The implication here is that we are constantly projecting all of our thoughts. You have a thought, any kind of thought, not just the ones you don't like (good, bad or indifferent), and you naturally reflect that thought into the world you live in. I will give you a few examples, and then you should generalize and see how this affects all areas of your life. Lets say for instance you have a favorite cousin and you meet someone who resembles him/her in physical appearance or mannerism. Isn't it true that you like this person even though you do not know much about him/her? The reminder of someone you love is projected onto someone you hardly know and you just like him/her. The same is true in reverse. If you meet someone who looks like the babysitter that you hated, then your feelings about that person may be negative. I used to hate people named Judy as a teenager. This was simply because a very pretty Judy tried to steal my boyfriend. She kept coming around for months. I could not seem to get rid of her nor my fear of losing my high school sweetheart. The jealousy I felt toward Judy caused me to hate anyone with that name. I literally felt nauseous when I was introduced to anyone named Judy... my fear and anger was mirrored onto her. As an adult I began working with a colleague named Judy and the mirror shifted to a neutral feeling about the name Judy. I healed that wound and the healing was reflected in my lack of response to the name Judy.

Now take this one step further, to a more abstract example. On your birthday how do you expect people to mirror their love for you? Most of us get cards, some cake, a present or two and long distance calls from family and friends. If your birthday came and went and none of these events occurred how do you think you would feel? As a culture we set up rituals to help us mirror how we feel about each other. When the rituals work we feel loved and the relationship is on good ground. But if the expectation we mirror onto others is not met, we feel unloved and hurt or perhaps angry and betrayed. All of these emotions are normal and most of us feel them. If life is a mirror and "thoughts begin in the mind of the thinker from which they reach outward" (Text pages 97-98 T-6.II.9), then the thought of not being loved based on other peoples' actions begins there too. I am suggesting that the feeling of not being loved because you did not get the calls or cards you expected on your birthday is a projection of a deep feeling of being unworthy of love. The feeling of being unlovable is in your mind first. It is a belief we carry and then we look to prove the belief. This thought is mirrored onto the people who disappoint us, but again here lies the power. That thought is the key to changing your mind about your self-worth. The feeling is a clue that you have a belief that you are not worthy of love. Behind the feeling is a thought and a belief. The belief that you do not deserve all the good things in life, or that you are really a rotten person and you deserve to be punished and rejected. The thought is there, and then we look for proof that we are correct in the belief that the thought has taught us. So when people do not act in ways that we expect them to, our belief is reinforced. We prove ourselves correct and perhaps we become annoyed, angry, or sad with the people who did not act as we expected. The day I can be completely ignored on my birthday and not have that impact my self-worth will be a fantastic day indeed. It will be the day that I know that I am more than the beliefs that I hold. It will be the day that I choose to reinforce the belief that the Love of God is all I need to be complete and that I am that Love.

I am not saying that we should ignore and mistreat each other, nor am I suggesting that we do not need people in our lives. That would be silly and leave us alone and isolated. The truth of the matter is I would be sad and angry if people ignored me on my birthday. The example is a metaphor. The message is that we have the capacity within our minds to change our thoughts about the world around us, and how we view ourselves. The power to heal your thoughts and to love yourself the way God loves you is within your mind. We ignore this and say "I am sad because you did…" Or we scream and yell for others to meet our needs and fill up all our loneliness. We mistakenly believe that the cause of our pain is due to the action or inaction of another. The cause of our pain lies in our deeply held beliefs… if we change the thought; the consequence of the thought dissolves as if it never was (Workbook page 192 W-107.1). To change the belief, we first must know what the belief and thought is. The process involves introspection. Projection helps us look within. When we see the thoughts and beliefs that we project, we have an opportunity to look at those beliefs. Many of us fear looking within. What are we so afraid we will find? I will discuss this fear of introspection in later chapters. I believe it is the key to unlocking our souls and truly touching the joy that comes with knowing your True Self.

## Repression and Denial

Denial and repression are defense mechanisms that people use quite regularly. Both denial and repression involve simply not remembering. When we cannot recall a memory we can say that it is repressed. Again I would like to expand using denial and repression from the level of defense mechanism to a normal way of thinking for humans. Denial is more conscious. I think it is easier to access things we deny. Repression tends to be a deeper forgetting and a memory that may be harder to retrieve. We forget things that we have knowledge of, such as phone numbers, anniversary dates, and dental appointments. Sometimes we just can't access the information. There are many reasons for this-- stress, being too busy, physical sickness and a dislike or disinterest in the event (like going to the dentist) can cause us to use denial. I often cannot recall the time of meetings that I have every week at my job in school. I have created a system to help with my recall of my weekly scheduled meetings. I rarely leave home without my date book because without that tool I can never recall the exact time of the meetings I schedule with teachers. I remember the meetings I schedule with students 99% of the time. Now if I could not recall any meeting times across the board, I would probably say that I had some type of neurological impairment, but I know when I am seeing students. For me denial is about the things I would prefer to avoid, or that I simply don't enjoy that much. I like working with the students more than with the teachers. I also feel guilty when I disappoint a student. I expect teachers to be able to take care of themselves.

Many of us repress painful memories that frightened us. When I was about 19 years old I had to drive my father to the doctor when he ripped the muscle off of his kneecap. My dad was hurt at home and he was in a great deal of pain. One of my sisters became very upset at seeing our father get hurt. In her attempt to help him she knocked him down and fell on him. He cried out in pain. We walked him to the car and I took him to the doctor and even helped him into the office. About six years later my sister was speaking to me about the day he was injured and I had absolutely no recollection of having been at home at the time he was hurt. I insisted that I was not there. She said, "Cath, you drove daddy to the doctor's." I just shook my head in disagreement and explained that she must have been remembering this incorrectly because I was not there. We each left convinced that the other was mistaken. Later that evening I was reading a book on my couch and in a flash the memory returned. I had driven my dad to the doctor and could again see the look of pain on his face. I remembered my sister, in her haste to help, tripping on him and the scream he let out. I thought about how afraid I had been. I had not felt much fear while helping my dad; I just did what I had to do. On the couch I was aware that I must have been very afraid of this memory to have blocked it so completely. I was amazed that I could repress so well and it made me curious about what other memories I refused to recall. I have developed a healthy respect for repression. To my surprise I was afraid to feel the fear that I was repressing about my dad's accident, and I did not realize the anger I was hiding regarding my sister and her clumsy behavior.

### Down and out... the repression projection rule

Whatever we repress, we inevitably project because projection literally is reflected in our perceptions (Text page 248 T-13.V.3.5). This again can be viewed as a psychological law. We repress what we don't want to know and then we project it out (Wapnick, Kenneth *Climbing the Ladder Home,* 1997*),* (Wapnick. Kenneth *Separation And Forgiveness The Four Splits and Their Undoing,* 1999). It's like throwing garbage out; you put what you don't want to see in the covered trash can (repression) and then you give the trash to the trash collectors (projection). It is an inevitable effect of attempting to hide things from yourself... you don't want to admit that these thoughts may be in your mind, but they are your thoughts, you hide them and see them in others. Then you convince yourself that this is where the idea came from to begin with. The belief is denied and the cause of the thought is the fault of someone else.

Let's look at the example of my father's leg injury. I repressed the fear of my dad's vulnerability and my anger at my sister's clumsy behavior. To see my father as vulnerable and open to injury caused great fear in me. When the memory resurfaced I felt intense rage toward my sister. What is the deeply rooted belief in the repression? Why would I repress this to avoid looking at it? I believe I felt murderous rage toward my sister for falling on my father. This rage was so intense that it provoked thoughts of violence towards her. The thought and feeling of wanting to harm my sister, makes my skin crawl, with guilt and self-loathing. Standing there as a 19 year -old, wanting to kill my sister for hurting my dad, is a pretty guilt -provoking feeling... nice 19 year-olds don't have such thoughts. Not knowing at that time what was causing my father such pain and seeing the color drain from his face as he screamed, left me with the vulnerable feeling that he could die. My family would have been lost without him and destitute without his earnings. There I was contemplating financial vulnerability and feeling guilty about that too. Again, a nice daughter would worry about her father's well being if he were injured; she wouldn't spend time wondering if she can complete college if dad is hurt. Taking it one step further since we are talking about defense mechanisms- Freud spoke of children having omnipotence of thought. He referred to the concept that small children believe that their thoughts have power. At some point in my childhood... although I cannot recall this... I, like all kids, became angry with my parents and wished them harm. Again we are back to the thought of violence or murder that leaves me feeling very ill at ease. Believing that those thoughts have power, I would have felt responsible and guilty for the pain suffered by my dad. Not wanting to feel the guilt and responsibility, I would repress the thought. (Just writing about it calls up the desire to repress it all over again)! I can then blame all of my discomfort on my father's injury and on my sister for falling on him. From the perspective of the world this is reasonable.

Then why did I need to repress the memory? What was so disconcerting to my psyche that I refused to recall the event at all? I had not done anything to cause harm to anyone, nor had anything tragic occurred that day. The fact that I blocked out this memory says much about the churning of beliefs that I had about that day. When I look at my beliefs, I recognize that the only power they have is the power I gave them through my belief in them (Text page 271 T-14.I. 3.3-4). When I see clearly, by looking at my beliefs, that some of them are ugly and unkind, I then have the option to challenge them. Without that insight, the pattern of repression followed by projection keeps repeating without my recognition. My fear of looking at these thoughts and my judgment of what they teach me about myself gives them power. To reclaim my power I need to examine and understand these thoughts from a different perspective. Thinking that encourages repression and projection of parts of ourselves (that we fear) keeps us stuck. The active refusal to look at our internal fears is the problem. I was able to look at the defenses that I used when my dad was hurt because I looked with the help of spiritual support. I accessed a part of my mind, which knew that my True Self is connected to Love and therefore, is loving. When I access that part of my mind, I have the spiritual support to look at what I fear with a compassion that knows no fear. The distance that is gained from this perspective provides me with a hopeful way home to God. It cuts through my personality and all of the defenses that I use to prove to myself that I am not capable of such ugly thoughts. I see things more aligned with the truth of my soul; I feel more connected to the Holy Spirit and to myself as God's Child. In this book I want to share with you some of the practical ways that I attempt to access this spiritual support. I am a student of this process and in no way feel that I have mastered the techniques that I am sharing. I simply want to learn how to help myself access this incredible Love on a more consistent basis. If the process in here helps you then that is wonderful. Your perspectives are welcomed, as we are in this journey home together.

Looking again at defenses, how would these thoughts be projected? Let's start with the thought that I would want to kill my sister. Please keep in mind that I have no intention of harming my sister. This idea is simply a thought that I repressed. At some point in our lives we become angry with the people we love and we have thoughts of violence against them. Most people in the field of mental health would say that the thought and feeling are common and the acting out of the thought and feeling is pathological. I agree with that premise, but I want to add that having the thought of murder accompanied by a split second of the desire is disconcerting to most humans... myself included. We repress and project those feelings quickly. And where perhaps

20

are they projected? How about onto the TV news or that highly rated "Cops" show? How about a good old horror flick, a football game, or a boxing match? A violent first person shooter video game does the trick for some of us. Did you love to see a schoolyard fight as a kid? Why is that? We as humans love to see the bad guys get what's coming to them. We thrive on sensationalism. The projection works. As a society, we honor the soldiers who do their duty and fight for our country and for causes worthy of taking a stand against. We are grateful for them and their protection. I too am grateful for them. In my heart I am thankful for their courage and for their deeds. The problem lies in how we glorify war in our attempt to respect their sacrifice. We become out of balance and paint the horror of war as noble. Violence as a problem-solving tool should never be romanticized.

One of my sisters used to live near an air force base. Her neighbor was an F-15 bomber. His job was to fly in the fighter plane and drop the bombs so that they accurately hit their target. My sister was friendly with his family and commented to me that he (the bomber) is such a nice guy. She was amazed that he could have agreed to kill to protect his country, drop bombs on people, and still be a good family man. He was very kind to her son who often knocked on his door and asked this man to "come out to play". My sister's son was often included in their neighbors' outings. My sister viewed this man as ethical, patient, tolerant and fun. She had some difficulty with the contradiction that he could be all of these things and he could choose a career where he agreed to kill people with bombs. I, on the other hand, was not surprised at all. It is reasonable to me that we all have the thought of murder within our minds and that thought is expressed in many ways. The protection of your country is an acceptable way to express that thought in this world. It is considered to be noble and is respected. We also have many other thoughts within our minds. This example of the F-15 Bomber demonstrates how easily an individual can be kind one minute, and become a killer the next.

We have a counter-culture that worships serial killers like Jeffrey Dahmer, Ted Bundy and Charles Manson. I don't even have to remind you of their crimes, you know them. We don't want to see that the thought of murder is within our defensive thinking. We can blame the next serial killer, drug murderer, or child abuser for all of the ugliness in the world. We say... I would never do that. Most of us wouldn't act the thought out. But the thought itself can overwhelm us, so we refuse to see it is within our ego. We repress it and then project it. We then think the thought is not ours. What we do not see is that the thought is reinforced by the acts of repression and projection. The first step to stop reinforcing the thought is to accept responsibility for it.

On a practical level keep in mind that we are only talking about thoughts and beliefs. We as individuals are not responsible for the actions of others. We do not look at the ugly things that occur in the world and say; " I am responsible for what is ugly because I have these ugly thoughts." Life can be difficult and people do mean, unkind things. What I am suggesting is that we each take responsibility for the thoughts and beliefs to which we currently adhere. I refer only to thoughts, not to action of any kind. We are responsible for our actions. We need to accept responsibility for our thinking as well. Our thinking will directly impact how we look at the world and at our self. Intra-psychic monitoring of your thoughts will always be the point that I am emphasizing for the purpose of this book.

As I attempt to look at projection and repression, I ask God if I can borrow His eyes, His vision, so that I can see the world as He does. I call God by many names. I refer to Him as the Holy Spirit and Jesus most often. I don't think it makes a difference to Him, by what name you refer to God. I don't believe that God has a religion nor that any religion has a corner on the market of God. If you have found a religion, or spiritual practice that brings you closer to God and to peace, then by all means stick with it. There are a million paths to the One goal of God. To imply that God has a favorite religion or name removes Love from the definition of God. I believe that the Holy Spirit is much more concerned with your state of mind and your happiness than He is with His name, His gender or the religion that you prefer for that matter. Every time I look at this world and at myself from the Vision of the Holy Spirit I am able to see my projections with gentle non-judgmental eyes. The experience is of the Holy Spirit or Jesus helping to heal the mistakes that I repeat… and that is the motivating factor for me.

Why is it that we are drawn to or repulsed by tragedy? Can you imagine asking Jesus to show you the six o'clock news from His perspective? Or telling the Holy Spirit that you are too repulsed to even look at the latest horror story on the news and asking Him why you have such a strong reaction to it? I am not suggesting that the behavior of enjoying a boxing match or watching an action movie should stop. The news is a daily event for most of us and I continue to watch and listen to it. On the contrary the behavior is not a problem at all. What I am suggesting, is that you ask about the *purpose or intention* of what you are doing and allow the Holy Spirit to show you a possible alternative view of your behavior. (Text page 67 T.4.V.6.7-10) The purpose changes when you share it with a new Teacher… a Spiritual Teacher who can help you heal yourself on the level of thoughts. God can help us look at our beliefs from the perspective of His beliefs.

22

## Rationalization and Justification

The defenses rationalization and justification are similar. When we rationalize we give our selves an excuse for a behavior with which we do not necessarily agree. We do not want to be judged by our behavior, nor do we want to behave in this fashion. We intend to behave the way we want to see our self ideally. We justify the contradiction in what we ideally believe and how we are behaving by making excuses or explaining away why we are acting in such a fashion. Contradicting our beliefs through our behavior can be confusing to us. What we are doing we do not condone but we do it nonetheless. We don't want to be condemned by another or ourselves for such behavior (as unconsciously we would) so we rationalize it. Justification is similar. When we justify ourselves, we are defending something that is done or acted out by others, that we would not support ourselves. In justifying any action we put ourselves in the role of the defender. It is not our fault, and if the world did not force us to behave the way we did, we would not have acted that way. Both of these defenses set up the defender, as innocent, and the guilt or fault lies outside of him.

Let's look at the example of my sister's neighbor the F-15 bomber. Now according to my sister he is a great man. If he were ordered to drop bombs on civilian or military targets he would do so. In his mind, and in ours, he is defending our freedom. This is a reasonable explanation to most of us. Still, most of us hold the belief that we should not kill. So we have to feel and believe that the dropping of these bombs is essential to our freedom. Maybe the bombings are essential to our national security and perhaps they are not. We need to believe they are, so we will view this country as a threatening enemy so that we do not feel guilty or responsible for violence, which was unjustifiable. We can manipulate facts to suit our purpose, leave out pieces of information that explain fully ulterior motives, and add subtle implications to prove our perspective. Our defense then is justified and our attack makes sense. The guilt is the responsibility of the enemy who forced us to defend. This is the purpose of the defenses of justification and rationalization... to place responsibility outside the self.

## Reaction Formation

What should we do about being repulsed by the six o'clock news or terrified by horror movies? The form of the defense does not matter; the thought behind it is the key. Repulsion can mask being intrigued by an event. Reaction formation is the defense that explains this. Reaction formation occurs when a person does exactly the opposite of what he unconsciously feels. It is a behavioral reversal in an attempt to prove to one's self that he is not afraid. A simple example of this would be someone who is living in a high-rise apartment even though he is deeply fearful of the height. He expresses his denial of the fear of heights by doing exactly what he fears. He is attempting to convince himself that he is not fearful. Again, we all access this defense. I will give you another example.

One way I have used the defense of reaction formation was in my work as a Hospice social worker. I was compelled to work at Hospice but I did not know the motivation behind the strong desire I had to work with the dying. Deep inside, and kept from my conscious awareness, I thought that I would learn to overcome my fear of death in this job. I surrounded myself with dying people, denying my fear of my own mortality. The job took great effort and I found that during my two and a half years of working for Hospice I was depressed, tired and I had very little energy to keep up with the things in life that I loved. I stopped bicycling and limited my social life extensively. I told myself that I was 'working off some karmic debt,' and in the end it would be worth it. I thought I was strong and I reveled in people's reactions to my work. I found that others acted as if I was 'angelic' for being strong enough to do this job, or they were disgusted at the thought, and avoided me with repulsion. For me the reaction felt powerful. I hoped that God would appreciate my suffering and sacrifice, and that I would benefit at my death. I continued to deny my fear of death. I was very drawn to the work and the draw served as proof that I was not afraid.

Well, over time I could no longer keep my fear at bay. I was scared to death (pun intended) of dying and the job did not help. My fear and anxiety increased and I had less and less energy to live a happy, fulfilling life outside of work. I gained weight, I isolated myself and I began to shake with anxiety if I watched violent movies or the news. I decided to be kinder to myself and I found another job. I quickly picked up my old hobbies and reconnected to friends. The energy that I was using to repress the fear was put back into the things that I enjoy. I began bicycling again, I joined a gym and I developed my old friendships. I admitted to myself my fear of dying. The anxiety from pretending that I was fearless dissipated. I know now that I was using the defense of reaction formation. At the time I did not know this. I can no longer fool myself about my fear of dying... but I have asked for spiritual guidance to look at my fears with the Holy Spirit as my teacher. I would not have had the ability to see the defense of reaction formation with out the vision of Christ. I would not have had the wisdom or insight to see this. I asked to see why I was so drawn to my work at Hospice. I asked to understand the purpose of the work. The answer was provided.

You know the irony about my work at Hospice was that a part of me was trying to connect to God. On one level I believed that to become worthy of God I had to pay some debt of karma. I believed that through my suffering and sacrifice I would find God more quickly. The goal of God is a great one and one I still pursue. The approach I currently take to connect to God is radically different. The spiritual connection of the Holy Spirit in my life has helped me to learn that suffering is a longer and harder road Home. There are gentler and kinder ways to attain the same end. It is this kinder way; a way that excludes sacrifice and suffering to which I am drawn.

When the focus is not looking within, it is because the fear is that this belief (any thought that you do not like) cannot be in the mind, as it is too "dangerous" or repulsive to accept. We don't want to see it and we can go to great lengths to deny that the thought is in our beliefs. Looking at some of the ugly beliefs and thoughts we harbor within our minds can be repulsive and frightening if we do it without spiritual help. It can be so overwhelming to look at these thoughts alone that, for the most part, we just don't look. We repress, deny, ignore, rage and project instead of dealing with our thoughts. Defenses take on many forms. Any time you feel that something or someone has stolen your peace of mind you are thinking with defenses. When you think through the eyes of the Holy Spirit nothing can prevent peace from remaining with you.

One of the ways we avoid looking at the fearful beliefs and thoughts within ourselves might be to control the environment around us. The need to feel in control in any way is a combination of denial, repression and projection. We still see the 'bad guy' who deserves to be punished outside of ourselves. We may not turn on the TV news as it makes us anxious and afraid. We may try to create a safe haven within our home- a place where the 'bad' things don't happen, keeping the focus on ambiance and creating a safe beautiful environment. Or we may prefer chaos at home to keep us from having the time to think too much. Keeping too busy is a great way to keep oneself mindless. But are we then anticipating that something will destroy the little that we have? Do we live in a state of fear and worry that although I have some calm now, some cash now, or some love now, it will be taken from me at some point in time? I have a tendency to worry every time my husband takes a drive without me. I worry that he will have an accident and be hurt or killed. When he is on a business trip that involves travel I have a tiny worry that floats around in the back of my mind. When I am with him in the car I don't worry. I sometimes think that he will be taken from me and I become afraid. I catch myself thinking that I would prefer to die with him, than to live without him. The worry is very subtle, but it is always present when he is on the road. Such constant worry and vigilance is my fruitless attempt to protect myself from the inevitable horror of worrying and waiting for tragedy to strike. Defensive thinking reinforces this. It takes a great amount of energy to keep your self defended. When our state of mind is contingent upon our environment in any way, we are thinking with defenses. One may find that he has certain preferences about how his world should be. That is not the problem. The problem lies in our belief that unless our preferences are met, we lose our internal calm. I prefer that my home be clean and neat. My need for a clean neat home is the result of a belief that the ugly world can be kept out if my home is clean and pretty. This is a faulty attempt to avoid addressing the belief that I am still fearful of how ugly the world can be. When my workdays get "ugly" my need for a clean home increases. If my husband leaves his mail all over the kitchen counter for a few days I feel troubled and slightly anxious about his mess. I can then blame him for my anxiety instead of looking at my beliefs. What am I not looking at and why do I fear looking at this belief? The "need" for anything to be exactly as expected or else becoming anxious or nervous about it, is a clue. If we must have things our way or become tense, we might be defending ourselves. Determining what we are defending may be the answer to helping us keep our peace regardless of our circumstances.

I began asking myself if I wanted to continue using this clean and neat defense. Now I do not have many complaints about my life. I like my life and I feel at ease for the most part with the way I have chosen to live. Still, I have not found a way of living that leaves me feeling peaceful in the world. Every time I achieve a goal that I set, I am left feeling a momentary satisfaction that fades. I then find a new goal, but I am left wondering what hole I am attempting to fill and why I cannot fill it. I do not have a constant feeling of peace and safety… these are the things that I want. I keep searching for a way to no longer be fearful. Understanding defenses is a good first step. Understanding what the hole is helps too. I believe that the emptiness I feel can only be filled with the Love of God. Any goal or human relationship that I have used to attempt to fill the void lets me down. When I allow the Holy Spirit to show me the problem through His eyes I am always full of hope and all goals vanish, for I feel complete and whole. That is the goal. Defenses are tricky; I often find that I prefer the hole to feeling whole.

Sometimes it is hard to recognize that refusing to watch the news is the same defense as loving to watch the news and seeing the bad guy get caught. Ken and the Foundation staff have helped me to learn this. Ken has taught many students about being neutral. I have heard him suggest that it is the reaction either of repulsion or the draw of something that is a clue that the purpose of your thinking might be defensive. We don't look within because we are afraid. Not watching the news is using the defense of denial. Its like saying, if I don't look this will go away. Watching the news and seeing that the unethical "sinners" are out there and believing that they don't have anything to do with how I think is denial too. We choose to feel empty and see the fears we harbor in someone else. So some of us keep looking outside ourselves at all the bad in the world to justify that we are not so bad; and some of us deny the whole thing in an attempt to pretend that the world is a safe place (my pretty home idea). Two expressions of the same problem (there are millions of ways to express this deeply held belief that reinforces denial). We all fear that the ugliness of life will invade us. We often refuse to look within. I am asking why? What do we think exists within our mind, which is so ugly, that we refuse to admit it is there? Why do we put so much emphasis upon and use so much energy into denying how vulnerable we believe we are?

I ask for help in this area often. When I am fearful about world events, when I refuse to watch the news with all of its horror, I turn to my internal Teacher and ask Him how He sees the situation. I recognize that my defenses have been poor teachers and I ask for another way to see the world I live in. It is inevitable that with this new view my fears and worries abate. My behavior may stay the same... I may or may not watch the news, and I will always prefer that my husband put his mail away, but the charge, the anger, the pain and the fear disappear. I wish I had words for this experience of calm internal knowing that my way of looking was a mistake. The vision that I can see with when I ask for guidance is more in line with the thoughts of God. My thoughts appear silly and foolish next to the wisdom of the Holy Spirit.

I think it is essential to note that this vision is not exclusive. It requires no special talent or degree. The gift of the vision of higher Wisdom or God is ours to claim. God has given it to us, and what He gives is given to everyone forever. It is our job to remove the blocks that keep this from our awareness (Text page 281 T-14.IV.9.5). We do not need to search for Love; we are Love. We do need to search for the ways that we have denied this truth, so that the defensive thinking (which is the building block that limits our awareness) is corrected. Your True Self is a gift that you can access upon the request of help for a different view. I am sure that I will make this point time and again. The Love of the Holy Spirit and His gifts are not denied to anyone who honestly requests them. God cannot be Love and play favorites... so ask for help, for insight into why you live in fear and so defended, for help in seeing the world through the vision of Wisdom and receive what you request.

## The failure of defense

Defense mechanisms do exactly the opposite of what they are intended to do. "It is essential to realize that all defenses <do> what they would defend. 2 The underlying basis for their effectiveness is that they offer what they defend. 3 What they defend is placed in them for safekeeping, and as they operate they bring it to you. 4 Every defense operates by giving gifts, and the gift is always a miniature of the thought system the defense protects..." (Text page 359 T-17.IV.7.1-4)]. Let's look at how and why this happens. We use defenses to avoid feeling or thinking about something that we believe is bad or fearful about ourselves. When we repress, deny, and project something we do not like within ourselves, we reinforce the very belief against which we are defending. The energy that is used to lie to ourselves, works on a conscious level. On an unconscious level, we are not so easily deceived. After all, it is our self to whom we are lying. So the liar and the lie are contained within the same mind. On some level we know that we are trying to fool ourselves, and that being both the liar and the deceived is silly. For most of us this awareness causes some confusion and anxiety. Why are we spending so much time deceiving ourselves? What is it that we believe which is so freighting that we have to hide it from the mind that has thought it? We have a choice when we begin to recognize our self-deception; we can put more energy into convincing ourselves that the lie is true, or we can look at the lie, recognize what it is, and ask to be shown the truth through the eyes of the Holy Spirit. If we continue to deceive ourselves we become fearful of the consequences of the false belief, i.e. we should feel guilty about being deceptive. The effort it takes to defend ourselves, in and of itself is a reinforcement of our innate belief that we are unworthy of self-kindness, compassion and the love of God. We incorrectly believe that God could not possibly love someone who deep down can't look at his perception of himself. We cannot even look at these beliefs to bring their validity into question. We have pre-determined that they must be correct. Why would we have gone to such great effort to conceal something if it was not hideous to begin with? We believe it should never be looked at. We reinforce what we fear simply by continuing to place our energy and effort into not looking at the beliefs at all. I cannot emphasize enough how we have deceived ourselves with our defenses. Our attempt to defend our fear-based beliefs, be it through projection, denial, repression, justification, rationalization or reaction formation, only reinforces the deception. The belief that we require defense mechanisms teaches us that there is something that we should fear. We mirror the need for defenses all over this world of ours. We have gone to great lengths to develop a national defense to protect ourselves from

28

outside enemies. An individual defense contains the same belief. We have gone to great lengths to keep our selves from our own thoughts... there must be something horrible within, from which we need protection. Without an enemy defense is not needed. But as I explained earlier the deceiver and the deceived are the same. Why do we require a defense from our own thoughts and beliefs?

I believe that history repeats itself over and over again because we have not yet come to recognize that defenses do not work. We continue to repress and project what we are afraid to look at, onto the world around us. We see the cause of our fear in the "bad guy" outside of ourselves. Then with great anger we attempt to psychologically, emotionally and physically destroy the person(s) who we see as the cause of our distress. This fails over and over again. We insist that we can figure out how to make it work. We do not recognize that what we want to "destroy" is our self -deceptive beliefs that we have projected onto the world. When we finally recognize that we do not know how to heal this self-deception and we ask for Spiritual guidance to look at our lies and correct them, then we have a way out of this seemingly endless cycle of self-deception.

There is a way out of this trap. We cannot escape this bitter reality alone. First we must ask for a different way to see the problem. This step involves being willing to be mistaken about what we believe (Text page 383 T-18.V.2.5). We start by admitting that perhaps the way the world attempts to solve problems is faulty. We acknowledge an openness to being shown a different way of looking at these problems. This will help us keep our peace of mind. With peace of mind being the goal we may find that we are a bit less invested in being right. That change of investment from insisting that we are right to putting our focus into the attainment of peace is the beginning of a journey back to the thinking of God. When we decide that we might like to begin thinking as God does, we then have one job... to get our thoughts out of the way. To be open to a new Teacher who brings a new perspective. To allow that perspective to work through us. We do not teach a Teacher; the Teacher teaches us. On a practical level this is giving up some control. For myself I find that I have to remember on a daily basis to watch how I am thinking, to monitor my thoughts and my beliefs. Then I take those thoughts and beliefs and I ask the Holy Spirit if there is a different way to perceive these thoughts. Then I try to allow His perspective to teach me.

### Guilt demands punishment

Being guilty in the world means that we are deserving of punishment. We project our guilt with great consistency to avoid the fear of being punished

(Text page 325-326 T-15.X.6). We can see how cultures mirror this idea all the time. Our formal and informal justice systems are based on the belief that if you have done something wrong you will be punished for it. Our courts are built on this idea. Child rearing, school discipline, speeding tickets, the death penalty and wars are fought, based on the idea that the corrupt will be punished and the good people will prevail. The belief, which we mirror, is that the guilty should be punished, for that is what they deserve. Then we as individuals do something mean to someone in our life. We treat them poorly, like a doormat upon which we may wipe our dirty feet. In our hearts we know that an admirable person wouldn't do that. This inevitably leaves us feeling guilty and guilt demands that we be punished. Ken has helped me learn from his lectures and his tapes that this idea is a psychological law so to speak. Guilt and punishment are joined at the hip. The belief is ingrained. If we believe in any way that those who have done wrong would benefit from being punished, we are normal egos. When we do something we consider wrong, we have just reinforced that we deserve to be punished. Then we wait and watch, with trepidation and vigilance, for someone to walk on us so we can stop (attack) them. We don't want to be punished. Who can blame us? The idea of it makes us fearful. We may let people treat us badly because deep down we hope that their punishment is enough. God then will know that we suffered, and will not punish us further. The cycle continues over and over again without our conscious awareness of it. This is a cycle that Ken refers to as the guilt-defense cycle. The desire to rid ourselves of the belief that we deserve punishment is monumental in psychological terms. The belief in and the feeling of guilt are excruciating and fill most of us with great fear. A fear that can be so overwhelming that we swear we will never look upon it. Guilt in ourselves fills us with shame, horror, disgust and stark terror. Guilt feels dirty and can leave us wanting to crawl out of our skin. We are repelled by the thought of it. Yet when someone else is guilty we want him to accept responsibility for his actions. The guilt defense trap: Guilt = fear of punishment = anger and defenses= thinking or acting out anger and defenses = Guilt...

This cycle can begin anywhere along its path. One may not even be consciously aware that he is using it. It is a seemingly endless cycle of self-deception. Defense mechanisms may be unconscious, but we utilize them to hide the truth from ourselves. On an unconscious level we know this. We cannot completely fool ourselves and the use of defenses reminds us that we are hiding. What are we hiding and from whom are we hiding? We cannot look at this destructive cycle without spiritual guidance, as it would only increase our fears and in turn, (as the trap points out) our defenses. Believing that we have more to fear will cause us to increase our defenses for protection. The vicious cycle can be seen globally. I like the process of looking at our global beliefs so that we can use them as an example of our individual beliefs. Individually we are just as trapped. We need to access the help of the Holy Spirit to have Him show us the way out of this guilt-defense trap.

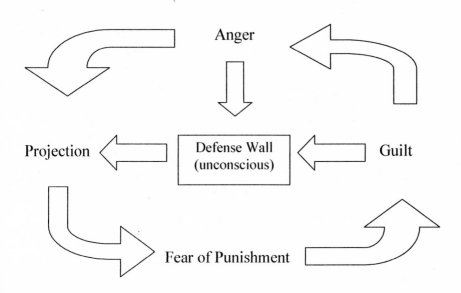

One way I go about helping myself that is not self-destructive (as defense mechanisms are) is by writing letters to Jesus. The writing of these letters helps me take a closer look at what my defensive thinking is. I look at the destructiveness to my peace of mind in my thinking and then I bring those thoughts to Jesus and ask His opinion on them. I believe that turning to Him as my teacher… the process of looking within… brings with it the correction from this trap of defenses that I foolishly rely upon for help.

So the question that remains with me, the one perhaps *you* are pondering, is "Why?" Why is it that we spend so much of our time and energy defending ourselves from our self? I will delve into why in the next chapters. How do defense mechanisms cost us a spiritual connection to God? The understanding of how we defend is the first step in gaining insight to the personal cost of peace that each of us pays by continuing to use defenses. It clearly makes no logical sense to defend our self from our own thoughts.

And when you think about it, defending ourselves from peace is insane. Yet defenses are a constant part of how we think. Are we helpless to change our thinking? Defensive thinking would lead us to believe we are. Defensive thinking is fear based. If we can move passed our fear, we will find an alternative to defensive thinking. We are fearful that if we really look inside we will be repulsed by who we are. We play a game of being in control. It is important to most of us that we view our self as psychologically solid, emotionally in control, important in the world and safe in our surroundings. We become anxious and fearful when we do not have some sense of control over our lives. This vulnerability is intolerable for many of us. So we choose not to think outside the box of defenses we have created (our life) and we remain on the treadmill going nowhere fast. We keep busy and occupy our lives in order to maintain the illusion of our self- importance and sense of control. As masters of self-deception we connect our restlessness with needing more... perhaps our restlessness is a call to end the deception. The Holy Spirit can help us to reach a state of truly being in control of our spiritual life, of facing mistaken beliefs that leave us empty, of ending the lies and of being honest. This is the purpose of looking inside. True control is yours to have; looking into your mirror will take you there.

# Chapter 3:

### Looking within

My experience of studying the *Course* feels like a journey within. This is a journey of discovering the power of my mind, of catching my mirror and gazing into it... the courage to look in liberates my mind. Ken and the staff at the Foundation speak of this liberation often. The experience of this liberation is immense and it contradicts holding on to *not* looking so drastically, that not looking and recognizing what that costs us becomes a source of anxiety in itself. The freedom comes from asking the Holy Spirit if He can show me my mirror from His perspective. The Holy Spirit does not think like a human; He does not judge or condemn. He is Love; gentle, kind, compassionate and He has great faith in my (and your) ability to achieve this goal. When we ask Him to show us the errors in our thinking and His perspective on our defenses, we hand Him the control to help us. His gentleness will cause us to smile sweetly, for how silly we have been to believe that guilt, punishment, sacrifice and sin could ever be the Will of God (Wapnick, Kenneth *Climbing the Ladder Home*, 1997). He challenges the belief that there is something so hideous within your mind, that you would vow never to look in again (Text page 420 T-19.IV.D.3.2-3). The effort you have put into defending yourself from looking at these mistaken beliefs will be redirected to allow the internal Wisdom of the Holy Spirit to help you find your True Self.

The healing is a process. Defense mechanisms are a very ingrained bad habit. Habits take time, patience, and devotion to correct. They are correctable. Many of us who have practiced the breaking of a bad habit know that we wax and wane in our desire to 'quit'. Change is a one-day-at-a-time adventure. As you practice defenselessness with the Holy Spirit as your Teacher, the joy you experience will reinforce the process. The first step is looking into your mirror. You must have a clear understanding of how you defend, what your bad habits are, prior to any ability to change them. The Holy Spirit will not help you with anything for which you do not seek help. If you do not see how you are defending you cannot ask for help to see the defense from His vision.

### Locus of control

People in the field of psychology speak of internal and external locus of control. Ken incorporates this concept throughout his teaching. An external locus of control exists when an individual feels that life happens to him and he is helpless to change the events that come his way. External locus of control is a giving away of one's power and denying the responsibility that one has for his thinking. It is a belief that we are powerless. Whenever we find ourselves blaming someone else for how we feel, we are acting from an external locus of control.

Again, please keep in mind that I am referring to thoughts and beliefs, not actions. If you have a car accident because someone ignores a red light and hits you they are at fault. How you choose to react to the situation is within your power. If you find that you are reacting with anger and pity that is when you turn to the Holy Spirit and ask for help to see this through His eyes. You don't deny the anger and pity. You look at what you feel or believe about the situation. You can ask for a different perspective on what you believe only after you have honestly looked at the belief, thoughts and feelings first (Wapnick, Kenneth *Separation and The Forgiveness The Four Splits and Their Undoing,* 1999).

An internal locus of control contains within it a belief that you have some power to choose. You will never lose the power to choose your thoughts. There are times in life when we may lose our ability to choose our circumstances; but never our thoughts. Ken often refers to the example of people in Nazi Germany who were placed in concentration camps and did not have much power to change their situation. Yet in the book *"Man's Search for Meaning"* by Victor Frankl, the decision to choose an attitude of hope and of life is clearly demonstrated. Mr. Frankl helped me learn that under the most adverse conditions we still maintain our power to choose what we believe. An internal locus of control indicates that an individual feels that he has some power over his life to change his circumstances. An internal locus of control is required here. It is essential that you believe that there is great power to heal your thoughts and beliefs within your mind. You will become an observer of your thoughts, and by watching and looking at them through the Holy Spirit with honesty and lots of laughter; the fear of those thoughts will dissipate.

If you deny what you are feeling and thinking about emotional pain that you experience, you reinforce defensive thinking. On a practical level if you are the victim of some trauma or suffering in your life it is essential that you have dealt with the complexity of emotions that accompany trauma before you can see the event through the eyes of God. People who have lived through the devastation of a childhood abuse, have been the victims of physical, sexual or emotional assault of any kind, need to come to terms with the feelings of shame, hate, guilt, disgust, horror and loss that accompany these events. To attempt to see your pain through the eyes of God before processing the pain of these events would not be helpful. The wounds of trauma can be devastating. People who have lived through difficult events often benefit from the professional help of a therapist. A good therapist can help you to process the pain and, over time, become comfortable enough with the trauma that you could ask the Holy Spirit to give you His perspective on the situation.

Most people can accept the idea that all of their thoughts begin in their mind (Text page 97-98 T-6.II.9). Here lies our power. The sentence sounds simple, but put some thought into it and you will see that within this idea lies incredible power... All thought begins in the mind of the thinker; therefore all change of thought begins in the mind of the thinker as well. I am asking that you do some intra-psychic work with this book. Some investigation of your own thoughts and how they impact your life, your peace of mind, your fears and your belief in yourself. I am asking that you have the courage to look within honestly. Human beings project all of their thoughts into the world in which we live - the happy and peaceful thoughts and the ugly, vengeful ones too. We all do this. Accepting responsibility that our life reflects or mirrors how we think returns the power of our perceptions back to their rightful owner... the mind that thought them.

### How can projection help me gain self-insight?

Projection puts the power of thought back into the mind of the thinker. Our culture is riddled with crazy thoughts that we rarely, if ever, question. Very often, we believe things, which are interpretations, as if they are facts. Earlier I referred to the *Course's* teaching that we project all of our thoughts and then we see the world from the perspective of these thoughts. Often we assume that our perceptions are facts. This is a common human error and one well worth discussing. *A Course In Miracles* states "Projection makes perception"(Text page 445 T-21.in.1). Still most of us believe our interpretations to be facts. Challenge that belief. Perceptions are interpretations and interpretations are not factual by their very nature.

Math contains facts that are proven. Scientists run experiments to test hypotheses in the attempt to prove facts. Our perceptions simply lie. In class Ken has often helped me to question my beliefs through his questions about perceptions. He asks many of the following questions to show that perception lies. Questions like, "How many of us believe that we have witnessed a sunset? It is certainly not as romantic to say I watched an earth rotate! Doesn't it appear to the eye that the world is flat?" Take this idea about perception verses fact one step further... look at our beliefs, our prejudices, and our self-images. What about our beliefs is fact and what is an interpretation and/or a perception?

Many of us misinterpret people's intentions every day. We take our expectations, beliefs or thoughts and place them on peoples' actions. If we don't get invited out to coffee with some work friends we assume that they did this because…. We read into each other's motives 'as if' we were mind readers and then we think that what we are told or what we say is a fact. We confuse our feelings with facts. Many people assume that someone was trying to get them mad, sad, or in trouble. We see our past pain in how we are approached in life all the time. We rarely live in the present, so our past experience and our way of thinking color all of our interpretations. I am a social worker. Part of my profession is based on recognizing that people only tell you their interpretation of what occurred in any situation. Rumors and a person's past are constantly being mixed into things that occur in our lives. We often misunderstand this and we make assumptions, judgments and decisions on what we claim to be factual information. Quantum physics tells us that nothing can be solid in this world. Atoms are mostly empty space and they are in constant movement. Things that contain within them fluidity and space cannot be solid. Still we believe that things are solid. Physics tells us that our perceptions lie. Why then do we continue to insist that our perceptions and interpretations are correct?

In general it is safe to say most of us believe that as citizens we need to follow basic rules of ethics. People should not kill is a value that most of us believe. We teach this to our children and we indicate that it is a law of God. It appears to be clear-cut and simple, but within this value there are many contradictions that send mixed messages. Many of us support the death penalty, while at the same time we teach our children that killing is wrong. We kill bugs, we eat meat and we may debate euthanasia or the abortion issue at length. Our movie heroes kill the bad guys and we cheer them on. It is the contradiction and the exceptions that leave us questioning our identity. If the rule is 'do not kill,' then how is it that we have exceptions to that. When we find ourselves making exceptions it leaves us confused about who we are.

Another belief that most of us hold is that stealing is something we should not do. The Ten Commandments list it as a request from God. Again, as individuals we make exceptions to this rule that may leave us questioning our identity. Perhaps we take paper clips from the office, or we fudge a few expense receipts for tax purposes. We make exceptions about taking from multi-national companies, rationalizing that they are thieves anyway so they are getting what is their due. I wrote a letter to God about this once when I was questioning who I am based on my ethics. I would like to share that letter with you.

*Dear God,*
*My thoughts yesterday are worth noting and getting your views on. At the time I felt eloquent and expressive. I fear that my writing will minimize the passion I felt yesterday about these thoughts.*

*I have fractured the foundation of this "self" I created. All the things I 'think' I am shake and falter. I note that my beliefs, morals, ethics and opinions can and do change on a whim- I am a woman who will be a chameleon based on my human convenience!! This thought fills me with shame and wonder at the same time.*

*I will judge a thief, and yet, if I am not correctly charged for things I buy, I will not speak up. I consider these things 'gifts'... I rationalize my thieving and judge others for acting as I do. I see these contradictions... they permeate my life. I feel less judgmental knowing more intrinsically that my judgments reflect self-condemnation and nothing else. NOTHING ELSE!!!?*

*Who am I then if not my beliefs, ethics, morals and opinions? I stand again in the shoes of a young adolescent-13 perhaps? I am "trying on self-concepts" like new fashion, and finding the style wanting. I am lost and left meeting a stranger within my own skin. This feeling is both disconcerting and wondrous. I am not concerned - it is a process of self 'S' discovery.*

*Who am I anyway? And if everything I believe I think refers to a whimsical self-concept; easily shattered, then what do my fantasies, dreams and bizarre unkind thoughts? The things I think that I will not share or even write of... what do they reflect about my self-beliefs?*

*They must reflect a lie. God would not create a Self who fractures and shatters on a whim.*

*Who is the I that you created God? I would like to meet Her.*

Questioning your beliefs can be great fun. You see when you believe something you start from the premise that you are correct. When you believe that you are correct you do not question. I ask myself why I believe what I believe all the time... it opens my mind and returns to me the power to change how I think. It expands my world from the inside out. Beliefs are multi-level. We have the obviously clear ones that are easy to define: killing is wrong, don't steal, don't lie and cheat. Pray every day, or, do unto others as you would have them do unto you. If we look at many of our beliefs on a deeper level we often contradict ourselves. We may believe that killing is wrong, but if someone tries to harm someone you love dearly, you might justify killing him to protect the person you love. If your country goes to war you might feel that killing is justified, you might be pro-choice or support the death penalty. Every belief we have is open to interpretation. Life is rarely clear-cut and most of us contain within our thinking, contradictions in our beliefs.

Beliefs affect us deeply on an abstract level. Many of us hold a belief in suffering as a way to grow or to find God. We appreciate martyrdom and feel that it too has its place in the road to God. We also hold a deeply ingrained belief that the sinners among us who make no attempt to redeem themselves, will be punished; that God will seek revenge and justice against the unworthy among us. Many of these beliefs leave us fearing God. If this holds any truth for you, then it is safe to assume that you have a fear of God that you believe in. The belief that we should fear God leaves us alone and lonely. It is no wonder we are so fearful to look inside at these beliefs when a part of the belief leaves us with no God to whom to turn for help looking (Text page 490-491 T-23.II.7.1-3). So many people today are abandoning formal religions because they teach opposing beliefs that confuse us i.e. God is love. God is all good until you cross Him; then he will destroy you. This makes no sense. God cannot be Love and be vengeful. One of these definitions of God must be mistaken.

### Button Pushing:

Let's work under the assumption that projection is not simply a defense mechanism, but a way of thinking. Thoughts all begin in the mind of the thinker (Text page 97 T-II.9.1). People often assume that others think the way they do. All people view the world from their own perspective. This is why you can watch the same movie with a couple of friends and you may all walk away from the film with a different view of the main point. Or why you and your sibling may have grown up with the same parents in the same home, but you both have different views of your family life. People add their own projection, or interpretation to what they see, hear and experience. It is a common experience for humans to categorize their thoughts. For example, my husband was trying to help me visualize where cyberspace is. He was speaking of webs and networks. In my mind the abstract idea of cyberspace needed something visual so that I could understand it. I imagined a highway with lots of headlights zooming about. I needed to categorize the new information to fit into things that I already understood.

When something or someone upsets you or "pushes your buttons" it can be understood that a defense that you use and deny using is being mirrored in what or who is making you upset. Keep in mind this idea that defenses are self-deceptive on a conscious level. Unconsciously on some level we are not fooled. Also unconsciously is the idea that we want our defenses to fool us consciously. We are defending our self from something we fear. We are using the defense to avoid the fear. Then someone comes along and his use of a defense reminds us (unconsciously) that we are lying to our self. Our lie is surfacing to consciousness and the fear is being exposed. We become uneasy at this point. We don't want to be afraid. We decide that the cause of our uneasiness and perhaps our fear is this annoying person. We dislike them, avoid them, attack them, gossip about them or do whatever it is we do to keep from looking within. The whole time our discomfort has nothing at all to do with the person who is annoying us. Our discomfort, anger, annoyance, and our dislike of people, who push our buttons, are our fears of exposing our self-deception. Our defenses are being challenged and we most often respond by building up more defenses. Button pushing seen through the eyes of the Holy Spirit is like exposing the Wizard of Oz. The Wizard in the movie was hidden behind a curtain. He was portraying himself as other than he was. Button pushing is an opportunity to allow a spiritual teacher to push back the curtain of defense for you so that the lie the Wizard put forth can be seen.

### Guilt and Punishment

We live by the belief that the guilty deserve punishment. This belief permeates our culture. Our court systems are based on this, school discipline has this belief at its core, parents teach their children that they will be punished when they do something wrong. Please note that punishment is an attitude of shaming and reinforcing guilt. It is the job of a parent to discipline a child. Discipline differs from punishment. When parents discipline a child they are teaching the child how to manage in the world. Teaching rules and right from wrong is the role of a parent. Rules and consequences in a culture are essential in the same way that good parenting is essential. I am not proposing that we abandon them. I am suggesting that each of us as an individual look at the beliefs upon which punishment is founded. What is the goal of punishment? Is the goal to teach, or is it based on revenge? When we act in the world from a stance of defensive thinking we reinforce our own fear. Looking at the belief behind your actions and bringing that belief to the Holy Spirit for His reinterpretation is essential to your maintenance of peace of mind. First you need to know what it is you believe. Punishment as revenge permeates our culture. Every aspect of our lives is filled with this belief. It is so ingrained into our thinking that we never question why we believe it. Nor do we understand that the purpose of the belief is to keep us from looking within. When we have the "bad guy" in the world we mistakenly believe (for a very brief moment) that projection worked and the ugly which "was" in my thoughts belongs to the guilty one, who is now going to be punished. We make guilt a fact and punishment the natural consequence of guilt. We never ask why we have built so many aspects of our culture around this belief.

Guilt is the driving dynamic of projection. We hate thinking that we may be the guilty ones. We connect being guilty with being unlovable. We believe that God sends the guilty to hell. We will do anything to avoid the wrath of God. So we project. We literally take this deeply unconscious thought that we are the guilty ones, deny that it is our thought, split it off from our self psychologically and see it in someone else. (Remember that all thoughts start in the mind of the thinker). Every time that we are angry at someone, every time we blame, condemn or are grateful that someone was finally caught, we are literally pointing an accusing finger and saying, "Look God... I'm not the guilty one who you should punish... But I found the guilty sucker for you". This desire to project our guilt outward, so that we do not have to accept responsibility for it being our thought, is overwhelmingly powerful. Guilt is the driving force in all of our blame. We will go to incredible extremes to deny that we believe that we are guilty (Wapnick, Kenneth *Separation and Forgiveness The Four Splits and Their Undoing*, 1999).

Let me give you an example of how even small children project their guilt. When I was a small child of about four and a half I was playing in the bathroom with my two younger cousins. My cousins were two and a half and three and a half. We were putting things in the toilet bowl and flushing them. This started out as innocent curiosity. We stumbled upon the idea with the toilet paper. The end of the roll was in the toilet and we flushed. We watched the roll spin around and around and we thought it was the funniest thing going. So we did it again and watched it spin. Then we put a couple of things in the bowl to watch them spin. Soon the toilet was backed up and the water was all over the floor. My aunt came in looking stern and angry. I was afraid of her as a kid. She was loud and she screamed a lot. I rarely crossed her and was most often well behaved in her company. All three of us knew we were in trouble and we were very quiet. My aunt demanded to know who did this. We all shut up. Then my youngest cousin picked up her Mrs. Beasley doll (a replica from the show Family Affair... the doll Buffy had), looked her mom in the eye and said, "Mrs. Beasley did it". My aunt stared at us. I waited in fear for her response. She began to laugh and with her laughter the three of us began to announce that it was of course the fault of Mrs. Beasley. My aunt left the room in hysterics. For a brief moment I thought we were off the hook. I was very relieved. Then she returned and told us that she knew we lied and she wanted the truth. My aunt told us this story when we were much older and she remarked at how confused we were by the idea that she knew we lied. We stuck to our story for a short time and then I guess we owned up. My aunt told us that she was psychic and knew things… that lying to her was a waste of time. At that age I fell for her lie and of course I now know that she just knew that toys were not real. We children believed they were, so giving Mrs. Beasley our guilt seemed like a brilliant idea from our perspective. The thing that tickles me in this story was that it was a two-and-a-half year-old, who picked up Mrs. Beasley and gave her our guilt. I gladly followed suit. I did not want the guilt and the punishment to follow any more than my cousins. The projection of guilt is so natural in defensive thinking that we just simply do it. We believe that by giving it to someone else we avoid punishment.

That belief which we deny lies in our thoughts. When you do feel guilty about something, what about that feeling causes such a strong desire to be rid of it? What about the belief in guilt causes such terror in us? The projection of guilt is like a never ending game of 'hot potato'. We insist that someone else is responsible for guilt. As humans we have minimized the impact of guilt in our minds. I have heard Ken say that psychology has not focused on guilt as a motivation for defensive thinking. Guilt is like an addiction with which we don't want to be discovered. We turn our backs on the so-called guilty, because we refuse to look at the hidden guilt that we harbor within our minds.

Think about how far-reaching this concept invades our thoughts. Guilt is one of those ugly, filthy feelings that many of us will do anything to avoid. It carries with it a feeling of repulsion and a desire to wash it away (figuratively and literally). Guilt accompanies deep-rooted shame and feelings of unworthiness. Guilt feels so uncomfortable that it is the root of the need to project. Projection begins and ends with this ugly feeling (Text pages 239-240 T-13.II.1). Our Judeo-Christian upbringings say that guilt is a fact. The religions state that we are born with original sin. This implies that at our core we are guilty; that our very existence is one of being unworthy of Heaven due to our guilty behavior that demanded punishment. God punishes Adam and Eve in the Bible and they are guilty. We inherit their guilt as original sin simply by being born. The interpretation of the Adam and Eve myth directly mirrors a society that believes in guilt. The belief simply is. It is never questioned. The story reinforces and justifies the belief. Every time you feel guilty you don't question if the feeling is part of reality as God sees it, you assume it is because you feel it. If guilt is ego-based, then perhaps God does not believe in it. We project our guilt onto Adam and Eve. The cause of our exclusion from Heaven is now outside of us and we are helpless to do anything about it (locus of control). After all, it was not our fault that Adam and Eve messed up!

Who could blame us for attempting to avoid guilt? We all despise the feeling of being guilty and the shame that accompanies it. I believe that life is a mirror and I still catch myself projecting my guilt all over the place. Daily I practice monitoring my thoughts to catch these projections. I don't attempt to stop myself from projecting my guilt. Projection is how we think. If the thought is there, the attempt to stop it is right back into defensive thinking. Ego -based thinking will reinforce the guilt. I simply watch and try to accept responsibility for the belief rather than my old habit of blaming. I ask the Holy Spirit to help me see this belief from His perspective. The fact that we project this feeling and belief is not the problem. I believe the problem is that we buy into the myth, which teaches that we are guilty to begin with.

Guilt teaches us that we deserve to be punished because of what we have done. We project this belief out, and we don't mind so much when others are punished; on an unconscious level we think our projection worked. But, we carry around the fear that we will be found out. This is because projection actually reinforces the belief that we are guilty. Remember the *Course* teaching that defenses reinforce what they are attempting to defend against (Text page 359 T-17.IV.7). So deep inside we believe we deserve to be punished for our "original sin". Much of this was explained in chapter two on defense mechanisms. So the attempt to project your guilt increases guilt within your mind. Then you are stuck in the guilt -punishment cycle. Trying to sort this out alone can make us feel very hopeless. The way out is not to attempt to understand this alone; the Holy Spirit has the way out of this trap. It is only through the perspective of the Holy Spirit that we are handed the key to escape. The key is a change of belief... but we cannot access that change without the keeper of the key.

I write letters to Jesus often. At times I feel very connected to Him and other times I experience that He is unreachable. I imagine we can all remember a time in our lives when we felt connected to a larger wisdom, a sense of God, whatever form He may take. My experience of connection to the Holy Spirit has led me to question why I believe in guilt at all. When I am joined with Jesus I enter a place of guiltlessness. These experiences fill me with hope and wonder. The sense of peace is profound, the joy and warmth are grand. The thing I recall most is the love of everything and everyone on an equal scale... the suspension of judgment and the freedom of knowing guiltlessness. If guilt does not exist from God's perspective, then perhaps our belief in it is mistaken. Perhaps part of seeing through the vision of Christ is the correction of our mistaken beliefs. If God does not believe in guilt then maybe we should not believe in it either. Can you imagine a life where the belief in guilt did not exist?

Perhaps God's thought process does not contain guilt, judgment and fear. Maybe God only sees what He is... Love. That is the thought within His mind and that is all God projects. Love would not know of fear, guilt, judgment, sacrifice or pain of any kind. If God is Love and my experience of Him is real... then why do I continue to believe on an emotional level that He is to be feared? Why do I continue to believe in guilt? What is the purpose of these beliefs? Who would I be if I gave up these beliefs? I ask Jesus these questions in my letters to Him.

When we begin to deeply understand this idea, we will recognize that all of the judgments we hold are an attempt to avoid the feeling of guilt, and to blame someone else for what we do not want to see within ourselves. When we ask the Holy Spirit to show to us who we are as He sees us, we then know that all He sees is the perfection that God created. In my experience, taking the Holy Spirit's hand as my teacher is a kind, gentle and most importantly, a fun experience. Who would have guessed that looking within at what I most fear would end up being fun?

### The Anger-Fear cycle

To help us understand some of the defense traps, in which we get stuck, I will use an example that I developed in my work as a counselor. How does anyone who is having difficulty with anger management see that anger is a projection? For the purpose of this book I want you to look at anger as a defense mechanism. Anger is defensive. It is a cover, to hide what you fear. We use defense mechanisms like rationalization and projection to justify anger, but in my theory that life is a mirror, anger is always defensive. It is therefore never justified. It is a loud attempt at projection. I believe this deeply. When we are afraid of looking at something within ourselves, something for which we don't want to accept responsibility, or that terrifies us, we become angry. Fear is the feeling that we are attempting to avoid every time we become angry.

Understanding this is one thing; putting it into the daily practice of living in another. There are many times in my life that my intellectual understanding greatly surpasses my emotional and psychological maturity and I find myself furious... a raging maniac, rationalizing my anger all over the place. I insist that I am right and I project the 'wrong' onto the person or people with whom I am angry. As I have said earlier, this is a bad habit, which can change only over the slow process of time and choosing the Holy Spirit as my teacher. I literally ask "Jesus... I'm crazy mad and I hate this or that... how would you see this situation? HELP". Sometimes I just feel like being angry and then I don't think to ask for help. As soon as I remember I try to ask. Sometimes I am too afraid to look within and then I may say "Tough luck Jesus... I don't want your help right now... but when I calm down some, will you help me see how you would look at what I am so afraid of". What I believe is that all of life is an intra-psychic process. When I am angry the first thing I attempt to do is see my mirror and take this mistake to the Holy Spirit or Jesus for His view and His correction. The Holy Spirit's view always calms me down and my anger dissipates. Then I can choose to go to the person with whom I thought I was angry and deal with the problem without the anger.

This does not mean that I do not correct things, people or events in my life. Ken has taught me that it simply means that I attempt to do it with the love of the Holy Spirit beside me rather than with my defenses. Let me give you an example. I am a school social worker and I work with kids who have trouble behaving in school. It would be unfair of me and disrespectful to them if I did not help them correct their mistakes. I would not be helping myself if I allowed an angry teen who was talking of a violent solution to a problem, to leave my room angry and plotting revenge. It would be unkind if I did not help teachers to develop behavior plans that increase a student's success in class. This is what I do for a living and it would be irresponsible to stop doing these things, using the cliché excuse that God loves you the way you are. That excuse is a hidden form of attack and unhelpful. When I ask the Holy Spirit to show me how He views my life, my behavior in the world looks the same, but the thought that guides my actions is one of love. My energy increases and things are easy... outwardly everything looks the same, but inwardly the energy that I spent defending myself is redirected. And I know that my actions are truly helpful... that is all the Holy Spirit can be. When I ask the Holy Spirit to show me the lesson that I need to learn I surrender the control and allow Him to work through me with ease. It feels as if I step back and watch my life as it happens. I am very much a part of the process, but I am the student and the Holy Spirit is the teacher. It takes a ton of energy to keep a self-deception from surfacing. The process of allowing the Holy Spirit to correct me is easy and fun. The fun is the part that always throws me. I have a belief that learning is work, and that God wants me to sacrifice for Him. The ease of this process has proven me wrong. My experience clearly says that God being Love is fun and demands nothing.

Most of us do not feel a strong consistent connection to God even though He is fun and undemanding. We maintain our control regardless of the fact that all evidence and experience of peace and happiness points in the direction of God. Life would be gentler, kinder, easy and flowing, if we chose to have the Holy Spirit as our teacher, but we continue to think with the ego just the same. We minimize the important impact that our thinking has upon us. We have to choose between thinking with defenses, and, thinking with God. We do not fully understand that this is *our* choice or the consequence we pay for minimizing the power of our thinking.

The desire to feel a bit of control over our lives is very real for most of us. I can't stand the anxiety that I can provoke within myself when I feel vulnerable or out of control of certain aspects of my life. I have begun to question my self-concept. My belief that my sense of control is essential to my happiness has begun to falter. I have begun to question why I choose against peace when a simple shift in my thinking can bring peace to me. I resist this shift in my self -concept. I have found that looking at my self-concepts and how I defend to maintain my sense of individuality is not an easy task. As I bring into question my beliefs about my judgments, ethics, and opinions I am left feeling as if I am walking on shaky ground. The guilt in my mind (and the fear of punishment that accompanies the guilt) surfaces if I attempt to manage this process alone. When I attempt to look at my concept of who I am alone I run back to the comfort of defending the self I believe I am. It is only with the help of spiritual support that I can look at these defense and beliefs and remain in control... peaceful, happy and in control.

Resistance is a defense mechanism, which I have grown to respect a great deal. It is a powerful force in the ego's arsenal of defense. Our desire not to be peaceful has a cause that we often do not understand. We have a fear of God that is strong even though it seems crazy. The resistance we put into avoiding looking at our fears is powerful. We value defenses and resist our happiness often because we do not understand our choices. We have mistakenly connected thinking without defenses to being vulnerable and weak. We believe that we will lose if we chose defenselessness. I imagine that the thinking of God is otherworldly. It is a type of thinking that we as people, thinking with defenses, cannot access without the help of a spiritual guidance. It is radically different from how we think. We need to be open to having our immature spiritual thinking revamped by a spiritual teacher whose thinking is spiritually mature. Let's take some time to recognize that how and what we think impacts our spiritual life. When we have a clearer understanding of our choices, (spiritual immaturity or spiritually mature thinking) we may be willing to have our thinking challenged.

# Chapter 4:

## Thoughts start in the mind of the thinker

As a social worker in public school I work with a number of teachers who are fabulous with angry or troubled kids. Often in their attempt to help they will tell an angry kid, "Think anything you want, but don't say anything you want". Now this is a good starting point, but it is misleading to all of us as humans. It implies that the things we think have no impact on us or on others. This whole theory is about how you think and with whom you choose to think. Thoughts directly impact how a person sees the world. A person communicates in a variety of ways through body language, words, and actions.

Body language has a great impact on people. Often I have to ask kids to stop using intimidating body language. My Dad had a look of disappointment and one of anger that could stop me in my tracks. Everyone knows when someone they love walks into a room upset, excited, afraid or angry... we don't have to ask, we read body language all the time.

Body language emanates from thought. Looking at and changing the way you think can have a direct affect on your attitude, mood and physical health. The teacher who informs a student that he has to begin with how he acts is not incorrect. That advice may be helpful to an angry teenager who has to manage his day in school. It can be helpful to all of us. How we act in the world has a tremendous impact on our lives. We also need to know that monitoring our thoughts and questioning how they impact our lives may be helpful. Medical science has given us many examples of how our thoughts directly aid in the recovery of patients. People taking a placebo who believe that they are taking medication have a greater rate of recovery. What we believe does matter. All of us who believe that we have been unfairly treated by the world would benefit from questioning that thought. We can all be tough in this department because we often err in the assumption that we are always right. As a general rule I rarely tell people that they are wrong. I offer them a "perhaps there is a different way to see this. Could it be possible that..."

## Thoughts do matter

Research has shown us that attitude can have an impact on the health and recovery of a person with a life-threatening illness. Thoughts have power. We all know that when we feel strong, powerful and are full of the joy of

47

life, good things seem to come with ease. When we are depressed and negative much of our life seems to not work well.

The point is that we initially need to accept responsibility for the fact that our thoughts contain more power than we currently recognize. Then we can begin to expand our minds by questioning the way we think, what we believe and why we are so sure that we are correct about our beliefs. I love to question these things. I find it awe-inspiring and mind-altering. It is a high that brings me closer to my True Self. It is a more uplifting feeling, than any I can remember, which brings me closer to my True Self.

### You cannot give what you do not own

Have you ever noticed that when you give love you feel more loving? When you are at ease and happy life seems to flow with the ease that emanates from within you. These are times that we have all had… when people want to be in your presence, opportunities fall into your lap and it is unnecessary for you to ponder and struggle over what to say and do throughout the day. Life can be this easy; undefended, gentle, calm and fun. This is how it feels when we allow the Holy Spirit to be our teacher… when the internal Wisdom that we hide within is welcomed into our conscious awareness. We all have accessed these easy days when we mirror the Joy that we have within ourselves. There is strength and power in this feeling that defenses cannot give us. This defenseless feeling of connection to God gives us a very different approach to solving problems. Let me give you an example that has been a reference point and a motivation for me to allow the Holy Spirit to be my teacher.

As a young woman in my early twenties, I ran into a High School acquaintance, a woman named Abby in a local bar... I was out with a good friend from college named Karen and I introduced the two of them. Abby and I had eaten lunch together during our senior year. We were sharing a drink and chit chatting. Abby asked about my High School boyfriend and I told her I had broken up with him halfway through college. She commented that she never knew what he saw in me to begin with. She became angry and for the next couple of minutes she told me what a fool I was for dumping such a great guy and how unworthy I was of him. As I stood there, listening I was clearly aware that life is a mirror, and that she was projecting onto me. Abby was speaking of herself and her beliefs about her own worthiness. My heart filled with love and compassion for this woman. I was aware for the first time that she was in love with my High School sweetie and she ate lunch with me all year and never gave this secret away. I respected her and thought how she must have hated eating with me every day. I cannot recall my comments to Abby, but I clearly remember the feelings. I felt only goodness, my internal happiness remained consistent. I felt love for her as a person struggling with mixed emotions... just like I do sometimes. I did not take her anger personally and I had a crystal clear connection to her plight. Abby walked away angry or embarrassed - I did not know. I turned to Karen and her face indicated that she thought, perhaps I was confused or dumb. She said, "Cath, do you know that that woman just ripped you to shreds"? I nodded and said, "I know exactly what just happened. Life's a mirror, you know, and her comments had nothing to do with me. She's just in pain, that's all". I had to explain to Karen that I did understand her view; I just did not see it that way... I explained my "Life is a mirror theory" and Karen, having heard this before, listened to the joy and wonder in my voice as I talked about this concept again.

There is no mystery in this example of choosing the Holy Spirit as my teacher. That evening at the bar I did not know that what I had done was to see Abby through the eyes of Love... asking that the Holy Spirit show me how He sees Abby. I know now that was all I did. No magic and no great talent and no years of meditation were required. The only requirement was a desire to see the world with Love and with a Wisdom that is not of this world. This story has been a lesson that I recall every so often, reminding myself that I have a choice in how I see the world. I can choose defensiveness and its consequences of fear and anxiety, or I can choose to ask for another view. This view leaves me easy and peaceful. Fear is absent and peace is mine. I am consciously aware today that I have a choice of teachers. Defense is the choice of the world; Wisdom is the choice of God.

I can tell you honestly, I still choose defenses most of the time. Silly, dumb and stubborn I know, but still, I do. I cannot trick myself into saying that I have no other choice. I know I have the choice. I know that whenever I ask the Holy Spirit for help (and mean it) that the support is given me. I ask the Holy Spirit simply to help me change how I think, not what I do. I believe that when your thinking is more in line with Love, what you do will flow naturally. Like those days of ease where you feel so connected to God and His love is your guidance. So my advice is not to ask, "Hey Spirit what should I do about...." Or, " Jesus please fix this..." I would suggest you ask, "Jesus how would You see this problem? Can you show me Your point of view?" If you allow the point of view of the Holy Spirit to flow through your mind then what you do will naturally follow.

Let's look more closely at my assumption of what Abby projected, and why it had nothing at all to do with me. We must start from the premises that "thoughts begin in the mind of the thinker" (Text page 97 T-6.II.9). All thought therefore reflects an idea and a belief that is held within the thinker's mind. People simply assume that they know how you think and feel. All of their assumptions are generated in their thoughts and those thoughts reflect their views. When you listen to what someone says you learn about how they think. When you watch how you respond, react and think, you learn about your own mirror. The idea here is to take yourself into your mirror. I believe that Abby projected onto me her fear that she would never be worthy of the love of someone who she thought was terrific. Her fear of looking at that belief was defended with repression. A thought like, "I'm not worthy of great love" began to surface. She became afraid of the ugliness of the thought. She defended the thought with anger and projected it out. At that point she made me responsible for the thought, i.e. she denied it was in her mind, she split it off and gave it to me- "only a fool not worthy of great love would throw a great love away... you must be the fool". Then she convinced herself that the original thought of not being worthy was mine, denying the responsibility for thinking the thought to begin with, and justified her anger by condemning me. This process reinforces the belief that she is unworthy of the love of an awesome person. Abby teaches herself, through her defenses that she is deserving of punishment by her attack on me. Remember the attack-defense cycle from the earlier chapter. We all know deep in our hearts that "ripping people to shreds," as Karen so eloquently put it, is not something that nice people do. Abby is teaching herself that she is guilty of ripping me to shreds verbally and therefore should be punished. A good love after all does not come to someone who deserves to be punished. Abby is not unusual. We all chose to reinforce our guilt every time we let our defenses teach us how to solve the dilemma of our unhappiness in the world. Defenses are poor teachers and they keep us stuck in a cycle that reinforces self-hate and which is deceptive. We have the option to stop this cycle. Ask yourself if you are happy with constantly using defenses, which teach you that you are guilty and deserving of punishment. Ask the Holy Spirit what His opinion is on that.

### Resistance Is Futile

The process sounds so simple. You watch your thoughts and recognize that any attempt to change them is a defense. So instead of changing or defending them you stop and ask the Holy Spirit if He would take over. You are then the student and the Holy Spirit, your teacher, shows you a different perspective. I have been a student of the *Course* for some time and I continue to experience great resistance in this process. Why is that? Why do I consciously and unconsciously resist a process that I know from experience will leave me happy and peaceful? The *Course* and Ken both teach that our resistance is based upon the fear of losing our individuality. We identify our self as being a body and having a personality. We think we are what we believe in. Our individuality is based on our beliefs, our thoughts, our personalities and our bodies. When we question who we are (as in my letter to God in the earlier chapter), we become afraid sometimes. I like this body and I recognize this personality. I am proud of the woman that I am. The Holy Spirit brings her reality into question… that terrifies me. When I am terrified about the idea that I may be wrong about who I am I resist the process. I will catch myself saying that the *Course* is too difficult and complicated, and I don't understand what it is asking of me. The fear I have that God will punish me is deeply rooted and strongly held. I sometimes think that that Holy Spirit is attempting to trick me into believing that I am something that I am not. These beliefs clash with the simplicity of the process of asking for help. I lack trust in the Holy Spirit and I resist His guidance. Ken puts an emphasis on this idea of fearing the loss of our individuality, as a critical theme in this work. It is why we stop practicing looking in. It is why the idea of looking within presents itself as a new idea… to the Holy Spirit, *within* is all there is. To those of us who believe we inhabit bodies, *within* means organs, tissues and blood. *Within* meaning a mind or spirit that is who we are, is a foreign concept with which we have to grow comfortable. I will explain this more deeply as it is so critical.

I am a *Star Trek* fan. I want to demonstrate the concept of losing our individuality through the idea of the Borg. The Borg are the archenemies of the Federation of Planets. The Federation of Planets, for those of you who are not fans of the series, are the good guys on Star Trek. They explore the universe in their star ships and they are ethical and good. You just love them and you always want them to win. The Federation has a strong belief in non-interference. This means they live and let live. They don't interfere with cultures or customs of others planet. The Federation has a strong respect for individuality and it encourages individuals to develop their potential in many arenas. In general the Federation is peaceful. Still, it will attack in self-defense. The members of the Federation are constantly thinking strategically to prevent themselves from falling victim to the Borg.

The Borg are brutal. The Borg terrify the Federation for many reasons. The most prominent reason from my perspective is because the Borg steal away a person's individuality. Let me explain the Borg so you understand. The Borg are part of a collective… like a hive. They have a queen who is the mind of the Borg. There is only one mind in the Borg collective… therefore there are no individuals. The Borg have one mission on the show. They travel the universe concurring planets and assimilating the species of that planet into their one mind collective. The Borg goal is perfection. By assimilating individuals they incorporate their knowledge, their technology, their strengths and their weaknesses. Once an individual is assimilated he loses his personality, his thoughts, ethics, values and any shred of choice or control. Choices are made by the one mind... the queen. She is in control and the assimilated ones are her drones. Borg drones walk around like zombies and they carry out the will of the one mind. A drone even loses his appearance as the Borg put their technology into the drone to enhance its strength and connect it to the one mind that will control it. The queen, after a percentage of a species is assimilated, knows everything there is to know about that species so that the assimilation of the rest is easy. Once the one Borg mind knows your species it knows your defenses, and has your weaknesses pegged. The Federation has to be very creative in its strategy to defeat such a wise and unconscionable enemy.

The drone is a fabulous ego example of what we think being connected to God and His one mind might be like. Have you even thought what in the world you would do in Heaven? A place where everything is so nice and there is nothing to fix or for which to fight. What cause would you believe in and what would you do? When I am thinking defensively, I think that Heaven might be rather dull. I have always believed that in Heaven I would still be Catherine.

The concept that runs through the *Course* indicated that in the true state of Heaven we are one with God. There is only one mind in Heaven (Text page 39 T-3.II.4.5-6). We don't have personalities, we lack bodies, there are no ethics or values required; there are no choices to be made as we are one, and we don't think, as we understand thinking. If we experienced a Oneness with God we would have no consciousness of a self that is outside of the One Self that is God (Wapnick, Kenneth *Separation and Forgiveness The Four Splits and Their Undoing*, 1999). I have no experience of what these words mean in Truth... when I think of this with defenses I see a drone. And I, like the Federation characters on *Star Trek*, fight with all my might to not be a drone. I love this idea of a drone and I will refer to it a number of times throughout the book. It is a wonderful example of how the ego fears and resists the loss of individuality.

So as not to throw the reader into a panic it is important to recognize that the Holy Spirit will never take away anything from us which we are not willing to put down. He is incapable of manipulation... a concept that boggles my mind. The letting go of our individuality in truth is not a loss at all. Ken defines it as a spiritual growing up. Small children have toys that they adore. They cannot imagine life without them. I was a great fan of

Barbie dolls as a kid. I always thought I would have a Barbie in my life, but as I grew older she lost her appeal and eventually the joy of playing with Barbie and her accessories faded. As an older child giving up Barbie was not a painful loss... it was a natural process of growing. It was natural, gentle and easy. The letting go of our personalities and who we believe we are is the same exact idea to the Holy Spirit. A growing up spiritually and putting down the toys of our limited personality; of defense and attack to which we have been so connected (Text page 623 T-29.IX.6). There is nothing to fear because the Holy Spirit does not require loss as part of this curriculum. As long as your desire to keep a part of your personality remains (regardless of the pain and cost), you will keep it. The Holy Spirit will use what you hold onto to help teach you (He is clever that way). So as your life drones on (pun intended), look at the resistance you experience in attempting to apply these principles and don't be surprised. Expect some resistance and know that at the moment when you are resisting you prefer life as an individual, and as you understand it, more then you desire peace. Then if you can, ask for some help.

## Spiritual PTSD

In my early twenties I began working with a man who had been a Hindu monk for about ten years. Five years prior to the time I met Robert, he had left the order of which he was a part. Robert and I became fast friends at work. We ended up spending a great deal of time together. Rob was a great teacher for me. He was the first person to introduce quantum physics to me. Through physics, Robert introduced me to the idea that the world may be an illusion. He taught me that nothing in the world of atoms is solid. Atoms are mostly space and space is obviously not solid. He has a way of making complicated ideas less abstract for me. Rob also taught me a lot about his life as a monk and about being Hindu. As our friendship grew I began to realize that Rob had an experience of God that I often dreamed about but of which I had little or no experience. His connection as a monk to a consciousness that was otherworldly amazed me.

Rob would sometimes speak of the experiences he had as a monk and meditation teacher. He had a vast experience of connection to a life force much greater than himself. He knew through experience that he was not a body and that the world is an illusion. Yet he was not practicing what he knew and he had consciously turned away from this truth. I was baffled about why Robert would have left the order when it brought him such peace and connection to a Love that was out of this world. I began to ask Robert challenging questions about this. Initially he spoke of not being able to live in the world anymore. Day to day living became difficult and as a monk and teacher he had trouble focusing on the task he was performing in the world. He felt that he was not a part of Heaven and he was finding it increasingly difficult to function in the world in general. What began to strike me was Rob's physical and emotional reaction to the conversations that we began to have. When Rob started to feel or deeply remember any experience that reminded him of his time as a monk, or about why he walked away from this life, he would sweat, physically shake and often get a headache or begin to cry. He would have to sit down and he often lost his breath. His heart would race and he would become red in the face. It was obvious that the loss of the life he had and the walking away from his Hindu Master Teacher were traumatic for him. Yet he walked away. He was not forced out of this order; he chose to leave. Rob's pain over this subject was great and I did not understand it for the most part. I did not understand why Rob, or anyone, would not choose to return to his order and his Master if he missed them so. To me He was so close to peace and the love of God and from what he told me he would be welcome to return. I can laugh when I write this now because I often do not choose the peace that I know I can have. I have a better understanding as a *Course* student, that we deeply fear losing our individuality so we resist the help of the Holy Spirit. Robert was very close to accepting that he was not an individual and he became afraid of the implication. He walked away. He was not ready. I know how to access the help of the Holy Spirit and I choose not to.

Rob and I are no different, although he has more closely experienced not being an individual than have I. Many of us say no to the love and peace that we can access. Not because we are bad or rotten people, but because we are afraid and perceive Heaven and the Love of God to be frightening and a bit dull.

Over dinner one evening my friend Lori told Robert that he seemed to be suffering with many of the symptoms of Post Traumatic Stress Disorder (PTSD) but the trauma was based on a spiritual loss and fear. PTSD is a mental health problem that many people connect to veterans or civilians of war or to people who have lived through very traumatic events, such as a natural disaster, a plane crash, sever childhood abuse, rape or incest. People with PTSD often suffer with a fear of looking at the trauma that occurred in their life. Yet the trauma resurfaces in nightmares, in familiar sounds that trigger a memory and in their dealings with life. PTSD causes people to be hyper-vigilant to events that may trigger their pain. They may go to great lengths to avoid, deny and fight the resurfacing of these all-consuming, painful memories. When a memory surfaces it brings with it the fear that was felt at the time of the event, or perhaps the fear of looking within in general. This fear can be so overwhelming that the body literally responds. The response can be one of fight or flight, it can be one of terrified helplessness, or any combination of defending that keeps the pain away. Rob's reaction to the spiritual trauma of keeping his connection to God was one of terror. Keeping the connection to God meant giving up his individuality and this frightened him. He became weak, pale and shaky with the memory of his connection to God. He reported great difficulty sleeping and he could no longer meditate. He suffered with anxiety and he developed many physical problems that keep him very focused on his body and the world. Rob is a friend who I adore, who has also has been a great teacher for me.

In my study of the *Course* I have developed a healthy respect for defensive thinking and the ego. I have come to recognize that I am very attached to my individuality as is my dear friend Robert. He and I are no different from each other. We both spend most of our time choosing defensive thinking. We touch peace once in a while and then we run away in fear of loosing the little that we believe ourselves to be. I have learned that the process takes time and that we are allowed to proceed slowly. Rob's Spiritual PTSD may be the result of him moving too quickly toward an end that he was not spiritually mature enough to accept. Rob has taught me to respect the process of growing up. Growing up takes time. If we move too quickly we may stunt our process.

### Finding your Voice... Power

I work with teenagers in a school. Often I am faced with an angry teen who wants to solve a problem with violence. I ask him to give me a little time to help him find a better way to solve the problem; a non-violent solution. I will ask for his promise that he will not resort to violence to problem-solve, until he attempts a non-violent solution. Nine times out of ten they reply with "You want me to just stand there and be beaten up?" They are always surprised when I say "No. I don't want you to stand there and allow someone to hurt you." (I usually add) "I sort of like you and I would not want you to get beat up silly. I'd never ask that of you!"

I am no longer surprised that many people have such dichotomous thinking. They think in two extremes; they see themselves as either the victim or the victimizer. They are baffled that there might actually be a third option. The concept of shared interest and win-win intrigues them and I often role- play how you can stand up for yourself without hurting anyone in the process. With teenagers I talk about Gandhi, Dr. Martin Luther King,

Eleanor Roosevelt and Rosa Parks. I work in a public school and I cannot speak of spiritual leaders but my spiritual role models are Jesus, Mother Theresa, the Dalai Lama and Buddha.

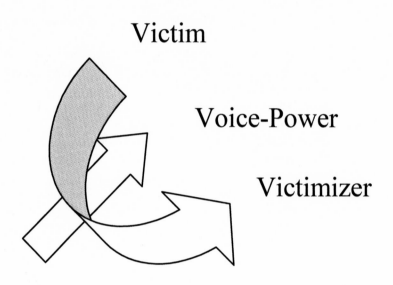

Victim

Voice-Power

Victimizer

How did great teachers find their strength? Where did Gandhi, Dr. King and Rosa Parks find the courage to stand up for their beliefs without being aggressive? How is it that they were able to find non-violent solutions to problems that foster rage in most of us? As a child I wanted to emulate the lives these people led, but I always felt too afraid. I did not believe that I could stand in the face of such adversity and hold onto what I believed. I felt weak and pathetic in comparison. I would think... I want to live with their bravery... then an incident would happen in school where someone was teasing another kid and to avoid being teased I would join in or walk away. I disliked this about myself, but felt too frightened to stand up and find my own voice.

It took me years to begin to grasp the idea that great spiritual leaders do not have courage as I defined it. Courage as I defined it is being afraid of your circumstances but living your ethics regardless. I often wonder in amazement at the courage of Dr. King, Rosa Parks and Gandhi, in tolerating the experience of such hatred directed at them. Courage in the face of adversity is a quality I respect, but which I find is limited within my life.

Then I began to imagine that these great people were connected to the Wisdom that I had the evening that Abby was upset with me. My experience is that fear is absent when I choose the Holy Spirit as my teacher. What these great leaders may have connected to was what I experienced in the bar with Abby... defenselessness. The absence of defenses as their teacher and the Wisdom of God as a guide to learning a different way of relating. I cannot answer how they may have been thinking, but the idea that we have a third option and a different Teacher has redefined my concept of courage. When I choose defenselessness as my Teacher, courage is not based on fear it is based on kindness. As Abby was speaking to me all I saw in her was self-doubt and her deep hope that this self-doubt was incorrect. Kindness flowed through me from a place of Wisdom that was much greater than myself. The Holy Spirit was in charge of my exchange with Abby. I had very little to do with the process. I was observing the exchange and allowing the Holy Spirit to give me His thoughts with which to think. We all have these experiences. Gloria Wapnick calls this "being thunk". Think back in your life and you will find one. Your kindness was not simply because you were in a good mood that day, or because you wanted something from the person to whom you were being kind- it was because you accessed a correction from the Holy Spirit. You can choose to do that again if you would like.

One of the most fascinating things about the movie *Gandhi* is the scene where Gandhi meets with the English leader. He tells this man that the English need to leave India, but when they go he would like them to remain friends. I was glued to the TV during this scene! I was amazed and confused that Gandhi made this request of the English. I can visualize the scene now as I write this and I can experience the wonder and confusion I felt from the dialogue. I could not fathom being able to honestly say such kind words to someone who I knew was oppressing my people. When I write about this now it appears to me that Gandhi was not using defenses as his teacher. I believe that he must have turned to God for guidance, for his thinking was beyond the norm of our world. What power was behind Gandhi's words? The strength superseded courage; it was the strength of Wisdom. If God is love then He must love the English as much as He loves the people of India. Gandhi had access to that Wisdom. The love of God, to remain love, cannot exclude and remain Love.

Great spiritual teachers do not think with their ego; they cannot exclude and remain connected to God who does not exclude. Can you imagine how Mother Theresa thought? How about Buddha or Jesus? Can someone who is without defenses suffer? I have brought this question to God in an attempt to understand my relationship to Jesus. I am a big fan of Jesus, but I don't tell many people this. I have this image in my mind that people who follow Jesus have to suffer, sacrifice and be martyrs. I don't want to do any of those things. I fear that if I tell people that I think He is an amazing teacher and a great companion, that they will see me as some suffering fool. Being raised as a Catholic I also have images of Jesus bleeding and dying because I was a sinner. I hate the guilt of that belief. The images repulse me and I reject them. I mean no offense to practicing Catholics. The Church helped me a great deal in my youth. I believe that the love of God is universal regardless of the form of religion or spirituality that you practice. As a young person I found a connection to God as a Catholic.

As a child I had a great relationship with Jesus. He was a constant internal companion of mine. When He was in my thoughts I was full of Joy. I spoke to Him all the time and even played games that I invited Him to join; like a childhood imaginary friend. I knew as a child that God was not connected to His name. That the quality of how you loved was much more important than the name you gave to Love. As a young teen some friends and I went to see the parish priest to discuss this. We spoke to him about opening up the youth group to kids from other religions. After all that *was* the kinder more Christian thing to do. The parish priest, who was wonderful man, agreed and our Jewish friends joined the Catholic youth group (I wonder how their moms felt about this)! Somewhere between the ages of fifteen to seventeen this idea of God preferring some people above others began to plague me. I became disillusioned with Catholicism. My strong belief that God could not pick favorites could not be compromised without great discomfort within me. I could no longer honestly say the Apostles Creed, as it claimed that there is only one way to believe in God and that God responds to only one name. I could not believe that Catholics had a corner on the God market. What about all the people who called God by a different name, but lived with His Joy on their lips? I knew that He loved them… or He was a lie. I left the church confused, angry and sad. I denied my experience of God and threw Him away. I threw Jesus out too… with the pride and arrogance of an adolescent. It did not occur to me that my relationship with Jesus had little to do with Catholicism. Perhaps Jesus agreed with my inability to believe that there is only one way to believe in God. I knew that God was not attached to His name. He did not care how or by what name you called Him… Mother Divine, Yahweh, Shiva, Buddha,

Allah or Jesus... The list is endless and God answers to all the names. Still I threw all of it away, the Joy of my relationship with Jesus along with organized religion.

I have to tell you that I missed Jesus. I felt lonely and more alone than I had ever felt before. I searched for a church where I would feel the connection that I was longing for and where I could believe what they preached. I checked out Hinduism, The Quakers, The Unitarian movement, Judaism, a Psychic Church, and Buddhism. I learned to meditate and I read many self-help books. I wanted to fill the hole that I felt inside my soul. I knew instinctively that no human relationship would fill me up. My career too left me wanting. Travel helped but it was very short-lived. I felt empty and I longed for the connection to Jesus that I had in my childhood. I was ashamed of the Jesus of Catholicism. I saw Him as the hypocrisy of the church and I did not want to pray to a God who condemned most of us and only favored a few. I checked out the New Age movement, studied psychology and began working at Hospice with the idea that perhaps I could find the connection that I was missing there. Where was the Joy I threw away and why could I no longer access it? People would comment and say that to be part of a church, you have to take the good with the bad of the religion. My thoughts always turned to "Why"? Why is it that we do not question these things? Why do we just say that others say it is so and therefore that we must believe it? Why do we trust the judgment of others more than we trust our internal Teacher? As a teenager I threw away my very real connection to my internal Teacher because I saw the contradiction and hypocrisy in the church. The church had nothing to do with my relationship to Jesus. I mistakenly connected the two and I spent the following ten years searching for something outside of myself to fill me up the way His love did.

Finally after ten years I turned back to Jesus and I asked Him "Why is it that I cannot find You? How come I cannot access your love? I miss you and I need your help. I want the connection to you that I had as a child." That evening I went to a psychic church (I was church-hopping at the time) and took a seat in the back, at the last row. I was feeling very lonely and unconnected. I was about ready to walk out when a woman asked it she could give me a psychic message. She told me that she saw me standing outside of a beautiful garden longing to go inside the gate. She described the garden in vivid color and explained that she saw an adult version of me outside the garden gate in dull gray clothes. She saw me as a child dancing at the garden in a beautiful party dress and shinny shoes (I loved shinny shoes as a kid). The child version of myself was reveling in the love and joy that the garden brought her. The woman hesitated and said the message I'm suppose to give you is: "if you would simply open the gate you could enter the garden". I began to look within; to reclaim what is my inheritance. I do not to this day have a formal religion that I believe I can follow, but the garden gate is open and I have walked in to find the love for which I was longing.

I began to study *A Course In Miracles,* and to connect once again to the Love that I left behind the gate. The *Course* is a spiritual thought system, which states that the world is an illusion. Buddhism says this also. The *Course* adds that we use defenses to keep the Love of God from us. That we can think with our ego or with the Holy Spirit. We cannot think without or apart from one of these two teachers (Text page 549-550 T-26.V.1.7-12). The Holy Spirit thinks without defenses. The Course says that in our defenselessness we are connected to the Holy Spirit. That defenselessness is where the safety of Heaven lies. Keep in mind that we are talking only on the level of thought. Defense mechanisms occur at the thought level. Earlier in this chapter I was explaining that teens sometimes have trouble grasping the concept that they have options outside of being a victim or a victimizer. To stand around acting defenseless and getting your butt kicked would not be helpful! That would simply be silly. Allowing one's self to be treated like a doormat in the name of God is not beneficial. It reinforces helplessness. I am speaking of the defenselessness that Jesus, Dr. King and Gandhi accessed, and they were full of power, action and love.

Let's take a look at Jesus. Perhaps He did not suffer, sacrifice and die for our "sins". Perhaps if we ask the Holy Spirit to show us the purpose of Jesus and His teachings we would realize a change in our relationship with Him. I am asking that you open your mind to alternative interpretations; that together we question the interpretation we placed on the life of Jesus and ask the Holy Spirit to show us if there is another way to see this. Think big, and suspend any prior beliefs. What if Jesus was spiritually aware enough of the option to think without defenses? If He was spiritually advanced enough to do this, and I believe He was, then He was not connected to fear of any kind. Can you suffer if you do not believe in fear?

Let's also assume that He knew that this world is an illusion, as stated by Buddhism and the *Course*. Well if the world is an illusion, then the self we believe we are, is part of the illusion. I have contemplated this idea for a number of years. I ask the Holy Spirit to help me understand this. If the world is an illusion and I am part of the world, then who am I? Who am I? This question is one of terror and wonder for me. It scares me, and it fills me with hope and great Joy. It has recently come into my awareness that perhaps who we are exists in defenselessness. Perhaps all we can be is found in the realm of Thoughts of God. Thoughts of God are by their very nature are without defenses. We always are searching to 'find ourselves' to become all that we can be, to uncover the mystery of life. Ken has introduced to me the idea that we may be looking for the answers in the incorrect place. The answers are not in the world; they are in our mind... our thoughts and beliefs. Jesus knew that He was not His body. He knew He was connected to God and in truth part of the Mind of God. As part of God Jesus knew that suffering and fear are also illusions.

Maybe, just maybe Jesus knew that His True Self was a defenseless thought in the Mind of God. If He knew this then He was not capable of suffering. He required no defenses, because there was nothing to defend. He was enlightened and knew that Thinking with God kept Him perfectly safe. According to my friend Karen, Abby attacked me. From the perspective I was sharing with Love nothing unkind was occurring. I think that great, spiritual, enlightened teachers live this every moment. I can access this state of mind when I choose to. The logical conclusion is that if I chose to access it all the time I would live a life of true peace that could not be touched, regardless of what was occurring in the world around me. Perhaps Jesus' message was not one of "you are sinful people; God is angry, so angry that I have to be sacrificed for your sins"... maybe that was the mirror of the writers of the Bible. Jesus may have been trying to show us that when you think without defenses you are connected with God. Then the world has no effect on you. He could have been saying that we are much more than this small vulnerable self that is so full of fear that it needs defenses. Jesus had Wisdom and Wisdom is a connection to the True Self we are as part of God. Wisdom does not require courage, for Love needs no defense (Workbook page 192-193 W-107.5). I think Jesus was teaching that we have the option to access defenseless thinking and we are not these weak and vulnerable bodies. I have accessed that experience of defenseless thinking. I know that everyone can. Perhaps all Jesus did was choose the Holy Spirit as His Teacher all the time. We too have the ability to choose the Holy Spirit as our Teacher and then to allow His thinking to work through us. Jesus was more advanced than many of us spiritually. His wisdom can be seen in His ability to only choose the Holy Spirit as His teacher. Most of us vacillate, choosing defensive thinking most of the time, fearing loosing our individuality and being drones with no differences and nothing special to separate us from other people; and then accessing the thoughts of God for brief moments. In truth I believe that we are just like Jesus. We have the choice between allowing defenses or the Holy Spirit to be our teacher. Jesus chose the Holy

Spirit one hundred percent of the time. Buddha, Mother Theresa and other enlightened teachers have done the same. The only difference between Jesus and each of us is the teacher that we are choosing. Then are we all just like Jesus? If Love cannot exclude and remain Love, then we are. We have His power within us. I ask myself how can I be exactly like Jesus and choose to think with such defenses? Why would I do that? Again I bring these questions to God and I ask. I am often faced with the image of a Borg drone in my mind's eye... Let me share with you a letter I wrote to Jesus about how I resist His love.

*Dear Jesus,*

*I took a kick boxing class this morning and as I was throwing a punch I realized that it was your face I was aiming for. In my mind's eye it was You I was pounding. And as I raised my leg to kick, the "Ehi-Yah" from my yell seemed to increase the force that I was using to slam in Your hollowed out chest. You stumbled backwards and I moved in to finish off the job. I hated You in that moment and I pounded your scrawny little body with fury. I kicked Your butt, by the way, and I felt ashamed and guilty the whole time.*

*How can I claim to love You and want the peace You represent when I can despise You with such abandon and rage? I confuse myself. I have been avoiding You often lately... feeling ok and not believing that I need your guidance. Hiding my fear of what You are teaching me and denying how afraid of the abstract idea of Mind I am. I am cold. I need Your help.*

*Love, Catherine*

This is when I know that I am feeling very attached to Catherine and I prefer my individuality at this moment. I don't mean this in a judgmental way. I am attached to being Catherine and to being part of the world in which I live. That is why this is a process for most of us. This attachment, like my attachment to Barbie as a child, appears impossible to live without. I cannot fathom the idea of who I would be, if I were not the individual that I believe I am. *A Course In Miracles* explains that we are spiritual children. This idea has helped me be gentle with myself along the way to growing up. I am a spiritual child and part of the growing up process includes vacillating between being ready to let go of my toys of individuality and my refusal to comply with that request. The request comes from me and is resisted by myself as well. Either way, Jesus is smart enough to recognize how to help me learn at the pace that I am able to manage without terrifying myself.

Now change is clearly a process; sometimes one that feels too slow and too arduous for my taste. The results of the process speak for themselves in my life. I am more peaceful when I surrender control to the Holy Spirit but that does not mean that I will always choose to do this. I have come to recognize that part of the process is taking a leap of faith that the Holy Spirit knows better then I do about how to help me keep my peace. Yet a leap of faith takes some trust and some experiences of peace. This is a catch 22 for me... without the experience my trust wanes; yet without the trust I hesitate to allow the experience to happen. Watching my thoughts and my resistance to admitting that perhaps the Holy Spirit knows more than I about spiritual matters helps me build trust for Him. The faith and trust that I have slowly begun to develop with the Holy Spirit has helped me to come to terms with the idea that nothing in this world works well for long. That is why all of us are left worrying and fearful. Life is good and things are comfortable, happy and we worry that this good life can be taken from us in an instant. All you need is one tragic event to befall this fragile body and we are done... our peace and sense of control is shattered. Peace this fragile is not of God, as God's strength cannot be shattered so easily.

With the Holy Spirit's guidance I have begun to admit that the defensive system that I have built my peace and my safety upon has a hollow foundation. I have come to question in my own mind that defensive thinking does not work. I see the pattern of making the same mistake over and over again with no end in sight. I have recognized that as a world we do the same thing. Any historian can verify how we continue to make the same mistakes time and time again. If you can see this pattern in your life even slightly would you be open to questioning that there might be another way of thinking that gives you a permanent peace? The peace of the Holy Spirit cannot be shattered; it is eternal. Defensive thinking creates a pattern of repetitive mistakes, anxiety, fear and apprehension. Would you perhaps be open to the idea that there is a different way of thinking available to you that is without any fear or defense of any kind? You can access this thinking; it is yours to choose. Recognizing how you can consistently access it is the challenge. Watching how you think, or monitoring your thoughts is a habit that helps (me) us to connect to eternal peace more consistently.

# Chapter 5:

## Thought Monitoring

I ask so many questions… Who would I be if I allowed God to be my guide all the time? Why do I resist giving Him control over my thoughts? Why do I believe that I need defenses? From what am I defending myself? What is in the way of me allowing defenseless thinking to help me all the time? How can I account for my experience of being defenseless and then justify my defenses? Who am I if the world is an illusion? What was Jesus trying to teach? If I am not my body, then what and who am I? How can I access a lasting experience of God? The list is endless. The questions are great fun to ask. I become alive with an expanded sense of my mind. I feel so connected to God when I question my beliefs.

*A Course in Miracles* asks that we resign as our own teacher as we are pathetic at the job (Text page 227 T-12.V.8 3-6). We are so stuck on that treadmill going around in circles and learning very little about how poorly we have taught ourselves. I was insulted and humbled when I first began to understand that the Holy Spirit was telling the ego (my defensive self) to resign. I have to admit, with a bit of thought I was in agreement. I go under the assumption that my defensiveness is a poor teacher. I have been badly taught and I need to be open to questioning everything I think I know. Every belief I hold is open to reinterpretation. Why do I believe that I am correct in my assumptions, perceptions and ideas? I will catch myself assuming something and then I will bring the thought to the Holy Spirit and say, "How would You interpret this?" Then I wait sometimes moments, hours, days, weeks and even months… perhaps years for my answer. If I were without fear my question would be answered prior to my asking it. My fear is a block that stands in the way of the answer I seek. I ask my questions knowing this and also knowing that when an instant occurs when I am fearless, that the answer will be accessible. I know that the Holy Spirit will not take away my fear (Text page 31 T-2.VII.1). *A Course In Miracles* explains that we have the choice between fear and love. For the Holy Spirit to take our fear away takes away our ability to choose. This would limit the power that our mind has. In asking for the Help of Christ Vision we are asking to learn the power of our mind and our thoughts. God cannot teach us about the power of our minds by limiting us. To limit our minds tampers with the law of cause and effect (Text page 31 T-2. VII.1). Cause and effect is another theme that runs through the *Course*. I will discuss cause and effect at length later.

God responds to me in silly and fun ways. Pop music plays in my head and I recognize the lyrics to be an answer to a question. Cartoons flash across my mind or enter my meditations and they lighten up my mood and correct my misinterpretation of a problem I think I have. I have had a number of experiences where in my insistence that I am right about things I hear the voice of Christopher Robin from Winnie the Pooh in my mind saying "Silly ol' bear". I connect Jesus to Christopher Robin and myself to Pooh bear. I know this sounds silly… and I think that is the point. Ken has helped me learn that when I take life seriously on the level of thought I am being defensive. As I take my thoughts less seriously I am able to access the correction with a gentle ease. At the point that I have accessed the correction, whatever I do in the world is coming from Love and it is kind and helpful. The best way for me to be a good counselor is to take my thoughts less seriously so that I can be defenseless and access Wisdom. As soon as my thoughts are connected to Joy my actions are always helpful. Being truly helpful for me is practicing a constant vigilance to recognizing my defensive thoughts so that I can allow God's interpretation work through me (Text pages 109-110 T-6.V.C.4). True power lies in defenselessness. This is not a common view in the world, but I think it is the key that unlocks the world of God that we have denied within our minds.

## Where does healing begin

Healing beings in the mind of the thinker. Unless we as individuals look inside and accept responsibility for the thought we do not like, we will never be able heal our minds. We live in a world where many of us are disconcerted by the constant repeating of history. Nothing ever changes. We fight war after war after war. We justify destruction and call it by many different names like national defense and progress. We create system after system in an attempt to help and to improve our lots as people of the earth. We rape the land, we rape nation states, and we rape individuals physically, emotionally and psychologically. We manipulate, bargain and deal. We create governments and power structures but we don't trust them. We fight each other over opinions on every topic imaginable. We instill rules, laws, courts and prisons. We attempt to stand for justice and we see the problem all around us and are overwhelmed by the chaos. We live in fear that life will get worse and we will loose the little that we have built up; our loved ones our money our health, our beliefs in our worth, our dignity. We are anxious and afraid, angry and lost. We are very lost. Many of us have lost hope.

I believe that humans are good… but we are pretty dumb. Like a dog chasing his tail we have wandered around in circles making the same mistake over and over again. Any good historian will tell you that we do not learn from our errors. World War One did not prevent the Second World War. World War Two did not teach anyone in Yugoslavia a thing about the insidious hell of war. The Arabs and Israelis may continue to kill each other well into the 21st century. We are pretty stupid when you look at our history… worldwide dummies we humans are. We insist that we will get it right at some point. But we never think about how we will manage to "get it right" when we keep making the same mistake over and over again. I don't think that we know what the mistake is, and that may be at the root of the dilemma in which we find ourselves today. We attempt to fix the mistake from a defensive stance. It does not work.

As nation states we currently have the ability to blow up the planet at least thirty times over. Environmentalists keep telling us that the world will not have the ability to maintain global homeostasis with in the next 30-50 years. We are setting ourselves up for an environmental disaster and we don't pay attention. We say, "That's the way it is and it will never change". We shut our eyes and say "they will know how to fix things by then…" Is this supposed to help us feel safe? In a defensive thought system yes it is. Does it work? Ask yourself if you feel safe in this world. Are you waiting for the balance that you work so hard at creating to crumble? Do you find yourself worrying, afraid and protective? Have you lost hope? I had, and when I insist that I am correct, my hope dwindles. When I ask to see these problems through the eyes of the Holy Spirit they look amazingly different. I don't pretend to have the answers to world problems. I do believe that when we think without defenses we see the world from a different view. Defenselessness includes the absence of fear. I am speaking of an individual intra-psychic problem that impacts, (much more than we can imagine), a world wide problem. As individuals it is essential that we begin with the healing of our own thoughts- each one of us. We cannot create peace without having a sense of peace from the inside out. The problem that we repeat is the belief that if we create peace on the outside we will have peace on the inside. We insist that outward peace is the answer. We are mistaken. We keep chasing our tails saying that, if we just get it right out here everything will get better… how many more conflicts does each person have to experience before he begins to question why this does not work? No one can do this for you. The question must begin in your mind and the Answer is there too. How many times in a day or a week do you become annoyed or angry with someone? People in your family, colleagues at work, the slow driver in the fast lane on the road, someone on line in a store? This is the place you begin. This is where you ask the Holy Spirit to show you how He would view your annoyance. Not how He would change the annoying person or how He can make your life better, simply how He would see the situation that is 'stealing' your peace of mind.

### How do you simply monitor your thoughts?
I learned to practice Transcendental Meditation about ten years ago. Meditation is a practice that I enjoyed immediately. I practiced two times a day for 20-25 minutes, for years. When I began to attempt to practice the *Course* on a daily basis I found that the practice of meditation helped me to watch my thoughts. When I meditated I was practicing noticing that I was thinking and not saying my mantra. When I noticed the thoughts, I was instructed by my meditation teacher to gently and quietly return to my mantra. If my resistance was strong and I found my mind wandering from the mantra I was told to simply notice this. Fighting the thoughts was not helpful in meditation. To fight, resist or judge the thought gave it power, and kept it in focus. This was in direct contradiction with the goal of non-resistance. The idea was new to me, simply notice- then stop. The goal was a quiet mind, but the gentle observing and watching of my thoughts and then turning to my mantra was a daily practice for me. My meditation teacher was clear about not resisting the thoughts in my mind. For years I practiced noticing and doing nothing about my thoughts... I simply returned to my mantra. That was the whole practice.

My practice of *A Course In Miracles* follows the same plan. I heard Ken explain this "formula" to practice watching your thoughts in a lecture and on his tapes. It sounded so much like meditation that it made sense to me. Ken taught that (we) I should live my life just as I always do. I can notice my thoughts and then instead of returning to a mantra, I turn to Jesus and say "Can I see this thought from your perspective?" Sometimes when I am angry or particularly irritated I just say "Help." The process is that simple. I just ask for a different interpretation of my perceptions. I assume that He knows better and I ask for help. No smoke, no mirrors, no big deal.

### Peace within the Thinker
No big deal- right. It's simple... but not always easy. There are times when this process freaks me out. I see the Borg queen coming to steal my individuality and I hold on like a toddler to her mother on the first day of school. I refuse to follow these simple directions and I believe that to follow them would leave me feeling like a Borg drone; without choices, weak, lost

and helpless. I become dumb, insistent that I am right and that the Holy Spirit does not know what is in my best interest. I am amazed at how stubborn I can be... like most of us! I am very much a student of this process and I have to practice on a daily basis. I forget to practice for long periods of time and then I become annoyed that I started practicing in the first place.

The process can be hard... old habits hold on for dear life from their point of view. I mean... who am I if I am not an individual and if I am not right about my view of the world? I truly do not know and that sometimes leaves me feeling unsteady. That unsteady feeling; the feeling of who will I be if I do this all the time, leaves me frightened and I resist the process. I do know that the more I allow Wisdom to be my guide the happier and more at ease I feel. I am more peaceful allowing the Holy Spirit to hold the reigns of my life... but I forget that sometimes and I take them back. Don't give up because you are feeling resistance. Resistance is a defense and we are in the bad habit of defending. That is all that is happening. It should be no surprise to any of us that the defenses we are so accustom to accessing in our daily life we continue to access as we look into the mirror of our thoughts. The key is in asking for help from something greater than yourself when you are less fearful. Just like my meditation teacher taught me. Don't fight your thoughts, just notice that they are there and then ask for help. If your resistance is strong, allow that to be and ask for help when you are less resistant.

One of the ideas that has helped me a good deal through this process is the concept taught by Dr Carl Jung about a collective unconscious. I will discuss the collective unconscious at length in the following chapter. The collective unconscious contains within it all of the thoughts that we share. Being unconscious we do not know that we share these thoughts but we do. Just like the Borg collective the thoughts are part of something much larger then this self that you believe yourself to be. This idea of a collective thought system has helped me simply watch my thoughts without getting caught up in the idea of what the thoughts (ones I find repulsive or fabulous) say about who I am. The idea that we all share these thoughts takes the passion out of the thought and the belief about who I am because I have the thought. This gives me the distance to look at the thought without judgment. I find it helpful.

As I keep this idea of monitoring my thoughts from a perspective of distance I have come to recognize that thoughts have consequences. They have power. This idea of thoughts having power is new to some of us and not to others. Learning about the power of thoughts and how to believe the idea that thoughts could actually have effects, was a reverse in how I typically see the world. I had previously believed that life happens and then the thoughts about life come after an event. The *Course* has helped me question the reality of this belief.

# Chapter 6:

**Question Reality**

A number of spiritual and religious thought systems teach that this world is an illusion. Buddhism teaches this idea, as does *A Course in Miracles*. If the world is an illusion, then we are all part of a dream so to speak. Carl Jung, the famous psychologist, coined the term 'collective unconscious'. Dr. Jung discussed that on the level of thought there is a set of symbols and ideas, which are shared by all the cultures of the world. Dr. Jung explained that there is a part of our unconscious that we share and to which we all have access; he referred to this as a collective unconscious. I have learned about the collective dream from the staff at the Foundation for *A Course in Miracles*. The teachers at the Foundation speak of the collective Hologram. I will give you my interpretation of what they have taught me. I view this world as a collective dream. We interact and relate to others all the time within this illusion. The connecting strand of a collective dream is the one sleeping mind that believes it is many individuals. We focus on one character within the dream and we refer to that character as our self. Our individuality is what we focus on because it is the desire of the sleeping mind to be an individual. I focus on the character Catherine... but she is a figure in the dream and the dreamer is dreaming her. Responsibility for our projections as part of our dream is a hopeful idea to me. It helps me to understand why we do not know who we are in truth. It is difficult to recognize that perhaps you are a dreamer of a dream and not the body to which you feel so attached and connected. It is even more of a challenge to grasp the idea that we are all part of one dreaming mind, which mistakenly believes that it is many. This abstract idea of being part of a collective that is really one is difficult to grasp. If we take this idea further into the unreality of the illusion, even the dreamer is still connected to God... so the idea of dreaming in itself is an illusion.

To better explain the collective unconscious and collective dream, I will return to the example of the Borg collective theme. The Borg are a collective; one mind controlling all the drones. When we think about not being an individual from the perspective of the ego, being a Borg drone describes the idea well. The irony of this idea is that we are already part of a collective mind. We simply believe that we are bodies. So in essence when we think with defenses and believe we are an individual body we are drones, but we don't consciously know this. Being a drone from the perspective of the *Course* captures my imagination. Ken has often spoken of the idea that, as bodies we are puppets. Our bodies take orders from a sleeping mind that has no conscious idea that it is asleep. Ken refers to these bodies and personalities as puppets. So I hate to tell you, but if this theory is correct, we are already drones being directed by a queen Borg (defensive thinking) only we falsely believe that we are the ones in charge (silly ol' bear). The power of this idea is that access to the queen Borg (ego) or to your Mind (Holy Spirit) is yours to claim. You have the power to choose. Drones have no option… but you are not your body, and the option to access an experience of this is yours if you want it. This idea fills me with humor when I feel connected to the Holy Spirit, and with great dread and fear when I think with the ego.

### Boundaries and accepting responsibility for our projections

New age thinking has placed a focus on peoples' ability to create within their lives. People with illness have turned to the power of positive thought. They focus on believing that they have health and the health follows the belief. People, who want a loving relationship, money, or a career-change, focus on affirmations to help create their desires in the world. Many New Age communities attempt to help world peace with these healing tools. The *Course* does not speak of changing the illusion that we live in. The *Course* puts the emphasis on changing our minds about the illusion so that we can awaken from the dream and know that we are dreaming.

As I learn about the power of my mind, I often practice creating things I want, within my dream. Initially, I would not allow myself to do this. I have a strong connection to the belief in sacrifice and doing without, as a way to connect to God. My attempts to change my dream and create things in my illusion felt selfish, and contradicted my belief that God favors those who do without. I also knew from my study of the *Course* that the spiritual process was not to make the dream better, but to awaken from the dream to find that you are the dreamer and not the figure within the dream. I saw it as a practice that would go against what I was trying to learn. I asked the Holy Spirit for help here. What is it I believe in and why do I believe that creating changes within the illusion is wrong? I was guided to practice creating abundance in my illusion. This practice has been a great teacher for me. I continue to struggle with this and I wax and wane on many levels. Sometimes I bump into my belief that going without will get me to Heaven. When I feel connected to Jesus and safe in His love, then creating abundance in the world does not hold my attention for very long, so I lay the practice aside. Then my fear of scarcity will flare up and I will find myself worrying.

I go back to attempting to create abundance to ease my fears. What I have learned is that our minds are powerful, and I was making too much of using this gift... not allowing myself to create abundance was mirroring helplessness and denying the power of my mind.

My ultimate goal is to awaken from this dream... but I am still a student and I attempt to follow the guidance of my internal Teacher. I believe there will come a time when I feel safe enough and have enough trust for my internal Teacher, so that I will not worry about what happens in the world around me. Currently that is not the case. I do worry, and pretending that I don't leaves me stuck. I am still in the process of discovering the power within. Learning about the power of my mind to create abundance has led me to ask some intriguing questions.

If I have the power with thoughts to change this illusion, then who am I? Does this body and personality create the form in the world... or does something of which I am a part but of which I am not consciously aware, do the creating of abundance? Am I the changer of the illusion? Who is the me who has that power? What is the power of thought? If this world is an illusion, then who is doing the changing of the dream? Where does Catherine fit into this? Some new age thought systems say that a universal power answers our requests for things in the world... are they correct? Am I part of that universal power? Who is the 'I' that can create form with a thought or an idea? And if I can create with thought when I focus on the thought... then is this world perhaps a focused thought?

I have thoughts about things that I would like in my life and about things I want to learn. Then these ideas and things show up in my life. I am amazed that this occurs. So the questions I then ponder are, how does this happen, why does this happen, and who makes this happen? The home I currently live in is a reflection of my pursuit of learning about the power of my mind to create. I wrote in my diary about the home that I was hoping to have. I put many details into my description. I requested things that I thought were luxurious and still I asked for a simple home with character. I asked for extra room where people could come to visit for extended periods of time and yet not invade my space. All of these features are in the home in which I live.

When I first was learning how to create abundance in my life I focused on getting a sailboat - A small catamaran. I was in graduate school at the time. I lived in a small apartment with two friends. I had no place to put a sailboat and certainly no cash to rent storage. But I visualized that I would have one. Well a month or so later I was on the phone with a friend of mine named Joanne. Joanne taught me to sail. We were teenagers and she had a small catamaran. I loved the feel of the catamaran. I loved being able to touch the water as we moved. Joanne and I were speaking of sailing. She has graduated to a larger boat that I could not handle. I told her that I missed the catamaran. Joanne gave me her catamaran right there and then. She said it was wasting away in her parents' yard and someone should be enjoying it. And just like that the 'cat' I focused on was there.

Let's look at the idea of lucid dreaming for a moment. Lucid dreaming is an experience some people have when they are asleep. While asleep the person has a dream. In the dream he realizes that he is sleeping and having a dream. Some other level of consciousness is awakened and the dreamer of the dream then knows that he is not the figure in the dream. I have had a number of lucid dreams. It is a neat experience. It is like being consciously awake during your sleep. When I have a lucid dream I usually defy the law of gravity and go flying. I love the feel of flying. I have told myself that the next lucid dream I have I will play more with creating things, but each time I become conscious in my sleeping dreams, the temptation to fly is so strong that I do not resist it. It is great fun. My friend Sean had a dream wherein a monster was chasing him. He realized that he was dreaming as he was running from this figure, so he stopped running and the character that looked like him turned to face the monster in his dream. He thought "crossbow" and just like that, the crossbow he thought about was there in his character's hands. He killed the monster. Perhaps our creating of abundance is similar to our lucid dreaming. Sean was able to create instantly in his sleeping dream. I was able to create over a period of months in my life. Are these two processes so different from each other? My guess is no, they are not. The mind is powerful and thought precedes form; the two can never be separated (Workbook page 29 W-17.1.3-6). In fact thought and its effects occur simultaneously (Workbook page 30 W.19.1).

Now I know that I can create within this life of mine. The process is not that complicated. I think the focus is about what you believe. The belief has the power of thought behind it. The rest is a matter of putting your senses into the experience. All of us have this power within us. It is simply a matter of our believing. It is not my purpose to teach how to change the dream that you live in. The point I am making is that what we believe is powerful in and of itself. If on an unconscious level we believe that we are not entitled to lasting peace, then we will not find it. So I return then to questioning what I believe. If my beliefs can create, then perhaps a closer look at what we believe is in order. I have a deeply rooted belief that God demands sacrifice and suffering in order for the goal of Heaven to be attained. I would gladly suffer and sacrifice here to have Heaven for eternity.

The thought behind this belief is that God will punish me if I am not 'good'. Why do I insist that this belief is correct? We are taught that God is Love at the same time that we are taught that God demands punishment for our sins. We believe that we are capable of sinning. *A Course In Miracles* has helped me to understand that there is arrogance in believing that we can sin. The *Course* explains that sinning implies that we can defy the Almighty and that even though He is all knowing and all powerful, He will be fooled, become angry and punish (Text page 405 T.19.III.8). These thoughts are so full of contradiction. How can the all knowing be fooled? Why do we believe that we have the power to anger God? What arrogance these thoughts contain! It is arrogant to believe that we can trick God and provoke love to forsake itself through anger. When you really put some thought into this idea you begin to see that it is ridiculous and full of arrogance. Prior to studying the *Course* I would not have had the idea to question that sin might not be a fact. Jesus explains in the *Course* that sin is part of the illusion and not real. The idea that God would have the need to punish us for our sins against Him implies that we have the power to offend the all knowing… to offend Love. Anger is directly antithetical to love. God being Love cannot be provoked to anger. To believe that we have the power to change God at His core is silly.

Earlier in the book I reviewed the anger-defense cycle. Anger is always a cover-up for fear. So when we say that God can be angry with us, we are saying that God will fear us and then defend Himself with anger. This is foolish. Love and fear or God and fear cannot coexist; one of them has to be an illusion. I have heard Ken teach this idea by explaining that if God is real, we must be illusory; if we are real, then God is dead. Anyone who has felt the power of the love of God knows that God is alive and well. So the question I keep asking myself is, why do I continue to believe that I, as a body and personality, am real? Is there an I who can create and change this illusion? Who is that me? How do I get to know that me? How do I access a part of who I am that I cannot see or touch? I imagine that I am asleep having a dream and asking, "How do I figure out who the dreamer of the dream is?" And as these questions 'drone' on I come back to the idea that I sometimes would prefer to be an individual body and to believe that I know who I am rather than investigating this abstract spirit of a self who is so unknown to me. Other times I want to know who I am as Spirit, and I soar within the vastness and beauty of the experience.

As I have said I have had some experience of lucid dreaming. During a lucid dream I am no longer strongly identified with the figures in the dream. I view the dream from outside of its characters- like watching a movie. What happens to the characters does not matter very much at this point. They are symbols of myself; they have nothing to do with who I really am. When I really grasp this idea, then the sleeping dream is a tool to learn what thoughts are buried deep in my mind. We have the option to do this in our illusion whenever we choose. The *Course* refers to this process as being above the battleground. I sometimes look around at what is occurring during my day from the viewpoint that I am dreaming. I look at how I am responding and reacting to my day to help me access the thoughts and beliefs by which I live. It feels great! I am not consciously aware of being in a dream, but I wonder. The wonder fills me with great feelings of Love... the connection to Wisdom. I catch a glimpse of awareness that this is an illusion once in a while and I am filled with hope. I am too fearful and too spiritually immature to maintain this awareness consciously. I am slowly learning that the 'I' I believe myself to be may not be who I am in reality.

How can the Holy Spirit help us to become more aware of who we are in the eyes of God? I no longer am convinced that God views any of us as bodies. I think that He only knows the 'I' of whom I am not consciously aware. The *Course* teaches that we are one with God; we are His thoughts... abstract formless and eternal as part of Him. How can we learn how the Holy Spirit can truly help us to have an experiential understanding of this Self?

Ken has helped me to understand this through the example of imagining I am the parent of a young child who is having a nightmare. I see the tension on my child's sleeping face and watch him toss and turn in bed. What would I do to help? Would I attempt to enter the dream and change it for him, or would I gently tap my child's shoulder and call his name reminding him that he was home, safe and sound? Would I worry about what my child was dreaming so that I could fix the dream? Most parents would choose to waken their child. God does not crawl into our dreaming mind and change the drama for us. We can decide with the help of the Holy Spirit what we should be doing in the dream to help us become aware of the dreamer. If the *Course* is speaking the truth, which I think it is, then this is only a spiritual, children's dream (remember how we are supposed to grow up spiritually). As we grow up spiritually and recognize that we are the dreamers of the dream, the need to change the dream will fade away. When we ask God, Jesus or the Holy Spirit to come in and fix our nightmares, they recognize a young child's request. The *Course* asks that we "put away these sharp-edged children's toys." (Workbook page 419 W-pII.4.5.2) The request for help to change the dream would be a sweet request from a small child. Can't you see a small child asking a parent to come into their dreams and make the dream feel safe and happy? As adults we would smile at a child asking us to do this. We would know that the option was ludicrous. We would not try and explain this to a very small child. We would simply waken them and comfort them when they woke up. The *Course* states that we are still in Heaven connected to God… but we are dreaming of exile. We demand that God enter our dream and improve it… ludicrous right? The purpose of the *Course* is to help us remove the defenses that keep us unaware of experiencing ourselves as the dreamer of the dream. To literally wake up and be a lucid dreamer. A lucid solution to problems in the world would be to ask God to make you more aware of the dreamer of the dream. That is where your power lies. Most of us do not have a conscious experience of living within an illusion… so naturally we attempt to fix the dream, not knowing that we are dreaming. This feels and sounds logical. The idea that the world is not real sounds nuts… psychotic even. Initially this idea sounded psychotic to me. It seems insane to think that this vast universe, not to mention my life, is not real. But perhaps, just maybe, the world is an illusion and all the hell, blood and gore, along with the death, suffering, and deceit of this place is an illusion too… doesn't that sound hopeful.

The focus of this book so far has been on the level of thought. Thoughts are where the problem is, so *thoughts* are where the Answer lies. Thoughts end up being beliefs. Looking at your beliefs about who you are is a question of monitoring your thoughts. Monitoring your thoughts takes patience and devotion. It is over a process of many years that I hope to deepen my understanding of my beliefs with the goal of awaking from the dream. I imagine that I would live without fear if I knew that I was having a dream. My lucid dreams are without fear. As a lucid nighttime dreamer I know that nothing at all is happening. I am watching a movie … a cartoon. Everything is intriguing and I am enthralled with the process of watching; not the process of participating within the sleeping dream. I hope that one day I feel enough trust in the Holy Spirit to allow my life to be more of a lucid dream. I believe that Jesus, Buddha and all truly enlightened minds are able to do this. That we are dreaming may be the joke of enlightenment. All this smoke and mirrors, all this pain and heartache… a dream. It sort of minimizes all the importance and seriousness we place on our lives. It makes me angry (frightened) just thinking about it.

I think my fear in this world emanates from my refusal to accept fully that my life is an illusion. This attachment to being a body and an individual in the world is what prevents me from accepting the Holy Spirit's view of this world whole-heartedly and allowing myself to wake up and be a lucid dreamer. I am attached to this idea of being 'Catherine'. I don't believe that

I am a drone with no real choice being dreamed by a mind of which I have no awareness. I am invested in my dream and I don't want to know, *really know* that I am mistaken. I vacillate with this idea often. I do want to know this and yet I don't. The devotion to monitoring my thoughts and asking to see the world through the Holy Spirit's eyes is the process that helps me change my mind. I see the process as a healing of many layers of guilt, fear and shame. The layers keep coming up as I heal a piece. The looking at my beliefs and asking for the Holy Spirit's Vision is the healing. This is a process that for most of us takes time. Unlearning the identity that you believe yourself to be takes patience, discipline and devotion. It is a simple process of choosing the Holy Spirit as your teacher; it is not always an easy process regardless of its simplicity.

Still we have to live in the world on a very practical level and my practice of the *Course* is practical. Life in the world remains the same for me as it has for years and years. My practice of the *Course* does not change how I live on a day-to-day basis. I go to work, shop for things, clean, cook, spend time with my husband, family and friends and do all the things that I have always done. My behavior is exactly as it always has been. The only change that has occurred is within my mind. I ask Jesus to be my Teacher through out the day and I catch myself being defensive and when I see it I say "oops!" And ask for help seeing this through His eyes again. That is all. Some days I am vigilant about this. Other days I forget to practice. My resistance to practicing can be strong. My insistence that I am a body and an individual permeates my life for the most part. I will set out to have a day of observing my life and then before I realize hours have passed and I have not thought about asking for help in my perspective at all. I have gone through periods of days refusing to ask for help. During those times I simply realize that I am too afraid that this may be a dream. I am convinced that God is demanding that I suffer and I would prefer to forget all that I think I have learned. I have found that to fight the fear is not helpful or kind to myself. I have a habit of saying "OK Jesus I am too afraid of you right now. You can hang out with me, but today I am being a body". This way I invite Love to join me, but I don't fight my fear. I maintain the illusion of control that at these times I require in order to feel safe.

Practical living as I practice the *Course* in my life is a balancing act. Part of me knows that my practice of the *Course* has nothing to do with what I do in the world. I can choose to change my dream or choose not to; it makes no difference. The *Course* is a tool not a religion; it is a way of thinking not necessarily of acting. So I go about living a normal life the way normal people do, but I live with a different teacher. I ask Jesus to guide me (and

Ken reminds me to be normal). Then I make plans. The caution is not what I do in the world but with whom I do it. I invite Jesus to accompany me throughout my life. When I am practicing with Him I smile more and I find that my peace is constant. My actions are more loving because that is who Jesus is. I allow Him to teach me by allowing Him to work through me. So how do I balance my planning and my belief of what is in my best interest from His? As a general rule of thumb I attempt to go by how I feel. The *Course* set this idea up as a gauge for students (Text page 494 T-23.II.22.6-13). If my peace stays constant then I can be reasonably sure that I am allowing Him to work and teach through me. I don't do the teaching; I am the student. I am sneaky sometimes and I decide that I don't have to ask about some of the more important things in my life as I know best… or I think I ask for help, but I really have decided already what I am doing. The text in the *Course* explains that this is a major problem for students (Text page 626 T-30.I.3.1-2). After I have decided, then I might say, "help me see this (what I decided is the right answer) from your perspective." If I am stubborn about being right about a point and see what I am doing I usually recognize that as an ego I am too fearful to allow Love in. Other times I don't see that I am insisting upon thinking with my ego and for a time I believe that I am allowing my thinking to be handled by Jesus. It can be some time before I see this. When I get "preachy" and insistent that I know how to practice the *Course,* I know I am fearful. At other times my defensive stance is less obvious. I have not come to terms with how to balance this. As I continue to practice I find that I am able to catch myself being defensive more quickly. I notice I am upset, needing to be right, fearful, anxious… any loss of peace more quickly. When I recognize the loss of peace the power of choice is again mine. Not noticing (or looking) keeps the power of choice from my awareness.

Jewel, the poet and singer, wrote a song that I use as the theme song of my life. (Any *Ally McBeal* fan will know that I borrowed that idea from the show! The therapist on *Ally McBeal* suggests to Ally that she pick a theme song, something to motivate and inspire her. A song that moves her spirit and stirs her soul). As I mentioned before, the Holy Spirit teaches me through music all the time. I will have asked for guidance, and a short time later I hear some pop tune playing in my head… and the words to the tune are the answer to my prayer. A common occurrence when I am resisting the help of the Holy Spirit in my life is a song. Sometimes it symbolizes that Love is going to stick around regardless of my temper tantrums and other times they are a message for me to relax and enjoy the process. I have grown to love that tune playing in my head! Jewel's song, on her CD *Spirit* is called *Life*

*Uncommon*. In the tune Jewel sings of not giving our strength to things that we no longer want in our life. She states, " No longer lend your strength to that which you wish to be free from". I love this line and I hear the tune in my head often. When I am focusing on how I dislike a colleague or feeling annoyed with someone on the phone I may hear the tune in my head.

Now I want to be careful here. The tune is a reminder that I have another choice. It is not a replacement for my angry ego thinking. When I hear the tune in my mind that is a clue that I have chosen defenses as my teacher. At that point I don't pretend to love the person who is annoying me and I don't try to fake it. I simply say "Hey Buddy (a.k.a.- Jesus) give me your view on this situation please… I think I hate this person, but I don't want to reinforce my defenses, so help me see this through your eyes". What I do practice, to the best of my ability, is taking my anger and talking it out with the Holy Spirit and not with someone who I perceive is the cause of my problems. My problem is the teacher I have chosen. My annoyance is the repression of a thought I don't want to accept as beginning in my mind and then the projection of that thought. The mistake is in the teacher that I choose. I choose to think defensively and my old bad habits rise up. I insist at that point that this is the only way to think and that the thinking is correct. This is the mistake. I do not need to fix the person with whom I am annoyed or the world at large. I need to change my teacher.

I repress my anger and rage often. I have learned that when I repress my anger it comes out in the form of my feeling physically cold. My acupuncture doctor helped me learn this. She kept telling me that all of the symptoms of being cold that I was asking her to 'fix' were about being fearful. She wanted me to look at my fears so that I could be warm. Initially I rejected her explanation. I understand reaction formation enough to recognize that this is possible so I agreed to allow her to help me release some of the fear. She did, and I became enraged and shaky with anxiety about how angry I was feeling. When I went back to see her she said that I was afraid of being angry. Again I thought she was off base, but after some time working with her on getting warm I began to see that the more at ease I was with being angry, the warmer I was able to keep my body. When I allow myself to be angry with someone I act emotionally distant and cold. When I repress the anger and deny that I am feeling it I become physically cold. Then I distance the feeling from myself. If we look at this from a perspective of thoughts only, I am distant and cold either physically or emotionally when I am angry. I am happier when I am warm, so repressing the anger is not the answer. Many times I remain angry (and cold) even when I think I am asking the help of the Holy Spirit. The lesson that I have to learn involves a process of looking at how I fear my anger and the out-of-control feeling that accompanies it. The fear of the anger or the belief that my anger is fearful and that I will lose control and act out my anger if I feel it, is the problem. I think that the Holy Spirit wants me to recognize that my anger is as much a part of this illusion as anything else... the only power it has is the power I give it. This is the balancing act I was referring to that leaves me feeling shaky. I believe that taking my rage out on others will only reinforce my guilt and my ego. I am tired of being physically cold and repressing my anger. The belief in and fear of my rage has the same effect of reinforcing my ego. Just like the example of watching the news or not watching the news I am reinforcing my defensive thinking by denying my rage and by expressing it... I fear it both ways. I don't have an answer here. I do now know that when I feel physically cold I am angry at something. I do take this to Jesus and say "Hey I must be ticked off at something... any clues you can give me"? I have not come to terms with this question. I do not know the answer, only the question. I continue to ask for Jesus' help and then I resist the help because I am afraid. As I notice the fear of my rage and allow myself to be guided by the Holy Spirit, eventually I will experience that the power I have given to my fear of rage is not real. For now I struggle with this lesson.

Acting in the world is how we have the opportunity to look at how we think. Continue to live your life the way you always have. In your life you may have many activities that motivate you and in which you are invested. At our jobs and in our lives we take points of view and give of our time and money to causes. Keep doing these things. There is no reason not to. This is the classroom of opportunity! This is how you begin to look at your investment and your beliefs. Let's say that you are invested in saving rain forests (or any other cause you believe in). You put your time into helping to prevent lumber companies from clear-cutting a forest. What are your thoughts and feelings towards people who work in the companies that clear-cut the forests? Be honest with yourself here. How do you think God would view these people? This is your opportunity. The world is our classroom. Live like you always have; ask for a new Teacher. This is when you look.

I think this is an important point and one worth going into. We have to start from the idea that this world is an illusion. If that is true, then the people and events in the dream are symbols that can create an opportunity for you to look at the unhealed interpretations that you project on them. We have to assume that there is a collective dream going on and everyone who believes that he or she is in the world projects his interpretations or her thoughts onto everything and everyone around them. So if I become angry with someone, it is not too helpful for me to yell at him or her if I no longer want to lend my strength to defensive thinking… like Jewel's song has taught me. I want to withdraw my projections and take them to a Teacher who can help me interpret them from a non-defensive stance. So I take the thought to Jesus… but I still live in the world, so then what?

## Cause and Effect

All thought is a reflection, or mirror, of my relationship with God. If the world is an illusion and everything in it is a symbol, then the symbols have to represent a belief we hold. I believe that the dream we call our life reflects our relationship with God. We believe, often on an unconscious level, that we are in conflict with God. That we have done something that has caused God to be angry (fearful). We are angry and fearful all the time. In our state of fear we look around and we say there must be a reason I am angry or afraid. Then we find a reason outside of ourselves. We blame the thing outside of us for what we feel inside. We literally reverse the cause of our fear and refer to the fear as an effect. *A Course In Miracles* explains that in this world we have literally reversed cause and effect and we see them out of order (Text page 450 T-21.II.10). We think that an effect (you made me angry when you cut me off on the road) is a cause (I feel angry). Jesus explains that the opposite is true. Let me explain this from the idea of a sleeping dream. When you are sleeping you have a thought within your mind. You then see a symbol that represents your thought. We call this a dream. In sleeping dreams the symbolic representation of a thought (what you see) is an effect of that thought. The thought comes first and it is the cause and the symbol or effect is the image in the dream.

Most of us can agree that in sleeping dreams that thought precedes the image we see. Maybe, just maybe this world is an illusion… a dream. Then this idea that a thought precedes an image takes on a whole new meaning. When I remember to look around during my day and bring into my awareness this idea that thoughts happen prior to images, I have the opportunity to notice the state of my thinking. How am I reacting to the world around me? What reactions am I having? My reactions tell me the teacher that I have chosen. I then have true choice at my disposal. Again I am referring to thoughts only. I notice the calmness or the chaos in my mind based on how I react and feel about my day. The idea is to notice my attitude and my state of mind; am I peaceful or am I anxious. I know what teacher I have chosen based on how I am feeling about the world around me. I do not try to change the world. I notice my mind and then I have the power to change my teacher.

Let's look at the idea of creating abundance in your life. When I thought about the boat I wanted, the thought of that boat preceded its appearance in my life. If we expand on this idea perhaps we will come to the conclusion that thought or belief always precedes form. The idea is clear with the sailboat. I had the idea that I wanted a sailboat I thought about it and put my emotions and feelings into the thought. I began to believe that I had this boat and then... Voila! I had one.

Let's take this idea one step further and think about other things that seem to happen in your life without your requesting them. Many of us feel that we are helpless to change our circumstance in life. We feel helpless and like victims of the world. I often wonder about this idea. If I can create consciously when I put my thoughts in that direction, do I create unconsciously all the time? Is this illusion the creation of a dreaming mind? What exactly am I responsible for within the illusion? And if I am the dreamer of this dream how do I access the part of my self that decides whom I am taking as my teacher? I end up not knowing who I am at all with these questions. Ken teaches that the part of our mind that has true choice is the decision-maker. I will refer to the decision-maker as the part of the mind that chooses for the sake of simplicity. The decision-maker is the part of our mind that can choose teachers... it is the part that holds all of our power. The decision-maker only has two things between which to choose- the Holy Spirit who will reflect the correction into the dream, or the ego that reflects defensive thinking into the dream.

I struggle with keeping a balance between being kind and doing what I believe is right. I may find that I lose my ability to stay peaceful and keep the Holy Spirit as my teacher, when I am in a struggle and invested in its end result. When I am invested in the outcome of a perceived problem I know that I need to pay close attention to my thoughts, my beliefs and the teacher that I choose to help me. I want to share an example of a parent being very angry with me because she believed that I had treated her daughter unfairly. We disagreed about her daughter's behavior and her ability to safely go on a school trip. I would not allow her daughter to attend the trip because she will not follow adult directions when she is angry. Her parents disagreed with my decision. They called my supervisor and, after my supervisor and I spoke, I called the parents back. I informed them that their daughter could not go on the trip unless one of them accompanied her. Again the parents disagreed with this and continued to be upset with my decision. They showed up at my office the following morning. I was tense, a bit fearful and angry. I concluded that the reason I was feeling all of this was due to these parents. Then I asked for Christ's Vision in this situation. I began to recognize that I was fearful and tense prior to our disagreeing on their daughter's behavior.

But if these parents were not the cause of my fear, then what was? If the thought precedes the image, then I was projecting my fear onto these parents... but the fearful thought was there first. What is the fear really about then? Had I become fearful that this might indeed be an illusion in which I believe myself to be? I am attached to this idea of being Catherine as an individual (you bet I am). I don't want to be part of something that does not include my individuality. I fear that not being this individual will leave me being a Borg drone. I often resist the concept that I may be the dreamer and not a figure within the dream. I become angry and resentful of the Holy Spirit... the fear is that if I keep looking at my life as if it were a mirror of the thoughts of the sleeper... then I may wake up and Catherine would not be so important. That thought combined with a deep-rooted belief that God (the Queen Borg) is angry with me and I should not awaken to Him creates great fear and resistance within me.

Now why would God be angry with me? The contradictions that we have learned as a Judeo-Christen culture haunt me. We are taught that God is love, but if you don't play by his rules he sends you to hell. Love then has the capacity to hate? He kills his bad children and picks out the good and special ones to whom he gives special favor. Then He sacrifices His Son because we are sinful. Deep down I fear this God. I hate a God who will set me up to suffer. I am troubled too by the idea that God chooses when we die. He steals our life (or our individuality). It sets God up to be ruthless. I am not satisfied or consoled by the idea that people are chosen to join God in Heaven. This idea puts God in the role of a vengeful unkind father. I don't believe that the God of the Bible is very loving. That is why a part of my thoughts that has the Biblical ideas of God embedded in it fears and resents this God. He cannot be love and do such hateful things. I think that the Biblical God is a symbol within the illusion. As a symbol within our illusion we have projected our thinking onto this illusory-God. All the contradiction and cruelty that we think but reject as our thoughts, we give to this illusory -God. Then we justify and rationalize our behaviors without taking responsibility for our thoughts and beliefs. After all this ego-God has justified our behavior! He rejected Adam and Eve and he rejected those who hurt his chosen ones. These symbols of the illusory-God reflect the state of mind of the dreamer, not the state of mind of God. This world is not a very loving place. We are brutal to those we exclude from our circle of special people. I don't believe that God could have created such a frightening place to 'send' his children. The sleeping mind mis-created this concept of God... and the unkind concept reflects the state of fear in the dreaming mind. We literally project our worst fears onto a made-up God. Because we believe that the illusion is reality, we believe that our made-up God is true.

Let's stretch your beliefs a bit and bring into question a myth that in our Judeo-Christian culture we often accept as the truth. Most of us believe that God created this world. The *Course* teaches that God did not create this world and that it is our mind that believes the world is real (Workbook page 23 W-14.1). We explain the horror of this place as our punishment for disobeying God and being cast out of Heaven. What if this idea was incorrect? Let's imagine that perhaps God did not create this world and that God, being Love did not cast anyone out of Heaven. What then could be the reason that we believe that we are here to begin with? Let me share with you my understanding of the myth that *A Course In Miracles* has taught me. In Heaven everything is one. There cannot be individuality in total oneness. Individuality and oneness are mutually exclusive. We believe that we live in a world where all of us are individuals. We see separation all around us. I fill up a space and I am limited to the space that I fill up. You occupy a separate space. We are not connected. Heaven would be the direct opposite to this. We would all be connected and where we began and ended would not exist. This is a state that I cannot imagine let alone accurately describe. Most of us understand at least intellectually that there cannot be two in the idea of one. For this explanation Heaven can only be a state of oneness. There cannot be anything in Heaven that is not totally connected to the All of God. And God is totally connected to everything. In a state of knowing God then we are abstract ideas that contain the totality of God within us. As creations of God, His Sons, we share all with everyone... because there is only one.

The staff at the Foundation has taught me to look at the Adam and Eve myth with an understanding that individuality is a tiny mad and unreal idea. They have taught me to see this story as a projection of defensive thinking. Cause and effect are out of order in this myth. The Judeo-Christian myth of Adam and Eve has reversed this idea of who kicked whom out of Heaven. (Remember that cause and effect idea). The Son of God (that is you and I) had an idea of individuality, or having two, in Heaven. The *Course* refers to this idea as the "tiny mad idea" (Text page 586 T-27.VIII.6.2). God knew this to be impossible and He smiled sweetly at the idea knowing that there can be no individuality in Heaven. There cannot be a state of someone having something that another lacks (isn't that idea beautiful). The idea of differences, lack and specialness cannot be part of life with God. The Son of God, who is One with His Creator God, liked the idea of individuality. The Son decided that He would like to be an individual. Again God smiled sweetly knowing that this was impossible. The Son took the idea of individuality seriously. In taking it seriously the Son began to believe that the idea was true. This is why the emphasis on what you believe is so important. The mistake in this myth is that Son's *belief. A Course In Miracles* teaches that a" tiny mad idea" crept into the mind of God's son (Text page 586 T-27.VIII.6.2). The idea was the thought of individuality. In Heaven this idea is considered madness, psychotic and literally impossible. The Son of God cannot separate from His Source (God), as there is no life outside of Heaven. The Son knew that God is only One. So the myth continues as the Son of God insisted that he be an individual and he made the choice to pursue this goal. He knew that to have two would mean that he would be separated from Oneness and that he would be different from God. This idea like an addiction compelled the Son. On some level the Son of God also believed that if there were individuality then Oneness would have been sacrificed. The Son of God began to *believe* that he separated from God. The thought of sacrificing Oneness or God caused the Son to feel guilty… but the smell of individuality is sweet, and the Son of God in an act of selfishness took what he desired. Then He fell into a deep sleep, prompted by a deep sense of shame, guilt, loss and fear. In His sleep He is dreaming that He has shattered the Oneness of God for His selfish desire to be an individual. If you look around the world you will see this theme reflected everywhere. It will include an idea that for me to live (physically, emotionally and spiritually) you have to die (be proven wrong, do without so that I have, or physically die). The theme accompanies a deep emptiness that includes loss, shame, guilt and fear. These themes that are reflected in our illusion are an *effect* of an untrue belief that we shattered Heaven. The cause is the belief… but (thank goodness) the belief is mistaken. God continues to smile sweetly at His sleeping Son… nothing happened.

Most of us have no conscious belief in this myth. We have no memory and no idea that this theme of shattering oneness is playing out in our minds. The idea is so horrific and causes us such pain that we cannot access it. We have to look around the world and notice the theme of "kill or be killed" (Manual page 45-46 M-17.7.11). We have to recognize the guilt and shame we see within ourselves and notice how unkind the world really is to begin to imagine that there might be some hidden terror in my mind that I am reflecting outside of myself. This is why the process can be rather time-consuming. It is too frightening to contemplate this thought. When I first read these ideas in the *Course,* and when I first heard Ken teaching these ideas *I* thought they were ludicrous. I had the thought that this was the stupidest thing I had heard to date. I defended against the idea by shaking my head and saying to myself that some of the ideas in this *Course* are so helpful, but this one is a joke. I still have trouble with this idea. I currently believe it has some value as it helps me understand why the world is such an unkind and violent place. It was made, according to this myth, on the idea that for me to have what I want you must be sacrificed. For me to live you must give me what I want. *A Course In Miracles* teaches that one of the beliefs we live by is the idea of one or the other. We both cannot have the same thing so if one of us has it the other has to do without. We live in a world of limited resources. Our economic principles are based on this idea of supply and demand... someone must loose for someone to win. According to the *Course* to give and receive is the same thing (Text page 540 T-25.IX.10). Again keep in mind the idea that this is on the level of thought. If you give away a dollar you might not get a dollar in return in the world. If you give away a state of mind that is full of revenge and hate you will get back anxiety, paranoia and fear. If you give away an idea that you are safe in Heaven and this is a dream worth watching right now so you can learn to heal your mind, you will get a feeling of safety and calm. To give and receive on the level of thought are the same thing consciously and unconsciously. This is why monitoring your thoughts, and not defending them so that they stay unconscious, can help bring you peace.

To believe that you can shatter Heaven, shatter God, contains the arrogance that we see projected in our belief that we can sin and offend God in any way in this dream. The violence (psychological, emotional and physical) we see projected in our world is merely a reflection of the projection that we separated from God (a violent act), and destroyed God in the process. We deserve to be punished for this selfish violent act of the murder of God. We in no way want to accept responsibility for the shattering of Heaven. That is why we do not look within. We believe that this myth is true. We reverse this idea in many of the religions of the world (to avoid responsibility) and we make God the "heavy" who will punish us for the sin of shattering oneness. The religions of the world don't do this out of malice; but they too believe that this dream is reality and religions base their teaching on this principle. We as the dreamer of this dream, the decision-maker who believes it is an individual, are terrified by what we believe we did to God. All of our defensive thinking is our insistence that we keep our individuality and not look at what we believe the cost was, for separation from our Source. Every defense mechanism that we use is set up to keep us not looking at our fears of this myth and to prevent us from realizing that we are still home in Heaven dreaming. How, do you imagine, life in this world would look if you knew on an experiential level that you were safe at home in Heaven dreaming of exile... just dreaming?

God knows that individuality is not true. We do not contain within ourselves the ability to shatter God. God has remained Himself. He is still One and we are still One within Him as His Child. Nothing at all has happened. We simply have fallen asleep and we are having a nightmare about individuality. The true God who is part of our True Self is still perfectly One… and in truth so are we.

Within the dream the fear feels horrible. We need something to blame for this uncomfortable feeling… so within the dream we literally dream up a conflict so we can say that we have a reason to feel so ill at ease. The lack of ease is the cause and it is present first. We don't know that we are dreaming so we look for a reason for our discomfort and an image presents itself within the dream to justify the feeling. Behind the feeling is a belief. If you change the belief then you change the feeling. If the belief is changed, to one of a kinder, gentler God, then the fear will disappear. The images within the dream may still be doing unkind things. The Holy Spirit will help you to change your mind about what you perceive; He will interpret the dream through the eyes of defenselessness and the absence of fear. When you have the experience that you are dreaming, all the fear of the dream disappears. No image within the dream has the power to take your peace from you. It is our belief and interpretation that the dream is real and having an effect on us that is the problem. The dream, if it were seen as such, would not be a problem. Looking at the dream in this way makes us one hundred percent responsible for all that we believe within the dream.

This does not mean on a practical level that we are responsible for all the figures in our dreams and their actions. That is not practical and I don't think it would be helpful. We are responsible for the way we act and react to the dream. When I am having a lucid dream images and events that appear to be out of my control drift by me. Crazy things happen like in many sleeping dreams. The power of a lucid dream is not controlling the images of my dream, I don't know how to do that, it is in knowing that it is not true and watching it. The power is in knowing that nothing in my nightmare can hurt me, because I am not in my nightmare. I am having the dream; I am not a character in the dream. I am beyond the dream in truth. That is the power and the lesson. Nothing at all is happening to me.

The dream tells me about the state of my mind of the dreamer. I can observe what happens in the dream and look at how the mind that is dreaming is thinking. This process can be rather disconcerting. This collective dream is insane. As I said earlier, kill or be killed is the theme of this illusion. Sometimes we destroy each other on a psychological level, sometimes on an emotional level. Often we physically kill each other. The illusion tells us all we need to know about the mind of the sleeping dreamer. The dreamer is terrified. The terror is symbolically represented by the figures in the dream. The thought comes first and the image or symbol in the dream is given the attributes of the thoughts of the dreamer.

This is the same process as my visualizing a sailboat in my life. The thought comes first and the symbol follows the thought. Why can we create things within our illusion? The answer is simply that our minds are powerful enough to change the symbols within the illusion. The power of our minds is a lesson that I am continuing to ask for guidance in learning. The reversal of cause and effect intrigues me.

## Tough Love… living life practically

How can we live normal lives and practice these ideas in the world? This is the practical stuff that I was talking about. I ask God "So now what? I bring my anger and fearful thinking to You, but I still have to deal with the person who is driving me crazy." I still have to live and function in the world that I believe I live in as Catherine. This is where faith and letting go of control take some practice. I want to give a practical example. In the school where I work in I am part of the crisis team. We are called in when a teacher cannot manage a teenager and needs him or her removed from the classroom. There are kids in school who have to be restrained if they are going to be violent to themselves or others. When the crisis team arrives we attempt to talk a teen down, or calm them down, with words. The goal is safety for everyone involved. A child who feels unsafe is more likely to act out his fear. We attempt to create a safe room for the frightened and angry teen. I will set limits and listen. Often I just stay quiet and let the child vent his anger in words. Other times I set quick, firm limits. If I can talk a kid down from a crisis, I will. If I can get him to leave with me safely, calmly and with his dignity intact, I will. If all my attempts are failing, I set clearer boundaries and explain the consequences of the child's inability to follow my instructions. I let him know that I will not allow him to hurt himself or someone else. I tell him in no uncertain terms that his safety is too important. If he cannot keep himself safe then I will. If a child still cannot keep safe, the team restrains him. A restraint can be done with Love as your teacher. It would not be kind to allow a child to hurt himself or someone else. When you let that happen you are reinforcing defensive thinking in the child. All teenagers know that they are not suppose to hurt people, so allowing them to do so is saying it is ok for you to teach yourself that you are a bad kid. You are also disrespecting them by giving them more power then they can manage. Adults are in charge at school. That is how it is done and that is how you create school safety. An out of control teenager is asking for help. My job at that time is to help him. I ask the Holy Spirit for guidance the whole time. I have had multiple experiences of restraining a teenager with Love as my guide. It is an interesting process to witness in your own mind. My presentation may look strong and firm. Within my thoughts I am calm and easy. I feel like an observer of the events taking place in the room. I can say at that time that I feel like I did with Abby... nothing that is occurring is personal, and my job is only to be as helpful as I can be.

I keep coming back to the idea that I am always referring to how we think and the teacher that we choose to help us in life. I have learned from the *Course* that we have two teachers: The Holy Spirit and the ego. We always choose one of them. The power of decision lies here. Will we learn from the perspective of illusions or from the perspective of Truth? That is our only real choice. Looking at your beliefs should be a practical experience. No change in behavior is required. You simply look; you ask the Holy Spirit to help you change your mind from what you currently believe, to His belief. Then you open your mind to the new belief. That's all. You stop right there. If God is love, then all of our fears of Him are part of the illusion. Fear is not any truer than any other part of our dream. Fear is a mistake. From God's perspective there is nothing to fear. From the perspective of the illusion this is a hard concept to believe. That is why we ask for spiritual guidance. The Holy Spirit knows that He is still connected to the Oneness of God. We have forgotten that part. We believe that the dream is real, so fear is real too. The Holy Spirit as a teacher is outside of the dream. He knows the Truth from the illusion and He can give you access to the Truth within yourself if you allow Him to help you. He knows that God is not angry. That Love cannot be deceived and that the nightmare, to which we are so strongly connected, is only a confused thought that has had no effect at all on your True Self.

Most of the time we don't want to know that this world, which we think is so important, is an illusion. That this personality and body into which we put so much time and effort is not real. Young children believe that monsters come to life at night. You can tell them that this is not so, but they will continue to believe in monsters. As much as they try to believe your comforting words, they still believe in their childish imaginings. Forcing the idea down a child's throat prior to their growing-up a bit, that monsters are make-believe is fruitless and silly. To please you a child may pretend not to believe in monsters, but the fear of monsters will remain. A child may need a parent to check his closet and under the bed prior to retiring to sleep so he is not afraid. You as the adult know that there is nothing to fear, but you also know that your child believes in the monster, so you ease his fear and check the closet and under the bed. With patience and kindness you check to ease your child's fear. You know that as your child matures she will grow out of the belief in monsters. Most parents don't worry about a young child being fearful of the dark as it is common in childhood. The Holy Spirit considers us just like a small child. *A Course In Miracles* makes multiple references to us as spiritually young children. We insist that the world is real; we insist that we are individuals. The Holy Spirit knows that forcing our young frightened minds to accept that this life of ours is make believe would be unkind. So he begins where we are, knowing that we will grow up and recognize reality at some point. He is endlessly patient; He will help us see that our fears and worries are based on false beliefs when we ask. The Holy Spirit will teach us at a pace that does not heighten our terror. Like a good parent he will correct our mistakes as we open up to correction. He does not believe in sacrifice or suffering of any kind so it is impossible that He cause any. He will not take from you, cause you loss in any way and He will not insist that you accept an idea that seems beyond belief to you. He knows that we are only having a nightmare about being individuals... but we don't.

As we grow and mature we will begin to let go of our childish beliefs and accept the truth. Our resistance to the truth can be intense! I know who I am in this illusion. This individual self might not always have it perfect, but I know her and I am attached to her. If the world is an illusion then I am not the individual I think I am. Who am I then? The search for the True Self comes to life with this question. For most of us this question causes great fear... and it gives us great hope. It is the beginning of exposing our self-deception. My True Self breathes a sigh of relief when I ask it... the defensive individual panics at the idea.

### Notice a thought 'float' by

There have been times in my job where I have been angry with a teenager that I am in a position to restrain. Asking for help at that point may take the form of my asking someone else to restrain this student right now. Good advice from a good Teacher. Acting out of anger is rarely helpful and can be hurtful to a child and to myself. There are times during a restraint where I will notice my thoughts are unkind or angry. Perhaps I feel powerful and find that I am enjoying the restraint. Once I noticed that I was getting a good upper body workout and I did not mind the struggle. These thoughts often can leave me feeling uncomfortable. They feel ugly. Just like allowing a child to hurt someone is allowing them to reinforce the idea that they are bad, these thoughts leave me asking who I am and what do these thoughts teach me about myself? I used to take these thoughts to heart and think that I was mean or dangerous. Today with the help of Jesus and Jewel's song I no longer lend these thoughts strength.

I spoke of meditation earlier. I mentioned that my meditation teacher advised me to notice a thought floating by and to watch it. He taught me not to resist that thought... simply to observe it. I have expanded the concept of observing my thought during a meditation to observing my thoughts throughout the day. I generalized the concept to help me expand my learning. Whenever I remember I watch my thoughts and notice without resistance the idea within my mind. So I have this ugly, unkind thought. I have a number of choices. I can choose to take the thought seriously and reinforce my defenses, consciously and unconsciously stating that such an unkind thought must mean that I am an unkind person. My self-hate is reinforced and my belief that I deserve to be punished is justified. I can repress and project the thought onto someone else saying she is the bad person and if she had not been so rotten I would not have such angry, hateful twisted thoughts about her. This justifies the thought and negates our responsibility for what we think. We are masters of deceiving ourselves; pretending that our thoughts do not begin in our minds. If I am not responsible for the thoughts that I think, if they are out of my control, then it must be that I am the victim of forces that I am helpless to prevent. The belief behind this kind of thinking is "it's not my fault."

I also have the option to notice the thought and simply not give it any strength. I ask God to help me see this thought from his view and then I stop. I stop analyzing, contemplating and judging. I just say "There I go again thinking defensive thoughts... what do you think about that Jesus"? It is essential that I accept responsibility for my thought and then ask for help seeing the thought through the eyes of the Holy Spirit. Taking responsibility puts the power back in the mind of the thinker.

I spoke earlier of my acupuncture doctor helping me to recognize that when I am physically cold it is because I am angry. I love the defense mechanism reaction formation as it is so sneaky. I don't want to be cold anymore which means that I have to look at why I am resisting being angry. I fear my temper and I fear that if I really let this temper out I would be vicious and out of control. I don't know about you, but I don't enjoy feeling out of control. There is also the social pressure of women being 'nice'... not to mention that I am a social worker by education and you know their reputation for saving the world and all that goody-two-shoes stuff. So my personality has bought in to the idea that I have to be nice. Being angry is not so nice so I hide this anger in my body. I give the anger great strength and reinforce it by defending against it. Now I want to reclaim my strength and stop giving it away in this defensive stance. Practically speaking, Ken's advice to me was that I have a couple of temper tantrums and recognize that they are no big deal and certainly nothing to fear. Here comes that balancing act again because I don't want to hurt others and in that process teach myself that my temper is volatile and to be feared. I asked for (and continue to ask for) lots of help with this one. It is a challenge to manage not replacing one defense with a different one. It is here that humility is essential in the learning process. I don't know how to do this so I cannot teach it. My faith is in the Holy Spirit and I have to hand him the reigns of my life so I can see an option that keeps me warm and does not reinforce my defenses. When I do this my temper appears to be silly. Many of the students I work with throw temper tantrums that may or may not be directed at me. I don't take them personally and I can watch them with the Holy Spirit and see within them a call for love, as the *Course* refers to it (Text page 217 T-12.I.8.7-13). The process is the same. I identify with Catherine as my self, but she is no different from any other character in my dream. The Holy Spirit has been able to help me observe my temper tantrums with the same compassion and kindness that I have for my students when they have tantrums. Compassion for others in the dream is the same exact process as self-compassion. Our focus is on this individual self as someone important and therefore somehow different from others. Seeing this difference is an ego deception. We are the same; individuality is the lie.

### You learn what you teach

Jewel's song "Life Uncommon" from her CD called *Spirit* has helped me come to terms with the idea that I will learn what I teach. What is it that I would like to learn... that is what I teach. The *Course* as I have mentioned before teaches that, on the level of thought, to give and to receive are the same. Where we put our focus then makes a difference in what we want to learn. I think in our lives the decision-maker in our minds can decide that we want to learn something... just as I am currently deciding that I want to learn *A Course In Miracles* so I am attempting to teach it to myself. The reflection of this is seen in the writing of this book and the devotion I have to studying this work. Catherine did not make the decision. It was made by the decision-maker and is reflected in the life of Catherine. The perspective and attitude we take throughout the trials of life always reflect the focus of learning the decision-maker has chosen. We drones follow orders.

I have contemplated sharing a story of mine that leaves me feeling vulnerable, but it has been such a powerful lesson for me that I am going to take the risk.... Part of my logic is that I know I can continue to learn from this lesson and I want to know the power and motivation of my mind. The *Course* instructs extensively about watching our defensive thinking, or egos as the *Course* calls it, so that we can choose the Holy Spirit as our teacher. If you are not aware that you have been defending yourself, then it is hard to stop defending. The first step is always to look. I have been referring to this as watching or observing. You observe a thought and then you bring that thought to the Holy Spirit and ask for a change of perception.

In my twenties I was in an emotionally abusive relationship. I allowed a man to treat me like a doormat and in the process I felt like I lost a vital part of myself. There were points in this relationship when I literally lost my ability to speak up for myself. I feared his rejection and the fear made me dumb. It was as if my brain shut off and I could find no words to say. I felt empty and I hated the person I was becoming. I began to believe that I was weak and pathetic. The relationship was a humiliating blow to my sense of strength. I had the image that I was strong and that image was shattering. I did not know myself anymore. I hated that man with a vengeance... and I allowed that hate to eat me up inside for years. (Remember I had to have the belief in being weak and pathetic first, then within my dream I find someone to prove that my belief is correct).

During my study of the *Course* I have been looking at the concept of life being a mirror on a much deeper level. I have taken the belief I developed in high school and expanded it to symbolism. If the world is an illusion and I am the dreamer, then why in the world would I put into my illusion such an unhappy event? Is that a part of who I am? What would be the purpose of seeing myself as weak, pathetic and speechless? I have brought this question to Jesus with great trepidation. You see the *Course* has helped me learn that the me I think I am, (the 'I' who can create abundance, not I Catherine), am dreaming. Part of my dream includes that I can be weak, pathetic and easily victimized. But along with being victimized there is a part of my mind that believes it is hurtful, unkind and will victimize to have its way. That man who I hated with such intensity is literally a figure in my dream; a part of myself from which I have split off because I do not want to look at how unkind I can be. The self-concept that believes that I can be cruel is not very pretty to look at. I took that victimizer, repressed it and projected it onto a man. Then I was no longer responsible for it. To heal these thoughts that frighten me, I first have to understand that I, the part of me that is mind and is dreaming, set them up. Then I have to take them to the Holy Spirit and say "Help... this frightens me. I don't like this part of who I believe I am... what is the purpose of putting something so ugly into my illusion?" The sleeping mind represents its thoughts in form within the illusion or within the dream.

Therefore everything within the illusion symbolically exposes a belief that the mind contains. Keep in mind that a belief is not a fact. A learned concept or belief is perceived and interpreted by the mind that thinks it. My experience of being connected to my Mind and the Holy Spirit is one of sublime peace, an absence of fear, need or judgment of any kind. Being connected to the world as a body is an experience that is full of fear, neediness, apprehension and a constant waiting for the little that I have to be taken from me supposedly by a loving God. These experiences contradict each other. They cannot coexist. One of them must be wrong. It is my hope that the fearful experience of being a vulnerable body is the mistaken belief. The identification that I have with this belief, that I am a body and an individual who can easily be cruel or be victimized, is strong and I am not willing to give up this belief in it's entirety. I do question it. I question my belief that fear is real? I ask Jesus "is fear real? Help me to learn your interpretation of my belief in fear". This lesson I would like to learn.

The part of this story that leaves me feeling vulnerable is not the idea that I was in an unkind relationship or that I allowed my hate to control me for an extended period of time. Losing my ability to speak up for myself does leave me feeling vulnerable. The worst vulnerability, the thing I hate to look at let alone admit, is that I am responsible for this theme being in my dream to begin with. It leaves me feeling crazy and dumb. Why on earth would I hurt myself like this? Why? I do think that we are often self-punishing in this world. We are so unaware of and so fearful about the myth of shattering Heaven for our individuality that we unconsciously condemn our self for this. In our individual selfish state we reason that perhaps self-punishment will help God forgive us our so-called sins. We attempt to punish ourselves so maybe God will see that we have suffered and he will forgive us. If this myth were true and God was angry for our 'escape' from Heaven, then suffering here to earn eternity in Heaven would be a logical thing to do. But if this is an illusion, then this idea of suffering to repay God for the sin of stealing life or individuality from Him is not necessary. If this is a dream and we are asleep then God does not even know about the dream. Like a parent who cannot enter a child's sleeping dream God cannot enter ours. (Perhaps when we wake up we can tell Him about it).

Let's look at this man that I spent so much time hating. He is a figure in my dream. Everyone in a dream is a symbolic representation of the state of the mind of the dreamer. The symbols of the dream all originate at the same place. They come from one mind that projects thought into form. Within my mind are a victimizer and a victim. I see them both in my dream and both of the characters are part of my mind. It is helpful for me to recognize that on a deep unconscious level I prefer to feel as if I am a victim of others and to deny the victimizer that is part of my thoughts. I take this insight to the Holy Spirit and I ask for help to understand it. On a practical level I am not responsible for the actions of any character within my dream outside of myself. I am responsible for how I act and react to the characters. On the level of mind, a level on which I do not live, taking responsibility for the characters at large may make sense. Currently I am still strongly identified with my individual self. I see myself as a body and personality inhabiting the world. Viewing myself as responsible for the actions of others would drive me crazy and would leave me feeling helpless. An internal locus of control would not be possible if this were the case. Perhaps as we mature and grow up spiritually we learn about the responsibility we have for all of the characters within our dream. I do not know. What I do know is that for now it would be impractical to accept responsibility for other actions. It is essential to the process that you take responsibility for yours.

I spoke earlier of the fear about God. I want to review this idea again as it is often hard to keep it in our conscious awareness. The Biblical God is the God onto whom we typically project this victimizing self. This is the God who threw us out of Eden. This is the God who punishes us when we are bad. This thought of victimization is a thought within the mind of the dreamer. This fear of God is there too. How and why did we ever come to fear God and see Him as our oppressor? And if the thought of oppression and unkind acts like murder are in the mind of the dreamer, how in the world did they get there? The *Course* explains that God is perfect oneness. Oneness cannot have two. Gloria Wapnick uses the term twoness in her teaching about the separation. In this illusion we have twoness or separation. You and I are separate and different. Twoness implies that oneness has been shattered. Something must have shattered Heaven because in our experience we see ourselves as individuals. We believe that we are separate from God and we never question if perhaps we are mistaken. What is two can never be one again. We do not question if being separated is true… we accept our perceptions as fact and we do not want to believe that we as individuals are responsible for the shattering of Heaven and, as a result, the death of God. Keep in mind that this is a myth. Nothing has happened to God and Oneness is still the truth. This mistaken belief that we are responsible for killing God, and that God (who cannot die) is seeking revenge, causes overwhelming guilt and fear within our mind. We will gladly punish ourselves and allow others to treat us unfairly if we don't have to take responsibility for shattering Heaven. Most of these ideas are unconscious. For the most part most of us do not consciously believe that we shattered Heaven, but we do symbolically act this out within our illusion. Within the defense mechanisms of this illusion it is believed that someone or something must have murdered God because we are no longer one. In the dream we see ourselves as individuals because we believe the illusion is reality. We believe that Oneness has been shattered. We know that God cannot die- after all, He is God. We do assume that this must anger God. We fear God's anger (the anger is ours with God for refusing to grant our wish for individuality). We project our anger with God onto Him. Then within that projection we begin to fear God's wrath (Manuel pages 45-46 M-17.7-10). This process is a major unconscious theme within the illusion. There is not one of us who would want to accept responsibility... or even remember that he is part of the so-called murder of God. This causes great guilt and as I explained earlier guilt is the motivation behind projection. Victimization is seen as outside of my body. It is not within myself. I would gladly be the victim of someone as long as I do not have to see the victimizer within. The thought that we are capable of great selfish acts of violence is powerful. Defenses hide these thoughts from our conscious awareness and this is why we defend. If I have to accept responsibility for shattering Heaven the guilt of that thought would be overwhelming and terrifying. Again keep in mind that an illusion is not true. Our defenses are defending a lie... nothing happened in Heaven and there is no world.

To many of us these ideas initially sound pretty far out there. As individuals we do not have the power to shatter Heaven. Keep in mind that I am not talking to the you who you see walking around in the world. That you is part of the illusion. I am speaking about the sleeping you, who thinks that you are an individual in the world, the decision-maker. This sleeping mind is full of a fear that is based on a false belief that Heaven was shattered by the thought of individuality. Thought creates form... like the sailboat I spoke of earlier. We see twoness because it is in our thoughts and we believe in it. Well, this sleeping Son of God is having a dream where Oneness no longer exists. The Son of God remembers Oneness and the love and peace that Heaven contains and is longing for it. This longing is mirrored all over our dream. We long for love, for that special someone to fill the void within our heart. We long for power, glory, adoration and pleasure. This longing symbolically represents our longing for the Love of God and for the Heaven that we mistakenly believe we destroyed. The Son falsely believes that He shattered Heaven. This thought fills His mind with terror, guilt and great fear, mirrored in His dream. God is not dead and Heaven has not been shattered. The Son of God merely has to waken from this nightmarish illusion to recall (with great hope) that He has been mistaken.

When I left the abusive relationship I had been in and got back on my feet, I swore that no one would ever again treat me so unkindly. I no longer would allow it. Those words are incredibly defensive and they carry with them great fear. They sound good in the view of the world and my mom would say "You go Girl!" but they are not easy or gentle. You see I don't know how I allowed this to happen in the first place, so I don't know how to prevent it from happening again. I still hate that part of who I am. I am repulsed by the part of me that loses my voice, and I fear it. My practice of looking at my thoughts and bringing them to God has helped me to have a calm peace and deep sense of completion in my life for longer and longer periods of time. I have begun to trust the process and I am eternally grateful for the guidance of the Holy Spirit. So I bring the question "Why do I lose my ability to speak up for myself?" to Jesus and ask to see this defense through His eyes. For years to come I imagine, I will continue to bring this fear to Him. It is the ugly (but untrue) part of me that the Holy Spirit can heal. If I continue to repress, project and fear it, I am lending it my strength. I no longer want to do that. So I have to look, or else I keep chasing my tail. When I look at this speechless vulnerable part of who I believe I am with the Holy Spirit its lack of reality becomes clear to me. I look and I see the dream. I recognize that nothing at all happened to the dreamer. The dreamer is not "I Catherine." To Catherine many things seem to happen... when I look with the Holy Spirit I am connected to my mind... the dreamer. As I allow myself to be taught that I am dreaming I recognize that nothing at all is happening. This process fills me with true hope-- hope that there is a way home; hope that helps me to remember who I am in truth; hope that feels as if I am skipping with the glee of a five year old on Christmas eve. It is a joyful hope that is shared with everyone.

I often find myself 'stuck' after an experience of hopeful Joy. I expect that the Joy that I feel will remain. It does not stay, and the harder I struggle to find it, the more lost I become. The process is like the peeling of a huge onion. I look within and heal some piece of guilt and some fear dissipates. Then I forget that I am within an illusion or I become frightened of losing my individuality so I deny that I am the dreamer and begin projecting again. I have seen that I project this fear of being victimized onto others. I see people who cannot stand up for themselves and I hate them. They disgust me. I have met this easily victimized side of my self-concept in other arenas. When I am around someone whom I put on a pedestal, I lose my ability to talk. Once I was stuck in a train station in Poland. I needed to buy a train ticket and I was having trouble communicating with the ticket agent. I began feeling overwhelmed. That weak and frightened part of me came to visit. I decided to try to find someone who spoke English and Polish to help me purchase tickets. As I tried to ask for help I knew that I had lost my voice. I stood around for two hours, feeling helpless and frightened. I could not find the words to ask for assistance. I was with some friends but the idea to ask them for help did not even enter my mind. My friend Paul showed up after two hours of wasted time and asked if I had found anyone to help us buy tickets. I told him I was overwhelmed and he took over for me.

The thing that troubles me the most about setting myself up to be a victim within this dream is how I lose my ability to think when I become voiceless. I lose my voice and my power to assert myself altogether. I play victim as "Catherine" based on the belief that victimhood is real. When I refuse to accept responsibility for my desire to victimize, I repress it deeply and act exactly in opposition to those thoughts. This is an attempt to prove to myself that these thoughts are not mine. That is reaction formation as a defense in form. Losing my ability to stand up for myself, and believing that I am helpless, is still a self-concept that I hold onto. I want to look at the reason why I choose her. My stomach is tight as I write this. I can feel the muscles in my back fill with tension… I am full of fear. "Help me see this with You Jesus.…"

On the opposing side of helplessness is the victimizer, the other side of this coin. I do fear the so-called power of my temper. I go cold with fear when I catch my thoughts wanting to hurt or control others. I am particularly repulsed when I catch the pleasure I can enjoy at another's expense. We all experience this in more socially acceptable ways in our everyday lives. How about when your team wins and you are psyched that the other guy lost, or when you feel better then someone because you out performed them at work. I have explained that when my hands and feet are cold I am literally holding-in anger. I try to control the power that I fear and it expresses itself as "coldness" within my body. It is a great metaphor to look at symbolically. I fear being cold to others; so I turn that inward and become cold. The deep-rooted fear is, if I allow myself to get in touch with my belief that I am a victimizer, that I will become dangerous. What I have begun to practice is noticing that my hands and feet are cold and turning to the Holy Spirit and asking for help looking at what I fear with His eyes. I am often not in touch with the feeling of anger when I am cold. I just know that I must be angry and I am expressing it in a way that hurts me. So I ask for help and slowly I get warm. I am giving this fear of my temper great power. The only expression of this fear that feels safe for me today is for me to get physically cold (when I am angry I become distant and emotionally cold). Now that I know what the coldness in my extremities symbolizes I can address the problem in a kinder and gentler way; with the help of the Holy Spirit at my side. I do not know how the Holy Spirit will help me experience that my fear of my rage is not real. Again I struggle with how to balance this. My struggle is my inability to trust that He knows best. If I were to simply follow the guidance of Jesus and allow Him to show me His perspective on my rage, then there would not be a problem to contend with any longer.

Taking all of our nice, pretty and kind thoughts to the Holy Spirit is all well and good, but the healing is in the thoughts that we hide even from ourselves. I try not to punish myself for my hate of the weakness and vulnerability in others. I know it is my mirror and my condemnation will not help me whatsoever. In my twenties and early thirties I tried that route of projecting my self-condemnation and it did not keep me happy or peaceful. The fear and the self-condemnation have remained with me. I can project them all I want... they are my thoughts and my beliefs. Projection or defending them in any other way only reinforces them. The Holy Spirit can heal them... but only if I bring them to Him. I cannot bring what I do not know is there. This is why this process is so intra-psychic. No one can make you do this. The choice and power is yours. Initially the process seems fearful, but the results will speak for themselves.

## Avoid Self-punishment

When I catch my thoughts judging people or myself for not being strong and tough, for appearing weak and vulnerable my old habit was to become annoyed and disgusted with myself or the person onto whom I was projecting. This is my old habit. It is the behavior that keeps me running around in circles, thinking that I am getting somewhere. If I catch those thoughts now and I would like them to be corrected without defenses I simply say, "There I go again." I notice; I observe and attempt to allow the Holy Spirit to do the judging. Then I move on with my day. Just like the meditation example that I gave earlier. I notice; I don't indulge or resist the thought. The thought just is. I am giving a number of examples of practicing the same process. Try a few on and see how they feel.

Keep in mind that being unkind to anyone, yourself included, is not helpful to healing. It will happen because it is a bad habit. If you can do nothing else, work on the kindness. Behavior that is unkind reinforces defensive thinking. Unkind behavior teaches you that you are not a nice person. This lesson will reinforce the exact process that you are hoping to heal. Bad habits die slowly. The process can take a long time. Patience is essential as you practice. If being kind feels like a lie I think it is best to keep quiet. Keep your projections to yourself. This can be tricky; sometimes the kindest thing you can do is to stand up for yourself. Again I know that the Holy Spirit knows how to help you best. It is His advice and guidance that should be asked for and heeded. He can guide you through your hate in the least destructive way. His guidance will not glorify or deny your experience. He will help and in the process you will challenge your self-concepts, your beliefs and your perspective. He is a gentle teacher who will never force you to accept His view on a situation. He explains that He prefers that we be happy; if we insist on being right... so be it!

Ken has taught me to recognize that the Holy Spirit teaches through contrast. When I compare the way He interprets the situation I am in with the way I had been looking at any event or circumstance in my life, I am amazed at how radically different His thinking is. I am also always happier allowing His thinking to dominate my life. In recognizing the contrast as a good teaching tool, I have begun to understand that many (and perhaps all) of my beliefs can be reinterpreted by comparing my thoughts and beliefs to His thoughts and vision. As I study the *Course* it has become clear that some of our basic beliefs, like the belief in sin, how we view compassion and how we automatically judge (in both a positive and a negative way) are open to reinterpretation. Even our thoughts on who God is at His core are viewed very differently from the Holy Spirit's perspective. I have revisited some of my beliefs about God, sin and empathy. I have just scratched the surface of the idea that there is a radically different way to view these ideas. Allowing this new interpretation to become a way that I think keeps me happier. The idea is simple but the process can be a challenge.

# Chapter 7:

### Forgiveness Revisited

In my study of A *Course in Miracles* I have been very moved by the section in Chapter 31 called Self-Concept versus Self. This section has helped me to recognize that my self-concept is directly connected to how and what I believe. My perception of forgiveness has grown as my understanding of this section deepens. The *Course* describes sin as part of the illusion and therefore not real. Because it is not real it is correctable. The *Course* counters this argument that sin is real in Chapter 19 in the section Sin versus Error (and in many other places) (Text page 402 T-19. II.1). I have written this section based on my understanding of the Self-Concept verses Self section and the concept of forgiveness that the *Course* has taught me. Forgiveness from a Judeo-Christian perspective involves seeing sin in the world, believing that the sin is real, and then deciding that the person who sinned is worthy of being forgiven. This is the ego's plan of forgiveness (Text page 169 T-9.IV.4-5). Sometimes this forgiveness can involve seeing someone as less than yourself either morally, financially, socially, physically or spiritually and then deciding that you should be of service to him based on your good fortune and the kindness that God has shown to you. You view this person, this sinner, as unable to help himself due to his circumstances. Their past or present circumstances evoke understanding in you. You may find that this understanding evokes pity (disguised as compassion) and your forgiveness of him is based on your belief that he simply could not help himself. The "sin" is not his fault; it is the result of his circumstances. (The poor slob is a victim of an abusive family, poverty, prejudice....)

Other times forgiveness is a process of seeing sin in yourself and in someone else and recognizing that you are both in need of redemption and doing your best to forgive yourself and the other sinner in your midst. Here you are attempting to have compassion for yourself. You recognize that you believe you are weak. You believe that you too are a "sinner". To condemn another would be self-condemnation. So you forgive another in an attempt to forgive your own self-hate.

At other times you may find that although you see "sin" in yourself mirrored in another, your self-condemnation results in your inability to forgive anyone for his mistakes. You hate yourself for being a so-called "sinner" so you are filled with hate and disgust at seeing the "sin" in others.

Forgiveness can also take the form of someone treating you badly and finding it within yourself to forgive him. All of these processes of forgiveness appear reasonable in the eyes of the world. In the eyes of the *Course* these forms of forgiveness make the dream real and continue the illusion. In all of these examples "sin" is viewed as a fact. It is not part of an illusion or part of a dream-- it is real. When you believe it is real then you believe that it is irreversible. When you break one of your dinner plates or a vase you may attempt to glue it back together, but the damage is done. It is not reversible. We believe that "sin" is an irreversible fact. What if we are mistaken? What if "sin" is as much a part of the dream as being chased by a monster was for my friend Sean? What would the world look like then?

To be forgiving can be extremely helpful and it is a path that the Holy Spirit encourages. First the Holy Spirit has to help you redefine what forgiveness really is if this world is an illusion. Ken's tapes and lectures have helped me to understand this idea that the *Course* teaches as forgiveness. It is different from the Judeo-Christian idea. I will explain it.

## Forgiveness to Destroy

Certainly if this is an illusion then there is no one to forgive. Practically speaking I still believe that I live here and I have much learning to do and the learning includes forgiveness. So what gives? How can forgiveness be redefined so that it is a helpful process? If you forgive someone for something, which you perceived as harmful, or, if you view another human being as less fortunate, or as a lost soul in need of your specific spiritual help, and that someone is a split-off part of your mind, then who are you forgiving and who are you helping? I am not saying not to be helpful in the world. We need people who are helping; people to bring back our hope and help us in the world.

Sometimes hate in the ego thought system is well disguised and called by names like love. The idea that hate and grandiosity are masquerading as love is not new to most of us. Sometimes what we do looks kind, but the purpose, intention or motivation behind the act is unkind. A sales person who wants us as a customer may or may not use this tactic. He may or may not care about your well-being and he wants the commission that your sale will bring him. It is difficult for someone outside of the salesman's mind to know if his motivation has some kindness behind it or, if it is only manipulation guised as caring. Let's take this idea to a deeper more subtle form of attack. Many students of the *Course* have a pamphlet that was published a year or so after the *Course* in an attempt to correct peoples misunderstandings of prayer, forgiveness and healing. The pamphlet is called *The Song of Prayer*. Forgiveness-to-destroy is an idea that is explained in the pamphlet.

Forgiveness-to-destroy is a subtle attack disguised as love. Let me explain. From the view of Heaven, God has perfect faith in us as His creations. His belief in us does not falter. He is incapable of doubting that we will recognize who we are in truth. At the same time He respects the fact that we are choosing to believe this illusion. He does not interfere with our choice. Within our minds lies every key that will lead us back to the recognition of ourselves as God's Sons. The Holy Spirit is readily accessible to us at all times. We are the ones who need to ask for a change in perception. It will not be forced on us. The Holy Spirit has God's faith in us and waits patiently for our request for His help.

This world we believe we live in is simply a mistake made by the Son of God. We are so confused by what reality is that we mistakenly believe that when we see sin in someone else that it is their mistake that is in need of correction. What we fail to recognize is that life is literally a mirror; literally a projection of the mind that is thinking. To judge another for a so-called sin is to judge ourselves. Forgiveness from the perspective of the Holy Spirit has nothing at all to do with making the illusion real. A dream is a dream and nothing that we wish or hope for can be made real in an illusion. The *Song of Prayer* attempts to correct our misunderstanding of forgiveness. To recognize that when we judge others for their role in this illusion we imprison our self. Our job in this process is to stop judging and recognize that we need to ask for our understanding of forgiveness to be replaced by the Holy Spirits who does not judge. In the *Song of Prayer* and in *A Course In Miracles* we are asked to allow the Holy Spirit to help heal our minds and to work through us so that we can see His work as a role model for the correction for others. In this model it appears as though you are doing something to help others, but the real work is in allowing the work to be done through you by the Holy Spirit. This will create a situation where you remain the student and continue learning, but you will be helpful to anyone who asks in the process. The *Course* states that we need do nothing (Text page 382 T-18.IV.7)… that is a challenge for me.

The idea worth noting is that every time you feel a need to forgive someone for something he has done to you or anyone else, you are attacking yourself. Every time you feel better than someone, and you want to help him without his request for help, you are condemning yourself to weakness and helplessness. Every time you allow someone to treat you like a piece of trash and smile thinking that you will deny your pain and forgive, you are enslaving your mind. God's Child can be hurt by nothing outside of Himself (Text page 659 T-31.V.15) and until we own this idea as an experience we need spiritual help to change our very twisted perspective and have that perspective corrected. Forgiveness-to-destroy is a difficult concept to hold onto. It contradicts everything we have been taught about being forgiving. People who forgive in the world see an error and believe it is real. This belief is proof that the Son of God can make mistakes. It is proof that we are separated from God. This type of forgiveness reinforces illusion. Don't fall into the trap of "making the error real" (Text page 215 T-12.I.1). There is no part of an illusion that is more real than any other part.

Forgiveness-to-destroy can be easily misunderstood. I have seen many people in the field of mental health mis-communicate an idea about co-dependency that is easily misunderstood, in a way that forgiveness-to-destroy can be misunderstood. Co-dependency implies that someone relies on someone else with an unhealthy level of dependency. Please keep in mind that children and teenagers by nature are and should be co-dependent. Parents accept the role of allowing their kids to depend on them until they are able to survive and support themselves without their parents. Adolescents are still co-dependent on their parents and adults however much they beg to differ. Generally speaking from an ego perspective, dependency breeds contempt, but co-dependency between adults can be okay with them and then it is not a problem. It becomes a problem when for example, one person in a marriage or partnership feels oppressed by the other's need for him or her. The partner who longs for more freedom resents the dependency. The dependent partner feels unable to act independently and resents his dependency as well. Dependency breed's contempt in most relationships and it is a subtle thorn in one's side that can fester into a raging infection if a couple does not monitor it. Many people in the field of mental health try to teach these couples that as individuals they are responsible for their own feelings. They are responsible to take care of themselves and they are not responsible for how their partner feels. All of this is true and all of this information can be used as a weapon if it is taught too quickly and too simply. I have seen both therapists and clients misunderstand this idea of being independent and not responsible for how another is feeling and use it to hurt others.

If you have been in a relationship where you are angry at being dependent, or fed up with being depended upon, it is easy to take the idea of self-responsibility and run with it. You can use it to selfishly abandon or condemn your partner and revel in the glory of being right about how sickly co-dependent they are. Why is it then that you have found yourself in a relationship with such unhealthy dynamics to begin with? Where is the wound within you? I don't mean this in an unkind way. It can be very painful to look within at what it is you gain from being in a relationship where you feel unfairly treated (Text page 563 T-26.X.4). Be gentle with yourself and with the others in your relationships. We are all stuck in our own way. In the early chapters of this book I spoke of how we are responsible for how we think, for our body language and for the content of our minds. Most of us need to deal with the complexity of emotions that comes with recognizing what this *Course* is asking-- that you begin the process of questioning everything that you have believed in (Text page 499 T-24.in.2). This includes but is certainly not limited to forgiveness; you may hit some times when you use the process as a direct attack on others. The Judeo-Christian process of forgiveness that we have been practicing, believing it was kind, is full of attack and resentment. It is easy for many of us to fall into the trap of using this process to abandon and condemn rather then to help heal your mind. Be patient with yourself and be gentle too. It is a common error and one that is fixable. When we forgive, it is our judgment that is being forgiven; it is our misunderstanding of what reality is and what it is not, that we are looking at with spiritual help. The Holy Spirit never implies that in the world we should ignore human suffering and not be kind and helpful to each other. Never does He expound on explaining to anyone that the world is just an illusion so they should get over themselves, and never does he advocate that you increase your level of fear or suffering. He does say that the process can be met with some resistance (Workbook page 69 W-44.5) (some... I have had a whole lot of some resistance)!

Again this brings me back to the purpose of resistance. Resistance is always the fear of losing one's individuality... of the ego-God, which I see as the Borg queen, coming to steal this individuality from us. Resistance is a choice for the wrong teacher. It is saying to the Holy Spirit, "I can handle this myself - thank you very much!" Resistance is the insistence that we are correct and that the Holy Spirit is mistaken. When we feel the strong desire to be in charge of our life and not allow in any spiritual help, we are fearful that by allowing the help in we will eventually find that this self to whom we are very connected is not so important. Hanging out with the Holy Spirit will leave us without a self that we know. The Borg queen is a great symbol of the ego-God. She hunts down her prospective drones with no regard for their life. She couldn't care less about what you need or want. She takes, with no thought of you at all. She is an invented queen and for me she is a fabulous representation of my fear of the ego-God and of losing my individuality.

## True Empathy

Empathy, in the eyes of the world, is a process of feeling someone's pain with them. It is seen as stepping into someone's shoes and imagining what they must be feeling so that you can understand their plight. Empathy is viewed as compassionate in the world. To be empathetic to the suffering of others is one of the focal points of many therapeutic approaches to helping people. Now as you may have already guessed, the *Course* takes this worldly idea and reinterprets it for us. *A Course In Miracles* reminds us that behind all of this smoke and mirrors of illusion stands the Son of God. The *Course* explains that the Son of God has in His power the strength and the will of His Father. Therefore He is incapable of suffering. When we look at a fellow human being in this world that is suffering and in pain, and all we see is this pain, we are denying that behind the illusion is the Source of all power. In this regard we are hurting ourselves because we are reinforcing suffering and weakness. In essence we are proving to the sufferer and to our self that we are weak by refusing to remember our connection to God.

Now I want to emphasize that to have compassion for people in pain is essential. Again I am referring to a process that happens on the level of thought and on the level of the mind; not on the level of the body. If you see suffering in the world and you want to help ease the pain of others, please do so. I know I have made this point a number of times and I will make it again. The world is a mess and we are suffering. It is essential that we have concern, compassion and that we offer help to ease this worldly suffering. *A Course In Miracles* would not suggest that we do not help ease the suffering of the world. What is does teach is that the cause of the suffering is the denial of our connection to the Mind of God. We should not forget this point as we go about the process of being human in the world. When we forget this connection and see only suffering we become sad or hardened to other's pain, or we use the defense of denial as a subtle attack by pretending that nothing is wrong. In essence we are saying that God is cruel and He is helpless to help...your suffering proves this to everyone who can see it. When we reach out with the empathy of the Holy Spirit we remember that behind the illusion lies great strength. It is the strength of God. We act like normal people would in the world. We do what normal people do; we let the Holy Spirit teach us that each and every one of us has this power within him. In recognizing this we do not limit access to the truth in ourselves or in others (Text page 330 T-16.I.1).

True empathy initially threw me the way many *Course* teachings initially do. This idea contradicted everything I believed about empathy. Being in the field of mental health I felt that I was pretty empathetic and I never felt that I was attacking someone by denying the truth within them. I did not buy into the idea that this was a subtle form of attack. I was on new ground with the idea that I had to look beyond the form of the pain and to the truth behind it. This process was one of faith for me as I did not believe that the Holy Spirit could teach me much in this arena (arrogant)! But as a student I figured I would at least give it a go, as He has been correct in so many other areas of my life. I cannot say that I can always employ this process of seeing the strength in someone regardless of his situation, but I have gotten better. In my job I tend to work with a number of students who are school phobic. I like working with phobic kids and I usually can help them if I have some time to work with them. I see the same kids for up to three years, so school lends itself lots of time in this regard. I do think that the success I feel in helping kids who are school phobic is based on the idea of true empathy. For some reason it is easy for me to see and believe in the strength behind the fear of school phobia. I see the strength that they deny in themselves and I know it is real. Once I see it, then nothing a student can do will convince me that he is weak. It is this belief in them that I feel the Holy Spirit lends them. I have found myself saying to these kids that they should "borrow my faith" in them until they have their own. Don't get me wrong I am not pushy with them as they are so afraid, but I do not see them as weak so I don't feed their belief that they are weak. In the world they are afraid; but nothing could make them weak with the power of the Holy Spirit behind them. Also I don't ever explain that they have the power of the Holy Spirit behind them, or any of that spiritual stuff. This is how *I* learn, and I do not preach it to others. I simply state that behind their fear is strength; I see it so I know it is there… then I challenge them to believe what I believe about them.

When we see someone in our life whom we *insist* is in need of help even when they are not asking for it physically, emotionally or spiritually, we teach them that they are weak. That is an attack. When we create a situations where the so-called weak are dependent on our strength; when we lack faith in someone's internal strength and rescue him, then we are buying into the idea that the Son of God is weak and helpless. We are also insisting that we can do the job better than God can so we will step in and take over. We are teaching others and ourselves that the dream is reality; our weakness, which the true Son of God is without, proves that we are no longer connected to God. God is indeed dead. When we don't see past the form of the illusion to the strength behind the dream, we have bought into the weakness of the ego. This is an abstract idea that has nothing to do with what you do in the world. We need a kinder, more compassionate world. To live in the world with compassion we should help the helpless, we are obligated to feed the hungry and correct the mistakes of violence and poverty in the world. On the level of Mind nothing is happening… because this is an illusion. It is when we overlook the truth behind the illusion that we are insisting that the weakness, illness, loss and helplessness are reality. Then we reinforce the self-deception (i.e. you are weak and helpless but I am favored by God and I will help you) and call it love. When you are convinced that you have the answer that will save someone, be careful. You're denying their strength and perhaps using reaction formation as a defense of denying your own strength as well. A truly loving act will help someone on the level of form (if they are hungry feed them, if they need a doctor take them to one, if you are a parent discipline your child). But on the level of Mind or truth recognize that they too are the Holy Son's of God who happen to believe that they are bodies. When we buy into the myth that we are the helpless victims of the world (vulnerable suffering bodies) we reinforce the self-doubt within our minds. This is a denial of the power of the Son of God's ability to change His mind. As we recognize the truth behind the illusion (at first intellectually) we realize that we are all the same with the same problem. We all believe that the dream is reality; we are all stuck and desperately fearful that we will never find Heaven again. We express being stuck and afraid in millions of forms but the cause of the fear is the same for all of us. (Workbook page 141 W-79.2)

### Being grateful for being wrong

One of the dangers about learning that life is a projection of your thoughts is the temptation to monitor other people's thoughts and avoid looking at your own. This is when you throw someone's mirror back into her face. You tell her that the only reason she did such and such is because she is full of fear and self -hate. You shove her defenses in her mirror under the guise of being helpful. Most of the time when you are insistent that someone look into his mirror or when you feel that you know what is best for him it is you who are full of fear. Understand that the true benefit of this theory is the intra-psychic work that it allows you to accomplish. It can be used as a defense in and of itself. When I was in high school and I first began to notice that people were always talking about themselves I began to shut up. Funny when I look back on it, but it was sort of like I did not want to hear myself talk about anyone, because I knew it was myself to whom I was ultimately referring. I became a young woman who watched and listened and then spoke. Anyone who knew me well could repeat "Yeah I know... life is a mirror" every time they were moaning about something silly. When they spoke about things that were truly painful to them I would not make that comment (I learned that one the hard way). It is not kind or helpful to tell someone who has just disclosed a painful memory or a pattern of abuse or abandonment in their life that they are reflecting a thought of their abandonment of God on people who will then abuse or abandon them. It is unkind to remind them that life is an illusion anyway so what is the big deal. It is mean, defensive, and arrogant and it reinforces your own guilt. For the benefit of your own healing, practice only looking at the mirror of yourself and allow others to heal their own minds. Having faith that you can heal your own mind with the help of the Holy Spirit will reflect in how you treat others about their mirrors. Believing that this is accomplishable will increase your faith in others' ability to heal themselves without your unsolicited help.

I am a clinician and I know that a part of therapy is starting where a client is. Much of the work I do reflects the beliefs I am practicing, but I can honestly say that working with teens I almost never speak of life being a mirror. Kids don't have a strong enough sense of who they are to take in this information. They are just beginning to develop an identity and they are too young for such an abstract idea. The concept of life being a mirror of our thoughts is an adult idea. Adults even struggle with it. It is abstract, and without a strong sense of who you are, looking at this idea is not helpful. I talk to teenagers about defenses. I teach the anger-fear trap, guilt and how it demands punishment; once in a while if I am working with a young teen who thinks abstractly, I teach him about projection. Older teens can grasp that concept much more frequently. The point is that it is easy to find yourself using this construct as a weapon. You can pound someone over the head with your newfound knowledge… it may be better to be quiet for a time and watch. It is your mirror that you are gazing into. If you find that you have a strong need to show someone his mirror, ask yourself why you want to do this. Then ask the Holy Spirit why you want to do this. Even your best intentions can be uninvited and therefore unwanted (Text page 380 T-18, IV.2.1-3). This is an easy trap to fall into. Be gentle to yourself if you catch that type of lecturing going on. Lecturing someone about his mirror does not make you bad, and it is not wrong or evil. You simply need to ask the Holy Spirit if it is kind and helpful. Most importantly don't beat yourself up for repeating the bad habit of seeing things outside yourself that need to be fixed… changing bad habits is only a matter of time. Be patient, kind, and laugh at your mistakes.

Sometimes as I am contemplating and monitoring my thoughts I find that I am laughing in a sweet and kind way at all the silly ways that I have been defending myself! I ask what am I defending myself from anyway? I have asked the Holy Spirit that one a number of times… I am still awaiting an answer. The *Course* says that we are literally defending ourselves from a God who we believe is maniacal. Well I agree that if the God of the Bible is the option for God, I am not sure I want to meet Him. The God of the

Bible is a pretty mean God. He drowns us, demands sacrifice, sends plagues to kill us and even has His own son crucified. The God of the Bible picks favorites and asks that we kill in His name. I am afraid of Him and I can see how my belief in a maniacal God led to me defending myself from Him.

When I feel a connection to the Holy Spirit the idea of defending myself from God on the level of thought seems crazy. It reminds me of my childhood experience of Jesus. The Jesus of my childhood was a consistent friend who filled me with Joy. This Jesus was my companion. I was a child, and my relationship with Him was childish. I denounced Him when I felt He was not answering my prayers fast enough. I spoke to Him often and turned to Him when I felt lonely. His Love for me never wavered. He was my guide. I loved the feeling I experienced when I felt His presence. I loved the safety and the absence of fear that was mine when He was with me. As a teenager the contradiction of the church began to confuse and anger me. Initially I took this dilemma to Jesus. Slowly I denied the experience of Him and the hypocrisy of the church troubled me greatly. I threw Him away when I left the Catholic Church. I denied my experience of His kind, joyful presence in my life and I believed what people told me about Jesus. I began to connect Him with the hypocrisy that I felt the church practiced. The Jesus I have reconnected to as an adult is the Jesus of my childhood. He is always kind, patient, and gentle and in his presence I am filled with a Joy that words cannot describe. I never feel judged or condemned in His company. So I believe that the church is mistaken. Jesus is not a hypocrite. When He says that God is Love and that He is part of God, He lives that. He does not choose favorites and I believe that He does not have a religion of chosen ones. Having chosen ones is exclusive. Love cannot be exclusive and remain itself. We have nothing to fear about Him. And I am convinced that most of the teachings about Him are colored with the defensive thinking of the writer. The writers of the stories of Jesus are not bad, sinful people. They were just people and in their writing about Jesus perhaps some of their defenses were shining through. Our defenses are only silly mistakes that the Holy Spirit or Jesus can help us to correct... nothing more.

So what of this angry wrathful God? Could we be mistaken about Him? Can God be loving and kind and send a flood to kill us? Can God be Love and choose one religion as being better than any other? Would a loving God ask us to suffer and sacrifice (Text page531 T-25.VII.3)? Why when we experience the Love of God do we continue to insist that He is a wrathful God? Why do we trust words in a book more than our own experience?

When I allow the Holy Spirit to guide me I feel fabulous and I have so much fun just being. So if that is what is available in a non-defensive thought system, then I am grateful that I have been mistaken. I am happy that I asked for the guidance and that I am attempting to find a different way of relating and living. Defensiveness does not make us bad or sinful. I think many, if not all of us, have had access to the experience of Love that is from the Holy Spirit regardless of the name you call Him. We then deny the experience and believe what others tell us to believe about God being angry, demanding and judgmental. I would say we are slow learners, stubborn... and kind of arrogant, but not bad. The more I practice thinking with Love the easier it becomes to access. The contrast between thinking defensively and thinking with the Holy Spirit becomes clearer and it is then easier for me to ask for help to look at how my thoughts get in the way. And then you know what I do... not to be too redundant, but I take those thoughts to the Holy Spirit or Jesus and I ask Him to show me the situation from His perspective.

Question what you have been taught about God. Sometimes we need to look at the validity of our beliefs. When you believe something you stop questioning. What I was taught about God, and my experience of Him, are vastly different. They cannot coexist. God cannot be both Loving and punitive. Logically if God is acting in a way that increases people's fear he is not being loving. If God is Love, and I believe He is, then the God of the Bible is mythological. I am eternally grateful for this insight. I am happy that I have been wrong in believing what the Bible teaches us about God. I am thankful for the Love that guides me back to a God who is not punishing.

I have to honestly say that the concept of an unkind God is deeply ingrained into my thought system. I resist Love often. I run back to the known of believing that I am an individual. I see God as the queen Borg and I fear that He will seek revenge on my blasphemous thoughts about Him being kind and good. The layers of guilt that I have yet to heal frighten and overwhelm me. I avoid looking and then wonder why? I think that the times when I resist Love are when I don't trust that God is Love. It is when I fall back on my old beliefs that God is mean and that we should have a healthy fear of Him. I remember hearing that we should have a healthy fear of the wrath of God in church as a child. Keep the cause and effect reversal in mind and look at this fear of God. The idea of fearing God is in the thought system first and then we reflect it into religions so that we can blame them for our ideas about God being so twisted. Religions of the world did not plant this idea. The idea comes first, its reflection follows. Everything about the thought of having a fear of God contradicts the times I experience the Love of God. When I am thinking defensively it feels as if I have never had any experience of God being kind, gentle, fun and loving. The *Course* explains that the two modes of thinking, one being with the Holy Spirit and the other

113

being with the ego, are mutually exclusive and have no overlap (Text page 110 T-6.V.C.4.7-10). We either think with defenses, or with the Holy Spirit. It is never both at the same time. We cannot be sort of both. We can wavier back and forth, but we are either in one camp or the other. The times when I am thinking with Love it is as if defenses are gone altogether. The times when I am thinking with defenses it feels like I have made no progress at all. All of my practicing seems for naught and that's when it feels like I keep making the same mistake over and over again. I get angry and discouraged. This is a great defensive trick. I have thrown the *Course* away for months at a time when I feel like this. Usually I just put it down for a day or so until I feel less fearful. But I have become very afraid of what it is teaching a couple of times and simply put it down and not picked it up for a few months.

The idea that the thought systems are not compatible at all is an important one. I have observed that a number of my friends who study the *Course* feel like they have studied the book for years and made no progress. I have fallen into this funk and wondered why I try to practice at all. This is the defensive trick that we play on ourselves. It is a time to ask for help. I have found myself there a number of times and refused to ask. In this defensive place I believe that if God finds me now I am in big trouble so I don't ask until I am a bit less afraid. I refuse at these times to contemplate compromising my individuality. I hold onto it at all cost. I have heard Ken say that it is as if there is a small voice in the back of my mind that says, "If you keep hanging out with this Holy Spirit fellow He will trick you and take your individuality... you will disappear into oblivion!" The fear can be horrific and I fight the idea by simply denying that the Holy Spirit is a part of my life at all. Again, be kind to yourself if this happens. It is not bad... it is part of the process. The hope is that as you can be kind to yourself the peace will follow. When you see that you are feeling too frightened or guilty to ask for help, you have gained insight. This insight is helpful in and of itself. Don't force yourself to practice when you feel this overwhelmed by the new ideas. That would be silly and unkind to you. Just recognize that you are frightened and that this is ok. When you are less afraid you will be drawn back to the study of monitoring your intra-psychic world.

### Defenselessness

How will you know that you are choosing the Holy Spirit as your teacher? What is it that the Holy Spirit is supposed to help you to look at? I have spoken of this observing your thoughts many times. I believe that the looking at your thoughts and asking for a different view... Christ's Vision, is an answer that can get you in touch with your True Self, the self that God created. The looking is not at your nice thoughts… or at all the good things that you have done. Looking at your thoughts is a looking at the thoughts that keep peace from your mind. These are the thoughts of annoyance, anger, frustration, disinterest, boredom, jealousy, manipulation, and selfishness. You know… all the things that you don't want to look at. The concept is that these are the thoughts, beliefs and feelings that keep you from Love. The looking is putting some emphasis on why we spend so much time focused on things that keep us from peace and then claiming that we want peace. If we wanted peace we would not spend so much time looking outward at all the people and things that leave us feeling annoyed, angry, frustrated, disinterested, board, jealous, manipulative and selfish. Peace is a state of mind, not a state of the world. Having the Love of God is a state of Mind. We claim we want peace and on some level we do… on another level we are fearful about having it because we connect God with Oneness and unconsciously we know that we would loose our individuality if we honestly choose God. We also have a deep-rooted belief that God demands that we suffer to get into Heaven. I would gladly suffer here if this suffering would lead me to an eternity with God. The idea of fearing the loss of our individuality is critical. If I choose God I won't be Catherine or a body. I will be some abstract concept of a Mind… a thought in the Mind of God and I don't know what that is (Workbook page 273 W-rIV.in2-3). I am not sure I want to give up what I am. So we don't choose God. I want to review one more time that God exists in a state of perfect Oneness. To be an individual there must be someone who is outside of us. This someone (or something) is the other. God being one with everything cannot have an experience of another. There cannot be individuality or another in God. When we choose defenses as our teacher we are insisting that oneness no longer exists. Oneness is the state of God. In our demand that individuality exists we believe that Heaven was shattered and therefore God was destroyed. Who among us, in honesty, would give up his individuality and along with it any conscious awareness of a self, if the Oneness of Heaven would be restored by this act? Not many of us can honestly say that we would give up our selves without resentment, sacrifice or fear to restore absolute Oneness. To avoid the guilt of that thought we make a million reasons about the loss of our peace and ignore the idea that the loss of peace preceded the image that we see in the world. We believe that if the world (our situation) were better that we would have peace.

I have to go back to this image of the Borg drone. Ego based thinkers cannot envision a world where they do not exist on some level as themselves. Borg drones from an ego perspective are without a self. Their individuality is stolen from them through an act of violence and a blatant disregard for them as individuals. This is the fear that we have of God regarding being in a state of Oneness. The Holy Spirit has been slowly helping me to see that He would never demand that I give up anything that I continue to desire, individuality included. Just like my childhood love for my Barbie doll I have a childish love for my individuality that I cannot fathom being without. It is incomprehensible to me that I can be other than an individual with my own thoughts, personality, ideas and my own body. I have no conscious experience of not having this self as who I am, so I am not spiritually mature enough to understand what is available to me outside of this self. The Holy Spirit, seeing me as a small child, teaches me at the spiritual level that I can understand. He makes no demands; He simply states that I will be happier if I allow Him to work through me as a Teacher, to show me the alternatives. His goal is that I have happiness and a more solid foundation of internal peace. When I am fearful I view Him as a thief setting me up for a loss of my so-called self. He is then the Borg queen sweetly tempting me to trust Him so that he can betray me. These are wild imaginings, like those of a child convinced that a monster is living in her closet. The Holy Spirit being a perfect parent moves at the pace of the learner and child. There is no force in this process, so move at a pace that is comfortable for you, recognizing that the process will include some bumps and bruises (self-inflicted by the way).

In my study of the *Course* the most challenging question that has come up for me is the idea of who am I if I am not a body… what is a thought in the Mind of God? I spoke earlier of my desire to create an abundant life for myself and in doing that, what I have begun to question is, "Who is the I that is able to change this illusion and make it more abundant?" This questioning of who I am in the eyes of God is at times threatening and at other times thrilling. I am amazed at how much I can enjoy the idea that I am not this body that I call Catherine. I really believe that this world is a mess and that history has shown that we are pretty dumb. We repeat the same mistakes over and over again. We do not learn from the errors of the past. I used to hope that we could make the world a better place. I doubted this but I wanted to believe it. I don't believe that we will be able to fix this place and make it better. I sometimes think, "I want off." I want to find a different way to live that does not include this world. I don't think things work here and I don't think they ever will. When I forget that this world is part of a collective dream that we are having then this idea leaves me feeling hopeless and sad. When I remember that the hopelessness of the world is based on hopeless frightened thoughts in the mind of a dreaming Son of God at home and safe in Heaven, I feel a bit better. I do believe that any healing involves a deep internal look at these thoughts and changing one's mind. I know that the world will not work... it is not real. The hope for me is about the gratefulness that I am mistaken, and that the love and kindness of the Holy Spirit are real.

Why is it that we as individuals, and that we as a world people keep making the same mistakes over and over again? What is it that keeps us repeating pattern after pattern and never learning from the mistakes that history and we as individuals make? I think it is our lack of awareness that there is a different way to think and to see the world. Most of us are not aware that we have access to a completely different thought system that leads us out of fear and ultimately out of the dream. We catch glimpses of this, but we don't know that the power to choose this Teacher is ours to claim. When you know that you have the power to choose a Teacher who can lead you out of fear you are filled with hope. The thoughts that we need to look at in order to stop lending them our strength and support (through defending them from our awareness) are selfishness, manipulation, attacking, defending, and not accepting responsibility for our actions. Let's look at them more closely and honestly.

The only way that I have been able to look at these thoughts that seem so ugly is with the recognition, however dimly, that they are part of a grand illusion. I can look at things that I fear, keeping the thought (the Holy Spirit is contained in that thought) that they are not real gently playing in the back of my mind. Without the idea that this is an illusion and therefore not true, these thoughts are too difficult to look at. I spoke earlier about how Ken advised that I practice having a temper tantrum or two, to learn that they are no big deal and to stop giving power to my fear of my anger. I struggled with this idea. I trust Ken's advice and I wanted to follow it but I believe deeply that to take my anger out on someone else is not ok. I have felt for years that anger is a defense and it is not justified. Ken was advising me to challenge my belief that anger is fearful and that I needed to deny it. I knew that he was not advising me to hurt anyone or to increase one's fear in a raging tantrum. I did not have a clue on how to do this. I did know that perhaps the Holy Spirit had a clue and that He could show me what I was not seeing. I asked and initially I could only have these tantrums in my mind's eye. Then one evening I became very angry with a man with whom I study the *Course*. I began to argue with something that he said and he was pushing the point and pushing my temper. I could see people in the room backing out of the conversation with worry. In the back of my mind playing softly in my ears was the thought that this is a game. I had the image that I was "trying on a temper tantrum" like a new outfit. There was awareness within me that this temper and this anger had nothing to do with who I am in truth at all. It was a fun experience. Never before have I had such fun being angry. I was clearly aware that I was not harming anyone. At the end of the meeting I spoke about how angry I was and some people said that they noticed. The man toward whom I had directed my anger remarked that he knew my feathers were ruffled but he did not think I was too mad. I believe that the Holy Spirit is often guiding this friend of mine and that he was able to see that I was calling for help through my anger. He did not see it as an attack... sort of like my story about Abby.

As we look we reclaim our power over the defenses behind which we hide. We question the defense's reality and we question the purpose of hiding behind it. We will look through denial, fear and projection to the truth behind the lie. Seeing the lie removes it as a block that keeps you from the Holy Spirit and the truth. As your defenses become more transparent you will be freer to have peace in your day. You may find that you still use the defense, but you will not hold onto it so tightly and you will recognize that there is another reality behind the illusion. The correction is a sweet process that is fun to experience.

As we become more aware of how our defenses play out we run into many obstacles that keep us resisting the help of the Holy Spirit. Most of us will run head long into our need to be right and feel as though we have control. This need to be in control is extremely common and when you see it within yourself be willing to laugh at the silliness of it. I know that I am stuck here when I find myself insisting or lecturing about a subject. We all have certain personality traits or self-concepts to which we cling. We connect these traits with who we are. Without this concept of ourselves we feel like fish out of water. If this part of our personality comes into question we may feel threatened. We may ask ourselves, "Who would we be without that trait." We have defined ourselves as bodies with personalities. As we question the reality of who we are we become threatened. Expect this so that it does not surprise you. Redefining yourself as an abstract Child of God is a process of questioning your self-concepts. When you become fearful about not knowing who you are if you are not this individual self, you will resist the process. That is expected, and do the best you can not to be too harsh with yourself for being afraid. I usually say "I'm too afraid of this God stuff right now Holy Spirit... today I need to be a body." Then I might invite Jesus or the Holy Spirit to come shopping with me. We have spent lots of time in Talbot's together when I am frightened. To expect myself to be spiritual at this point would be like expecting me to take off and fly to Mars.

I need to be in the world as a body and an individual at these times. I need to feel that my feet are firmly planted in my life and not in abstract concepts of a self that I do not understand. I invite the Holy Spirit to join me so that I can learn to trust Him more. I just live doing whatever it is I do and I hope that the fear that I feel will be short lived. Don't fight your resistance. Accept where you are and as you become more at ease with an expanded concept of yourself, you will continue to grow.

We all project this illusory sin-of-selfishness (that we would shatter Heaven to get what we want) out into the world. It should come as no surprise then that we are selfish as a species. It is safe to say that if things don't deeply impact our lives we just are not that interested in them. Many of us have things we believe are worth fighting for. We have those things we love. Generally speaking we put humans first and we put the humans that we love above all others. Most importantly we put our individual self first above even the humans that we adore. There are some exceptions to this but in general there are not many people for whom I would die. I don't think that I am an exception to this rule.

I had a colleague who went to visit her family in Liberia a number of years ago. She was gone for over a month and upon her return she told us that the nation had experienced an overthrow of the government. Her family was comprised of some high-ranking government officials. She had just lived through a war and no one in the office where we worked had heard a thing about it. If it was reported on the news or in the paper it was given so little coverage that not a whisper of it was leaked to any of us. We were shocked. Her family had to escape from their homeland and a number of them were living in her home. It was not safe for them to return to their country. Now this is important news when it is happening in your living room. But for Americans at that time Liberia had little or nothing to offer us politically speaking. The news just was not relevant so it was not reported. This is a common event... we are not interested in events that do not affect our lives. And the suffering of some people in a nation that we don't know much about is irrelevant. This is how this selfishness masquerades. It's our "Yeah... so.... And what does this have to do with me" attitude that we hide selfishness in (Manual pages 45-46 M-17.7). Don't get me wrong, we cannot save the world and there is too much news going on to be aware of all the horror stories that occur in this world. I am not trying to suggest that we do that. What I am saying is that the theme of selfishness plays out in all of us, however subtly. It is not that we are bad, rotten people who should feel guilty for being self-centered at all. The problem is that we forget about our collective consciousness as egos. The collective ego thought system contains within it thoughts and beliefs that are selfish and say "it's you or it's me babe and I plan on making it me". We believe in thoughts that say only the fittest survive here. This collective theme of selfishness is part of the whole thought system so, of course, it will be reflected in your illusion. Expect it because you are part of the ego collective consciousness. Don't indulge it and remember the ego thought system is an illusion... so if the thought provokes guilt that is only because you believe that the illusion is reality. It is not. In truth the Holy Spirit knows that to give and to receive is the same... He knows that selfishness is impossible in Heaven (can you imagine that...wow). So since there is nothing outside of Heaven and selfishness cannot exist in Heaven it cannot be real. That we believe it is real is obvious. That we have the option to question this belief should be equally obvious at this time.

We may love the sensationalism that sells a story on the media, we may be amazed at the magnitude of suffering and we may even do what we can to help. Then we forget it. Now many of you may argue and say that you care about lots of things, people and causes. I believe you. Part of who we are is connected to the Holy Spirit. That part of us is connected to the collective consciousness that loves the way God does. We are capable of great good and of great acts of kindness and selflessness. I am not denying this at all. But like I have said before *A Course In Miracles* is not concerned with the part of our mind that connects to the Holy Spirit. The purpose of the teaching is to help us look at the motivation we have for not doing that all the time. If we always chose to access the collective thoughts of the Holy Spirit the world would not be so strewn with disaster. It is helpful to know the experience of accessing the thinking of the Holy Spirit. It gives me something to contrast the times that I reject that thought process. The point is that the problems occur when we don't access this love and we have to understand why we choose against it in order to make a different choice. The defensive part of our mind is tricky. I challenge you to look at why and what your ulterior motives may be regarding the intrigue or repulsion you feel about sensationalism. What defenses are you accessing as you are drawn to or repelled by things in your life? There is a saying that most of us need an enemy. Why is that? What is the purpose of seeing an enemy outside of one's self?

As Americans we can be nationalistic in a time of military invasion, but when the crisis is over we may go back to a behavior of separating our political interest from a different group that we had previously been aligned with only weeks before. We transfer our allegiance based on our immediate needs. We do that on an individual basis as well. We may exclude one group from our list of friends until we find out that they are involved with something or know someone from whom we want something. We all do this. It is not exclusive to any one of us. This is the beauty of looking at these ideas. It is not as if you have a corner on the selfishness market. Selfishness and greed are some of the very reasons that we as individuals are unhappy and not at peace. We have this constantly unsatisfied, selfish, greedy idea that floats around our mind. As a culture it is easy to see how we do this. In America we foster a belief that the pursuit of wealth is the answer to peace and happiness. We struggle to accumulate wealth and will sell out our ethics and values to have it. We hold in high esteem people who have money and then often, behind their backs, we hate them. We kill for money... literally and figuratively. Again we don't question why. Keep in mind the premise that the thought of scarcity, or that we lack something essential that will make us whole, is a belief that we hold within our collective ego mind. We project that thought onto the world and look for the answer to fill up our feeling of deprivation in the form of wealth. The true scarcity comes from the illusory belief that we have shattered Heaven (Text page 11 T-I. IV.3.1-5). We believe that we are no longer part of Heaven. This loss is huge and so seemingly irreparable that we are left longing for something that we just cannot name in this world. The emptiness that we feel demands that it be filled up, so we pursue completion of ourselves in money, relationships, power, fame and addictions. In the tape series *Climbing the Ladder Home*, Ken discusses the idea that Dr. Sigmund Freud spoke of four forces that motivate people in their search for happiness. I am not quoting Dr. Freud directly. Generally speaking he theorized that people are motivated by money, physical pleasure (Freud called this the love of a woman), power and fame in their pursuit of happiness. All of these activities are full of the concept that we are incomplete and that we need something outside of us to make us whole. When we ask for help looking at this feeling of being incomplete with the Holy Spirit it does not mean that we have to give up what we are doing in the world. It simply means that we choose another Teacher to guide us in healing these misperceptions.

### Winners and Losers

Look at our concept of heroes today. Many of the role models in our nation are exposed as basically selfish people who will walk over any and everyone to keep them on top. We call them independent and rebellious, with the killer instinct of a businessman. What do we think this will accomplish? The one who dies with the most stuff does not win. There is no winner. The person with power gets his way and the rest of us hope that we are on the side of the one who got his way. A belief that permeates our world is one of kill or be killed (Text page 465 T-21.VIII.1). We act this out psychologically, emotionally and physically. We believe that our self-worth is determined by how much we "win". To win it is essential that someone loses. In the world of defensive thinking we will always have winners and losers. As I mentioned before we sometimes refer to the survival of the fittest. We hold a belief (that we never question) that we must kill or we will be killed. This is just the way that it is. I had a conversation with a good friend of mine a few years back about how America as a nation could feed the world. But we don't want to drive down prices for farmers, so we pay them to let their grain rot in a silo when people around the world are starving. I was appalled at this idea. My friend who is a scientist and thinks very logically said that the problem with feeding the world is that then people will breed and we are already overpopulated. If we keep feeding them the problem simply continues and worsens. He suggested that we continue this policy as a nation, allowing our grain to rot, because the solution of feeding these people will simply prolong the problem. To my friend allowing these people to starve seemed like the most reasonable solution. He did not think that education on birth control would help much as having children defied logic in his mind to begin with. Now I was furious at him at the time and I thought he was crazy... but he thinks like an ego... and for the most part so do I. He is a good guy and a dear friend. He simply believes that this reality is the only one we have. He is feeling lucky to be on the side that is winning (so to speak). He has access to food and water so he can calculate population control with very little emotion. To win at the cost of another is not a victory for anyone in the eyes of the Holy Spirit. Actually the Holy Spirit, according to the *Course* cannot see loss, as He does not believe in it. To give up the belief in loss... that idea takes my breath away. The Holy Spirit sees only gain (and maybe even grain) for everyone... loss in Heaven is inconceivable. Inconceivable... I can't imagine that. The idea of a loser and a winner is so ingrained (pun intended) in my mind that I really cannot imagine how everyone can win. I would like to catch a glimpse of this concept on an experiential level, but currently it is simply an idea that I pray is true. I am so tired of worrying and watching the pain of loss in this world. I am so tired of being fearful that I will be on the losing side. I am so tired of fearing my thoughts. I am ready for a new vision on this idea.

We don't ask how the Holy Spirit might view beliefs that we don't question. We just accept that this is simply the way that it is. These ideas of loss, scarcity, a winner and a loser are so ingrained into our thinking that we simply accept them as factual. How would life change if we no longer believed that only some of us could win? We see the effects of this belief mirrored all over our illusion. Some people have and some do not have. Some of us are winners and some of us are losers. If I view myself as lucky it means I need to see someone as unlucky to make a comparison to myself. The focus is on seeing one another as inherently different. They are different and we are the winners. They will starve because we need grain prices to be maintained and we have the power to maintain them. Plus we decide that the population needs to be controlled. Now we make these selfish decisions from only one perspective that we assume is the only perspective that there is. We happen to have more power as a nation at this time, and we make decisions that cause great suffering based on an unconscious belief that we are inherently God's chosen ones. Slavery was based on this premise. Every invasion of one nation by another one is based on this idea; they are different and we are their betters. They have something (oil, gold, water, and free labor) and we deserve it. Selfishness is a defensive way of thinking. If life is a mirror these thoughts mirror the defense mechanism of reaction formation. They are full of deeply hidden feelings of inadequacy, unworthiness, and murderous rage. People, who are peaceful within, do not oppress or repress. There is no need to do so.

Inadequacy, unworthiness and murderous rage are pretty ugly thoughts to look at. Without the gentle help of the Holy Spirit looking at these beliefs is overwhelming. We must look at them to reclaim our power against repeating the mistake over and over again. We can only look with Love by our side. I am asking you to contemplate an idea. If you brought these ugly, unkind thoughts to the Holy Spirit and He said… This is not the real you. God made you and you do not contain any thoughts of inadequacy, unworthiness, rage or murder. If only for a moment you believed Him, then I promise you that you will no longer fear these thoughts. They will be silly. They will have no power over you. The fear of them disappears as you reclaim your power over your thinking and your beliefs. When you look at them with the help of Love they are nothing.

The Holy Spirit does not believe in selfishness. He sees only shared interest. He cannot recognize differences. Love sees only the inherent sameness that we share. How do you think this sameness would look? How would you feel if you could look through the Holy Spirit's eyes at how very much the same we are? We all would win, have and share. We would not need to compete because there would be no need to take. I am not talking about an ideal world… I am speaking of a state of mind. It is unimaginable; I cannot envision it. I hope one day to be able to see this-- To move past my personality and into my True Self. This self is eternal, created by God, and contains a mirror of God Himself.

Attack is another defensive stance that most of us cannot fathom living without. We are constantly braced for attack as individuals, groups, states, nations and as a world. We set up national and worldwide strategies of attack. America has the largest military in the world. Some of us consider ourselves the police of the world. We justify our attacks simply by saying that it is essential that we defend ourselves. We don't need much more than that for an explanation. Attack and defense walk hand in hand. On an individual basis we feel that we have the right to attack people who annoy or threaten us. People who fail to show us the respect we think we should have, or those who enter our space are open to our attack. We defend our beliefs and morals through attack; sometimes in the name of God. What we fail to recognize is the idea of respect, having space, being offended, or overlooked and even our moral sense of good and bad are our perceptions. We set up our belief system within our illusion. Our fragility is constructed by our beliefs. This sense of who we are based on our beliefs is open to change each time we contradict what we say we believe. I know I discussed this earlier but to clarify any confusion keep in mind that beliefs are open to reinterpretation throughout a lifetime. This leaves us questioning who we are. We say that we believe in a value but over time we may find that we contradict this value in some of the ways we live. Some of us struggle with this and some of us don't. Let's say we have a strong belief that people are deserving of respect simply because they are alive. Then in a family argument we disrespect our partner or our parent. This contradiction can leave us feeling fragile on the inside.

Change your beliefs and your perception has to change. Can you imagine the internal power you would connect with if you allowed the Holy Spirit to redefine being respected from the point of view of God? Do you think you could perceive being overlooked by a family member or a boss if you could see through His eyes? Imagine if you allowed the Holy Spirit to show you how greatly you limit yourself through your expectations of how life should be. Our expectations limit our options, increase our fears and stunt our spiritual growth. Imagine how much we could learn about God if we allowed our perceptions to be healed. We live in a violent culture where spousal and child abuse is not considered unusual. Teens kill each other on the street and in our schools. We search for answers and we skew statistics to help make things look like they are improving. We have tried to fix the world throughout our history. The world of form is not correctable. We each need to look inside and ask to learn how to perceive the world from a non-defensive stance. As we heal our perceptions we will see the truth. The desire to heal the illusion will slowly be replaced with the acceptance of the truth.

Jesus was spiritually advanced enough to think without defenses. All of our enlightened teachers are able to do so. The concept of courage that I spoke of earlier is part of defenseless thinking. In an earlier section of this book I spoke of the idea of forgiveness-to-destroy. I want to discuss forgiveness again. In the world we believe that forgiveness is based on someone overcoming adversity and then finding it within his heart to forgive those who committed 'sins' against him. I think that the Holy Spirit views forgiveness from a very different perspective. Let's review the idea of having a lucid dream. In a lucid dream you recognize within your dream that you are the dreamer and not the characters in the dream. If you are having a lucid nightmare you will watch the dream from outside of the figures within it. You may do, or have committed against you, unspeakable acts in a sleeping dream. All of these acts are happening within your dream... in your thoughts. When you awaken you may be grateful that what occurred was only a dream! Nothing really happens in a dream after all. Perhaps you are relieved, that you were only dreaming. Maybe you feel troubled about the images, but there is no one to be angry with and no one to forgive... it was your dream. Jesus knew that the world is an illusion. He knew He was having a dream. He knew, as a lucid dreamer, that He was home in Heaven safe and sound. Nothing at all happened to Jesus' True Self. There was no one to forgive because when you have a dream nothing happens. Forgiveness in this sense is not about other people being absolved of their unkind acts. It is about forgiving yourself for believing that this illusion is reality. It is a process of saying there is no life outside of Heaven (Text page 493-494 T-23.II.19). There cannot be individuality regardless of how fiercely I demand that I am a body living in the world. It is about looking within and asking for the means to return to Heaven and the Oneness of God. Forgiveness is the gentle process of reminding yourself that the world is an illusion and that going home to God is your right. You do not have to earn His love and you do not have to condemn in His name. Forgiveness is the process of removing our defenses as they keep us from remembering that the Love of God is who we are. Be kind and gentle to yourself... it is only a dream... the road home is yours to reclaim with a strong and true Guide to lead the way.

A subtle form of attack is to make someone dependent on you. As a nation we do this with money. We lend money to nations to make them indebted to us. As individuals we do favors, support and perhaps buy someone gifts and then we feel that they owe us. If someone we helped out does not return the favor when we feel we need support we see him as unworthy of our friendship in the future. Some of our favors are conditional and set up to form dependency and obligation. This form of attack can often be hard to see because it looks like kindness. The clue is the obligation or expectation that you place on others. When you expect something in return from someone, whether you know it or not you are attempting to manipulate him, so you are attacking him. Again don't feel bad about this... we all do it. When you look at this without Love by your side it can be very overwhelming, ugly, and cause you great distress. When you look at it with Love by your side it is much easier, because Love does not acknowledge attack or defense. So you say to the Holy Spirit, "Help me look at this..." and when you see it though Christ's Vision it transforms into a call for Love (Text page 128 T-7.VII.7.4-8).

Looking at our kind and squeaky-clean thoughts seems like a lot more fun doesn't it? Easier too. I have no problem letting others and myself in on how nice and sweet I am. I can play the role of being a good-girl rather well. In my professional life I have chosen the role of a social worker and you know how sappy and goody-two-shoes our reputation can be (enough to make me sick to my stomach)! Thinking in terms of the collective has helped me to be gentler and kinder as I attempt to notice my unkind defensive thinking. Often I run head long into my desire to avoid looking, as I often feel guilty when I look. The Holy Spirit can reinterpret guilt for you and that reinterpretation does make the process a bit kinder. Examining the belief in guilt can make your relationships kinder too. When you ask to see guilt from the Holy Spirit's view it becomes what the *Course* refers to as a call for love and nothing more. Wild how this feeling of guilt with all of it's disgust and repulsion can lose it's power simply because I ask to see it from a different perspective. Guilt becomes a symbol of choosing defensive thinking. The Holy Spirit has no symbolic representation for guilt, as He does not believe in it so it simply does not exist when you allow Him to show you how He thinks. All of our beliefs and the symbols of this world can be seen in this light. The process always leaves me amazed in its simplicity and its profound results. I would have never guessed that a simple request, and my permission to have the request granted, could bring such happiness. I love the results although my permission to have the change is essential and I often withhold it. I accept responsibility for my withholding permission to change my view and I have come to respect the idea that nothing in this process will be forced or rushed. That part is ok; silly and foolish but ok nonetheless.

# Chapter 8:

### Call for Love

In Mother Teresa's book *"No Greater Love"* she speaks of knowing that each of us have Christ within. Mother Teresa knew that Christ was trapped within individuals. That we were lost with out the recognition that within us was the power of God. She indicates that early in her career she understood that Christ was within all of us, but that Christ no longer knew Himself and felt trapped. Her vision was the motivating force in her life's work. From the perspective of the *Course* Mother Theresa had true empathy. This empathy was reflected in the faith and love she could give to the people for whom she cared. She did not pity them. She knew that the strength of Christ was within them. The strength may have been hidden to them but she saw it, and from that sight she had to know that Christ is no pathetic weakling. He obviously is lost, frightened and confused. He needs help finding and remembering Himself but within Him lies the power of Heaven itself. Mother Theresa had the ability to see beyond attack and defense to the call of Love behind it. She connected to the Holy Spirit and stayed connected as it appears to me. She was aware of the power of Christ with herself just as Jesus was. Many of us access that Wisdom for brief periods of time. Then we turn back to defenses and we forget that there might be another way to see this world (Text pages 627-628 T-30.I.12.3).

The *Course* explains that all attack is a call for Love (Text page 128 T-7. VII.7.4-5). Now in theory this sounds nice. We are all calling for help and when we think with defense or attack we are asking for help. Well, on a practical level this always sounds like a touchy-feely excuse. You see when someone is treating me like a jerk or when I myself am being a jerk to someone else I don't see a call for love, I see a jerk. So I ask the Holy Spirit from time to time what this means. I don't understand this completely but I do have an idea of what this implies (from my perspective).

I have mentioned earlier that all attack is an attempt to get rid of guilt. Guilt is the motivating factor behind projection. Keep in mind that everything you see is a projection- *all images*. Projection is how we see our thoughts. Therefore all images contain at their base the belief in or the idea of guilt. The Holy Spirit does not project. When you allow Him to work through you the *Course* teaches that He extends His Love. When you think with Him and are defenseless you do not project (Text page 129-130 T-7.VIII.1).

Keeping this point in mind, think of someone who is very defended. He is angry and fearful. The *Course* teaches us that we are never upset for the reason we think (Workbook page 8 W-5). Prior to whatever it is one believes is the source of his anger, some guilt surfaced or bubbled up in his mind. With the guilt comes the belief that the guilty deserve to be punished. Being punished frightens us. We look for something outside of our mind onto which to project the guilt. It becomes his fault that we feel this way and he is the one who should be punished. So we project, attack and defend. The guilt comes first and it is part of the illusion. Guilt is a feeling and feelings arise from beliefs.

The call for Love is hidden in projection and attack. It is always a mask over a fearful request. The request is for reassurance that guilt is not a part of who I am... and in truth it is not! Empathy and forgiveness from the Holy Spirit's perspective have helped me to begin to see that attack, regardless of how my defensiveness perceives it, is always a plea that is asking "Help me to remember that I am worthy of the Love of God. Please don't let guilt be part of who I am". This request can be granted from the Holy Spirit's vision.

As selfish people who are constantly feeling as though we are being attacked and saying we have no choice but to retaliate, we constantly rationalize and justify our unkindness. We tell one another and ourselves that we had to return the attack because the other guy was the aggressor. We scream that we are the innocent victims of the brutality of another and we pretend that self-defense was our only choice. Again keep in mind that I am speaking on the level of thought and mind. I have implied all through this book that perhaps we are much more than we realize. That there is a part of our mind that is much larger and more powerful than the body we believe ourselves to be. The *Course* teaches that we all have the ability to choose this decision making self and view our illusion with it. Within your mind you are closer to your natural state of being. Do you think that Mother Theresa and Jesus knew in a more experiential way that they were part of a larger and more powerful mind?

Behind all of this acting-out in the world is an unconscious idea, the one that we are projecting all over the place, of worry and terror that if God catches up with me He will kill me for stealing life (individuality) from Him. I will ask again as I did earlier, why is it that we do not make the simple and happy choice to follow the guidance of the Holy Spirit? Unconsciously we will blame anyone and everyone for that stealing of individuality. We won't give it back mind you... not without a fight. The Star Trek Federation fights the Borg for everything they are worth... the idea that we will kill to keep this body alive is real for us... myself included. The insistence that we are individuals and any recognition that perhaps we are not is a pill I cannot swallow. I have very little experience that would help me learn that I am not an individual. I have to go on faith with this one. The theme that we will go to great lengths to protect this individual self is easy to see in the world. On the level of mind I don't understand the mirror. What I do know is that this crazy, insane thought system is keeping us stuck in a prison that we created... we have the key to unlock it. Looking at our attachment to being individuals with bodies and personalities plays a big part in unlocking this prison house according to *A Course In Miracles*. I honestly don't know much more than that although I am asking to understand this more clearly.

Ken has taken the idea that we believe we owe God, and helped me see how we mirror that idea all over our dream. The idea of sacrifice, bargaining, compromise and suffering come into play with the thought that we owe God for what we stole from Him. From the ego's point of view we unconsciously believe that we stole the power to "make life" from God. We don't want to give that power back but we recognize that we have to pay for it to appease God's wrath. We see this theme of paying for what we take from others mirrored all over our lives. We call it by names like compromise... you have to give a bit to get is a belief that most of us hold as reasonable. Compromise is something that we do in the world. Compromise and giving to get something that you want is a theme that is considered a normal part of a healthy family life. When the compromise feels like a sacrifice it is a payment. When the deal works out to feel as if you are getting more than you are giving, then we feel that we have won. To win means that someone else had to give something up. I will bend on this one but I expect something in return. Psychologically we do this all the time, with partners and lovers, friends, family, colleagues and bosses. We give to them but we expect something in return. It is bizarre that we call this part of love. It is so ingrained in how we think and so viewed as normal, that it is never brought into question. We even assume that God Himself must think this way and expect that we pay Him with atonement, penance, sacrifice and some suffering along the way. We earn the right to be in Heaven this way. This idea makes God an enemy who will expect us to be in pain for His Love. Looking at this with honesty is initially a bit disconcerting. It is not a pretty idea and it does not sound very loving. The ego thought system is not very loving because it was begun with fear, thieving, attack and murder as its core. It is only logical that when we look at it we see the themes that it was built on playing out within the illusion. The themes, ugly and hateful as they are, are not a part of who you are as the Son of God. These themes are the blocks that keep you from remembering who you are as God's child though. Looking at them without judgment with open eyes and honestly is the key to reclaiming their power. Recognizing that these ideas are part of the theme of the ego thought system has helped me to stop taking the ideas as my personal fault or my personal weakness. I have had to recognize that when I buy into the ego thought system I buy into all of its beliefs. The themes of being manipulative and hateful to get what I want are in that thought system. Then it is no surprise that I see myself being an ego.

## The Freedom of a Collective

There is great freedom in seeing the ego thought system and the thought system of the Holy Spirit as a collective. I have found it immensely liberating to stop pretending that I am nicer than I am feeling inside when I am too afraid to listen to the Holy Spirit. I have uncovered the beauty of being able to be honest with myself and admit what and whom I hate, or that I don't mind that a bad thing happened to a certain person or group of people; or that I hate Jesus or the Holy Spirit for the moment, because their teaching will lead me down a path where my individuality will become less and less important to me. I have found when I don't indulge my anger, and by that I mean take it out on others, but I don't pretend it is not there or that I am more spiritually advanced than I am. I am relieved at the release I feel. The irony of this for me has been that the things I am looking at used to cause great shame and guilt in me. Now I expect that when I choose the ego all of the ugly comes with it. It is not personal and the ugly part of this thought system is not me. It is a collective thought and for the moment I have chosen it. So the ugly part of this hate-filled thought system plays out in my life and I find myself fearful and feeling ugly, unkind thoughts. Then a part of me remembers that this is the package... the ego package comes with all of the accessories of hate. I am free to pick this package or to choose the Holy Spirit's gift. Sometimes I choose defenses but the freedom of not being able to justify it and the understanding of the collective mind prevent me from forgetting (for very long). I no longer have to lie to myself about how much I defend and how much I have hidden hate under these defenses. It is the most liberating feeling. It is ironic to me that I can look at the ugliest thoughts that I harbor and find that it is these thoughts that help me feel so connected to the Holy Spirit. It is these thoughts, always remembering the collective as I look at them, which are liberating me from this prison. It is these thoughts that I am grateful to see. Go figure? I did not believe the *Course* would give me this through looking at the ego. The book says that it will, but I doubted. I practiced and I continue to practice... and sometimes I continue to doubt. I can say that the experience is wonderful. You look at the ego collective thoughts and say... Yeah, yeah it's this collective defensive ego again... no surprise. You can stop thinking that because you have such ugly unkind thoughts it must mean that you are an ugly unkind person. The idea that you are ugly and unkind is part of the ego thought system. You have the ugly unkind thoughts because you connected to the ego-collective that is all. You have another choice to connect to the Holy Spirit's collective too. In the thought system of the Holy Spirit you are not capable of ugly unkind thoughts... then who are you?

The idea that the Son of God has to compromise, bargain and suffer to have love is a joke; we don't see the joke yet so it appears to be the only way to fill up the hole we feel in our soul. We have been greatly mistaken. Ask to see this idea of compromise and bargaining for love from the Holy Spirit's view and see what He shows you. The contrast from his view as a Mind to ours as bodies and personalities is extreme. The contrast from the defensive collective thought system to the Holy Spirit's is extreme as well.

The *Course* teaches that we are all suffering from the same problem. We are all stuck in the same bitter thought system of defensive thinking. We all desperately need a new Teacher to lead us out of the misperceptions that we have come to be so attached to. Can you imagine living and no longer believing in attack and defense? Who would you be without the belief in defending yourself? What about your thinking would change? How would the world look? Part of how I attempt to negotiate the subtle traps that defenses lead me to stepping into and then blaming someone else for is by the recognition that we all have the same problem. All of us at one time or another feel lonely and trapped in this crazy mixed up world. All of us walk around fearful that we will be hurt emotionally, physically and spiritually. All of us struggle with the purpose of being here. All of us at some point feel that we are out of place in this world... we just don't feel at home. Many of us are searching for a road that gives us answers. I don't believe that the answers lie in the world. My hope is internal where my Teacher of hope and Love resides. Together we can take a path home to God. We all need and want the same thing... to find a way home to God and out of the fear that this world provokes. We don't have to continue to destroy one another to have this; it is counterproductive and keeps us stuck in fear. We have been stuck on this seemingly endless treadmill long enough. If we could choose a different Teacher we would no longer see others in our classroom as our enemy. The people in our lives are our teachers. They are the ones onto whom we reflect our mirror. Through an honest look within the mirror (keeping the concept of this world being an illusion in our minds) we can remove the defenses that keep us from the Holy Spirit and find our peace.

## Defenses and our relationship with God

Part of the beauty of recognizing that this world is an illusion is that it returns the power of decision to the dreamer of the dream. The *Course* has taught me that God did not make this world… there is no world as this is only a dream. God being a good parent still cannot magically crawl into our dream and fix it for us. This idea contradicts most of our ideas of God as our rescuer. God cannot rescue us from a dream with which he is not involved. I still forget this idea in my practice of the *Course*. I find that my old habits of asking the Holy Spirit or Jesus to change my dream for me are dying hard. I want the dream to be a nicer and kinder place. I get angry that God cannot do this, as He is not also asleep. When I hear Ken saying that God does not even know about the world, let alone about my individual self, I get angry with him for bringing up such an uncomfortable topic. This idea that God does not even know about my dream is so frightening sometimes and I deny the power of my mind by demanding that the Holy Spirit make my dream better.

Generally speaking in the Judeo-Christian upbringing we were taught to expect that God would help us in the world. We pray to God for world peace, health, to save and keep the ones we love safe. We speak of God as having a plan for us. We refer to events and circumstances as act of or the will of God. We ask God to provide for us and to be the fixer of our fortune or misfortune. We set God up in this regard because when things don't go our way we get to blame it on Him. He becomes the one who lets us down and we fall prey to His lack of compassion, His wrath and His "mysterious ways" (Wapnick, Kenneth *Separation And Forgiveness The Four Splits and Their Undoing,* 1999). I believe that recognizing that this world is an illusion puts the power of redemption or damnation back into the dreaming mind. This gets God off the hook as the destroyer or provider of our happiness. It puts full responsibility on us for all the things that happen in the dream. Again we are not responsible for what others do in the dream, but we are responsible for our reactions and how we handle what they do. Most importantly we are responsible for choosing our Teacher. This is the only true choice, the choice between truth and deception. If we do not choose the Holy Spirit to help us He is powerless to do so. He needs our request and we need to ask for His guidance and wisdom. No one can force us to do this. It is our responsibility. I think this point is one of the things that make the *Course* such a unique spiritual thought system. I have learned through my study of the *Course* that it is myself that I pray to (not my body self but the mind that is asleep… I pray to the dreamer of the dream, the part of this dreamer who remembers the Holy Spirit). I pray that I choose the Jesus as my teacher. When I am stuck in defensive thinking without Him, He is powerless to help me (unless I ask). I don't ask Him to come into my dream and change it... I ask that He help me change my mind about who I believe I am so that I recognize that I am the dreamer. If I really knew that I was the dreamer and still one with God in Heaven the dream would contain no power over me.

Putting the power back into the mind that is dreaming has helped me recognize how my defenses directly mirror my relationship with God. In truth we have never left Heaven and we are still connected to the One Mind of God. Think back to the myth of Adam and Eve demanding that they be individuals and God simply smiling knowing that this was not a possibility. Adam and Eve demand that their request for individuality be upheld and in their fear of demanding this from God they believe that they forced the wish to be reality. I have explained this using the *Course's* symbol that they have fallen asleep and began dreaming that they were individuals. Nothing at all changed in Heaven... but Adam and Eve (also symbols) think that something did. God does not know what they are thinking as they sleep for all continues to be One in Heaven (Text page 236 T-13.in.3). Adam and Eve (that's all individuals including you and I) believe that they pulled off the impossible and destroyed Oneness. Their proof is that fact that they see themselves as having bodies and their bodies are separated. Seeing separation around them they believe that God must have been destroyed, as oneness cannot exist in twoness. In the myth the *Course* teaches that this is the birthplace of sin. As the *Course* has shown us earlier the belief in sin causes guilt and a fear of punishment. Guilt is the driving force in projection. Sin does not exist in the Holy Spirit's thought system. Without the belief in sin there is nothing to be guilty about; then there is no guilt to project.

So... all this time that we have bought into this idea that we live separated from God we have been deceiving ourselves. We simply fell asleep. We cannot exist outside of Heaven ... nothing can (Text pages 493-494 T-23.II.19). The thought of separation and individuality is a deception. Ken uses the wonderful example of having your dreams analyzed to expand on this point. If you went to a therapist who interpreted dreams they would teach you that everything within your dream is literally a symbol of yourself. Dream symbols are visual representations of your thoughts. Let's imagine for a moment that this world and the symbols that are included within it are representations of your thoughts. The last thought that you had in Heaven (prior to falling asleep as all thoughts must be taking place there because we never left) was the one of demanding your individuality and being willing to destroy Heaven to get what you want. Within this dream we as a world and as individuals mirror this idea in everything that we do. It is helpful for me to watch what I do with people in my life when I am annoyed or insistent that I am right and then to recognize that within my relationship with them is my relationship with God. I want to give a clear example of this.

Within my illusion I have recognized a theme of learning how to forgive myself for feeling victimized by people who are very demanding and have narcissistic tendencies. I call these people 'high maintenance'. They have a strong demand to have all of the attention focused on them and they can be brutally competitive if they are not in the limelight almost all the time. For a number of years I have seen this pattern of many narcissistic people in my life but I have had a hard time recognizing the mirror. I kept saying, "Jesus I don't get it. I just don't think that I am very narcissistic, but this lesson keeps popping up. Can you help me see what is going on from your perspective?" I have been very resistant to accepting the answer that Jesus has provided and I make snail like insights. High maintenance people annoy me a great deal. I find them to be too much work. They do not do well with entertaining themselves; unless you are oohh-ing and ahh-ing over how great they are they are ill at ease. They have no interest in anyone else (really) and unless you fill up their insecure emptiness and shower them with attention they negate you. They demand your attention to avoid that ill at ease feeling. I can never relax with these people and I depart tired from any event that I share with them. They never approve of things that others do because they always have to top you. There is no point in having an honest conversation with them but God forbid you ignore them... there will be hell to pay. Narcissistic people bore and enrage me... yet in an odd way I feel that they have some authority over me because of how demanding they are. I resent the demands and my feeling is that if the demands are not met I will be negated and treated as if I am irrelevant in their presence.

I cannot see the mirror. Am I narcissistic and using the defense of reaction formation? I only know that narcissistic people can push my buttons faster than lightning and my rage and fury come out with full force in their presence. I hate these people and I like it that way. I have recognized that I prefer to revel in the hate that I feel for them, than to have the peace of God that I have the power to choose. Insane perhaps, but I have not been willing to bend on this issue. This is not because I am a sinful rotten person, but because I become too fearful of looking within. I fear that if I forgave this problem, that the personality to which I connect myself would lose the self-importance that I have attached to being 'low maintenance'. I think this is a clear example of how I use reaction formation. I have repressed my desire to be the center of the world deep down and then I project in onto people who conveniently take on these personality features that I have rejected.

I recently began to realize that from the perspective of defensive thinking I view God as a narcissist. He would not share the limelight and give me my individuality. Unless we follow His rules He has the power to negate me to hell. The ego-God is the ultimate authority. I am not a 'high maintenance' person because I set up this dream to show this illusory God that I would not steal too much of His limelight. Then I see others who appear to have stolen more and I rage at this idea that they have more i.e. I rage at the idea that God refused this request for individuality. The demanding people in my life are the victimizers and the thieves. I only asked for a tiny bit of attention, but those 'sinful' people took more than their share. The ego-God will be angry with them too and I will be off the hook. Whew! My rage and boredom have nothing at all to do with the 'high maintenance' or narcissistic people in my life. My rage is at God for not allowing me to have what I demanded. My boredom might be a mask that I place over the thought of giving back what I stole (in the illusion…. Remember nothing happened in reality). Every time I find myself dreading, hating, resenting or being disgusted by the time I am spending with a good old needy narcissistic person, I have an opportunity to pray that I choose the Holy Spirits perception of this theme that plays out in my life. I rarely choose His perception of this. One day I might be less fearful and more able to experience the truth about this fear. When I choose His interpretation the investment I have in seeing them as the cause of my anger and fear will disappear… I remain hopeful that this moment is only a choice away.

### Symbolism

On an abstract level all of the figures in the dream are a piece of you. On a practical level what does this imply? I have heard Ken put emphasis on careful understanding of this point as it can be greatly misunderstood and cause great pain to people trying to practice this thought system. It is important that we recognize that on a practical day-to-day level we are not responsible for the things that people in our lives do; even if they are pieces of ourselves. Let's say that you were a victim of rape, assault or incest, you as a person in the world did not cause this to happen because of your bad thoughts, and you are not responsible for the actions of others. What you are responsible for is how you act and react to the world around you.

When you recognize on an experiential level that the world is an illusion you are then consciously aware of being the dreamer of the dream. This conscious state includes the absence of fear and a lasting connection to God. At that point in your spiritual maturity you would recognize that the victim and the victimizer of any situation are symbols of the same mind. To attempt to live in the world with this belief when you begin your journey of accepting responsibility for your dream can be very destructive. As your awareness of your Mind increases it is necessary that you learn this lesson. Keep in mind the illusory state of this dream as it is a major theme. It should not be a weapon to increase your guilt, shame or fear. People can fall into the trap of using this idea as a weapon against others. I have heard Ken caution people about this easy trap in many of his workshops. An example may be to tell someone who is physically ill or in emotional or physical pain that the world is an illusion after all and nothing is happening. Or to encourage them to accept the truth that this is a dream and their pain or their illness will go away. Ken explains that people in pain of any kind (emotional, physical or spiritual) are in a heightened state of fear to begin with and it is not very loving to slam them over the head with something that will increase their fear. It is an attack disguised as love (forgiveness to destroy). In general this thought system is a private issue between you and the Teacher that you choose. The Holy Spirit will wait for your request for a change of perception prior to providing it. He will do the same for people in your life; your job is to change your mind and to have some faith that the Holy Spirit will do His job and help everyone who asks.

It is a bit comical to me how often we believe that God is in need of our assistance in order for Him to get things done around here. Many of the motivating forces behind our desire to feel in control we call the 'will of God'. In our desire to be helpful, which can be a force that the Holy Spirit accesses to work *through* us, we often take charge and decide how the help should be allocated. When we allow the Holy Spirit to help through us it is an effortless process that does not have much at all to do with who we are as individuals. When we are invested in being helpful, and in the outcome of our help we may be fooling ourselves. These ego tricks are so subtle that it is easy, and for me inevitable, that we will fall into at least one or two traps a day. We are conditioned to be independent minded and to think for ourselves. The Holy Spirit says that we are small children who do not know much. He explains that we are the students and not the teacher. In the workbook lesson 155 he encourages us to step back and get our desire to be in charge out of the way so that He can teach. He does not need us to teach Him a thing or two. He does not require that we show Him how wonderful and kind we are. He knows that when we are connected to defensive thinking we are not kind. He also knows that we are the Son's of God full of grandeur and beauty. We do not have to convince Him that we are worthy of His love or of salvation. We do have to recognize that as the ones in need of salvation we are not the teachers. We need to practice stepping back and allowing Him to guide (Workbook pages 291-293 W-155. 1-14). This takes some practice and some patience. When I first learned this idea in my study of the *Course* I would invite the Holy Spirit in to help me with very mundane things in life that had to do with what I did in the world. I would ask Him about something I should buy or where I should drive to avoid traffic. When it came to what I considered the more serious life decisions I left Him out of it. I would take my decision to Him when I had made it already and ask Him what He thought. Then I read the *Rules for Decision* in chapter 30 of the text and I became so angry about what the Holy Spirit was asking me to do that I threw the *Course* away for a few months (Text pages 625-629 T-30.I.1-17).

When I picked up the *Course* again a few months later I read the *Rules for Decision* again and I incorporated these rules into my daily meditation in the morning. This section of the *Course* explained me to a tee. I would make a decision and then ask the Holy Spirit about the decision I made as if I was asking Him to help me make a decision. Jesus explains in this section that this is a big problem for those of us who believe we are bodies. We are used to making decisions about what we do all the time. Now I was asking to be taught and having a bit of trouble giving up my insistence that I know best. I am the student and students follow the direction of a teacher. What I was doing was judging a problem from my perspective and deciding what should be done about it. After I had decided what should be done I would ask the Holy Spirit how he thought I should proceed with what I had determined should be done. I felt that I was asking for help... but I was really fooling myself and not allowing the Holy Spirit to help me. So, as a typical human who believes that I am right, I had a struggle with the idea that I needed to be guided prior to my deciding what the problem is. I simply had to surrender the entire day and the entire process to the Holy Spirit if I really wanted to learn. I don't always do this. Sometimes I do and sometimes I fool myself without any awareness that I am fooling myself. Other times I outwardly don't care what the Holy Spirit thinks and I do what I want even thought experience has taught me that I would be happier listening to Him.

I have a strong attachment to being Catherine and I have no intention of not keeping her... I also have an opposing desire to find a peace that the world cannot shatter. Like a bad thunderstorm these contradicting ideas explode in my mind and I fight my best interest and myself. I take this a bit less seriously then I used to (except with those narcissists) and I find that as I ease up on my self-condemnation for such conflicting ideas I am happier.

Very often I still insist on making decisions without the guidance of the Holy Spirit. What I have learned is that if I practice the *Rules for Decision* well, then the little things that I used to ask for help with, such as how to avoid traffic or anything like that, never comes into play. I simply have no need to even think about these things as my day meanders on. The days are easy and the thought of what to do about anything is rather irrelevant. It is as if the Holy Spirit drives and I am a passenger in the process. It is fun.

All of us are searching for happiness in one form or another. We all want the same things pretty much. How we see ourselves accomplishing the goal of happiness may vary but the idea is universal. We want to be without fear and we pursue this goal of happiness by searching for something or someone in the world. I have noted a number of times that the goal of happiness is a fine one but that perhaps the avenues that we are walking to achieve this goal will not get us there. I have advocated that we continue to pursue the goal but that we request a different teacher as we continue on with our lives. I believe that all of our relationships reflect our relationship with God at their core. Therefore a careful examination of the purpose behind any and all relationships, with people and with goals, might be helpful in the process of looking. It is impossible to bring something you do not see to the Holy Spirit for His interpretation. So let's look a bit more closely and honestly at our relationships.

# Chapter 9:

### The Circle of Specialness

The *Course* goes into great detail about the idea of specialness in the world. Specialness is an ego weapon that is heavily (and somewhat heavenly) guarded by defenses. Sometimes it is difficult to see as a result. My understanding of specialness has deepened through my study of the *Course* and through the teaching of Ken and the Foundation staff. Specialness is how we delineate whom we will love, whom we like, for whom we don't have any feeling at all and whom we hate. It is the logic that the ego uses to get what it believes will keep happiness in its grasp. Specialness involves the inclusion and the exclusion of people from your life. Special love is a small circle of people who are liked, loved, needed or wanted in your life. Special hate is the people we blame for our misfortune; those who we feel have victimized us and whom we may exclude from our lives. People who fall in the category of special love can just as easily become objects of special hate. Having our demands and needs met by others is a requirement of specialness.

All specialness is an attempt to maintain happiness within your life. This goal is a great one; the means to attain the happiness is flawed. When we look at how we attempt to keep happiness in our lives with specialness as our tool, we begin to recognize why we have been so empty and why every worldly goal we reach in life leaves us unfulfilled in the long run. Nothing in the world works forever, nothing lasts and that worry about losing happiness leaves us fearful. We will never attain the goal of happiness and peace if fear is the thought behind it.

The pursuit of happiness is an attempt to avoid pain and fear. The search for that which will keep us happy is a statement that says without something I am unhappy and in pain. An example to help us understand this idea is easily seen in our relationship to food and water. Hunger and thirst are painful. Our bodies remind us that we are thirsty and hungry through pangs in our bellies and aching in our throats. To avoid the pain of starvation and dehydration we eat and drink. We then feel better. Emotional needs take the same form. We feel the pain of loneliness or the emptiness of sorrow. We look for the object or person who can ease this hunger and soothe the pain. We believe on an emotional level that we will die if we do not find something outside our self to fill us up. We search for the thing to give us the happiness that we believe we lack. Believing that we are incomplete is the ego's baseline. The baseline began with the idea that we lost God when we shattered Heaven by insisting that we be individuals. Worldly things cannot fill this emptiness of missing and longing for God. From that point we attempt to find completion outside of ourselves. This implies that if the special object from outside is not found that we may be in pain for our lifetime. I am in no way attempting to imply that we pretend that we do not need the love of others in our lives. Research has shown that infants fail to thrive without external love and affection. I would be lonely without others. We are social beings and giving and sharing our time and our love is one of the ways to keep peace in our hearts. Still every time we feel the hunger of loneliness and the thirst for fulfillment we are ultimately longing for God. Any other answers to that call will leave us wanting.

The fear of not finding or doing without the correct external specialness object can become so great that we will walk all over people to get what we believe we need to attain happiness. The belief in scarcity plays a role here. In this world we believe there is only a limited supply of love to share (again I am talking about thoughts not things) and if we do not want to lose, we better make sure we win. Someone has to lose… this is what we believe. There are those we consider winners and those we consider losers in life. We do not think that it would be possible for every one of us to win. Because of this belief in scarcity and competition, we worry about losing what little we have. So when we find the happiness that we were seeking we wait with trepidation for it to be stolen from our grasp both figuratively and literally. We attempt to bargain with others to keep what we have found. When the bargain works special love continues, when the bargain fails special hate takes the place of special love.

The ego teaches us to guard the little we have… a fear-based thought. Fear cannot be at the root of happiness. True happiness cannot coexist with fear; they are mutually exclusive. The goals of happiness in the world are always centered on the needs of the body. The needs of the body will never be satisfied (Text page 58 T-4.II.7). The mind connected to God is completely satisfied and without needs. We continue to insist that if we can meet our needs in the correct fashion that we will attain lasting happiness. It takes great learning to recognize that this will never work. All of our needs contain at their core fear and emptiness. In and of themselves, pursuing goals and meeting our needs are not bad things. It is fine to be famous, powerful, and wealthy and to have great love and pleasure in your life. The belief that these things are the keys to lasting happiness is the mistake. The belief that things outside of the Love of God can keep us feeling complete, whole and safe is a mistaken belief. To believe in and pursue these goals does not make us sinful bad people, but it does indicate that we are confused about where

140

happiness can be attained. First we must understand what it is we believe then the mistake can be corrected with spiritual guidance.

## Substitutes for God

Fame, power, money and pleasure are the substitutes we use to replace the Love of God that we feel we have lost. Most of us, looking with some honesty, will recognize that we tell our self that if only we had the right partner we would be happy. Or we work diligently to climb the ladder of financial success believing that the things that money can buy will bring with them peace and happiness. Many of us believe that power and fame are the answers to the emptiness that we feel deep inside. We rave about our successes with bravado hoping that we can convince our selves that we have found the answer to peace. Power is no substitute for Heaven, and God cannot be replaced with any of the goals that we have placed as blocks to keep His love from our awareness. A world that is so full of pain and suffering, and a species so confused about how to acquire peace is hell. The *Course* has taught me that there is no substitute for the Love of God that will keep any of us satisfied and peaceful. A small piece of Heaven (power, money, fame or pleasure) cannot come into hell and make it Heaven. The only answer to the call for the Love of God is the Love of God (Text pages 630-631 T-30.III.2).

We believe in scarcity. This belief creates great fear within us. For certain things in life we would rather kill then contemplate how we could manage without them. I was not surprised to hear that as Y2K approached Americans stocked up on guns, canned goods and water. Now in a practical sense it is smart to be prepared and take precautions. Having some canned goods, water and batteries just in case was a fine idea if it was helpful to ease your mind. But gun sales were at record highs. Why was that do you think? I believe that this is a great example of how we will defend ourselves to keep what we see as ours. It speaks to how fearful we are that someone will come and steal from us. We will defend our things as if they are our selves. We see our things as if they are our piece of so-called Heaven. On the level of mind we defend our individuality to the death.

Many times we don't even know what it is we long for. If you knew that it was the Love of God that you longed for then perhaps your approach to how you sought happiness and peace would be curtailed. Generally speaking we do not recognize that we have a mind, soul or spirit. We don't recognize that the longing is for a connection to that more honest part of whom we are. Part of the purpose of looking that I have found helpful is that I now am clearer about what I am yearning to have. It is not of this world that my

141

longing is stemming. I still confuse this when I am afraid; but even a tiny bit of clarity through which the Holy Spirit may teach through is enough.

We believe that we can substitute the love of God with things and be satisfied and content. We make an ego-God out of money, power, fame and pleasure. We attempt to attain these things believing that they will make us complete. If someone attempts to take our money, lure our partner from us, squash our sense of power or deny us our glory, we will psychologically and even physically kill to keep what we see as ours. We speak of playing "the game" of love or of having the business "killer instinct". We refer to people who can maintain their political power or who are skilled in keeping the public interested in their fame as successful and lucky. We believe that if we had what they have we would be happy. Substitutes for God will always fail us. The ego sets up these substitutes and leads us down a path of "seek and do not find" (Text page 223 T-12.IV.1). We are looking for the benign goal of happiness and an easy, internal-contentment. We find unsatisfied goals that become cancers that eat away at our peace, bring us discontent and fill us with hopelessness. Happiness that lasts evades us and to ease our feelings of pain and suffering we seek again only to discover that we are just as lost and in just as much pain as before. We will compete, manipulate, lie, cheat, steal and kill to reach our goals. We can become so lost in the pursuit that we never stop and ask what it is we believe this goal will truly bring us? We are out of perspective and unclear how to change our view.

### Special Hate

Let's look at special hate more closely. It is easy to see what we hate and despise in life. It is easy for me to recognize that I would prefer to exclude 'high maintenance' narcissistic people from my life. They push my buttons and I give them my peace. I blame them for my feeling of being ill at ease and then I can justify that my discomfort is their fault. When I can, I avoid them with purpose and intention. Our special hate partners are the ones that we blame for our misfortune and unhappiness. We feel like they will victimize us, or that they have victimized us already. A parent who did not seem to love you the way you needed to be loved; a group of people who committed crimes against humanity; the child abuser who lives next door; family members who drive you crazy and have mistreated you. You see special hate in racism, sexism, anti-gay and lesbian protests, pro-gay and lesbian protests, pro-choice and pro-life violence, political stalemates and the fear of the mentally ill. The list can go on and on. When you can clearly delineate a person or a group of people as different from you and either worthy of your rage or not worth your time, you are looking at special hate.

They may be the people you live with and judge harshly or they may be people you have never met but whom you decided are less that you. Special hate can take millions of forms; the intention is always to see yourself as different from, better than or more worthy of love than someone who you have excluded from your love (Text page 500 T-24.1.3.5).

### Special Love

Special love is much more subtle and tricky to recognize. As people, who believe that we are bodies and that the world is real, we have concluded that we have certain needs that should be met in order for us to be happy. Let's break this idea of needing down to a survival strategy. We naturally require some daily nourishment if we are to survive. Things like oxygen, water and food are things that are essential to daily living. It is easy to see in these examples that we find something outside of ourselves and we 'take it in' to meet our needs. We are glad that it is there and we appreciate that we can take it as we see fit. We don't consider the impact that it has on others or on the world; we need it for survival and we take it. As I said before the same process that sustains us physically we believe is required for our emotional sustenance. We find special love partners who we believe will fill us up. We pursue careers that are supposed to satisfy our hunger for learning and accomplishment and exceed out financial requirements; and we seek glory and fame so that our greatness can be adored and our name can live on without us. We crave power that we may make a difference in the world and or that our desire to control others is satisfied. We seek passion and pleasure in our bodies and the bodies of others. We believe that passion exists with great lasting joy in one or all of the above goals. The bargain of special love is the exchange of something that you have, that another sees himself as needing. If he fills the need in you, the bargain works, the exchange is made and we say that we are happy. The happiness is conditional on the unspoken deal that was struck (Text pages 112-113 T-7.I.4) (Text page 451 T-21.III.1). Meet my need or I will withdraw my love is at the root of all bargains. It is conditional, selfish and full of demands. In truth a bargain of conditional love is not very loving. Behind the bargain is the fear of loss (not a bad person, just a frightened one). Peaceful happiness cannot be maintained with fear of loss at its root. This is what the world calls love.

Most of us say, "Well that is just the way it is." Your job in a relationship, in your work and in your family is to meet the needs of someone and if you don't, you will lose him. This thinking is the logic of the ego. To attain lasting peace and happiness this must be questioned and reinterpreted by someone with greater wisdom than we humans currently have. We accept this as love. We see it as factual. It is insane. Why don't we believe that we deserve to give and receive unconditional Love? I am not suggesting that we choose to treat people like doormats and demand that they love us unconditionally. Or that we accept being treated like dirt and not standing up for what we believe to be just and right. I am also not suggesting that we not do nice things for those we care about. Getting stuck in the form of what these words are saying is easy. Special love is an attitude and a belief. It is not what you do in the world. Being unkind or withholding of love in the world would not be helpful. It would be foolish and it would not help. We can find thousands of examples of these attempts in life and they bring with them pain, loneliness and suffering. It is important to behave ethically, kindly and with peace as your goal. The cost of reinforcing unkind, hateful, angry behavior is self-suffering. The goal of this practice is peace and happiness not more pain. Conditional love causes pain to both the giver and the receiver. It is not the road to peace. The recognition of this is essential to the process of bringing this problem to the Holy Spirit. He has the Wisdom and experience to help us see the futility in this practice. I want to share some practical examples to help bring this point to light.

When I graduated with my bachelors I had no clear direction regarding my career. I knew two things: first I wanted to have a secretary and second I wanted to be rich. It was no accident that I decided to work for a Wall Street firm and pursue my series seven license as a stockbroker. I began by working for a couple of brokers so that I could learn as I was studying. I had the books for my test and I was setting up a study schedule. I really liked the job in an exciting sort of way. I worked for two brokers who were big into option trading. Trading options is like betting on horses. The pace is fast and the action is high. It was fun. One day one of the brokers, Jim, who had an office down the hall from me did not show up or call into work. This went on for a few days. No one knew where he was. A few days later the branch manager announced that Jim was dead. His burial had been the day prior to this announcement. The cause of his death was not disclosed. As you can imagine many rumors began to float around the office; suicide or a drug overdose were the top two. His family requested that no flowers be sent to their home as their arrival upset his children too much.

I had a bird's eye view into Jim's office. I was not yet a broker... I was a secretary. The position of my desk was such that I looked directly into this man's office whenever I raised my head. The reaction of my colleagues to Jim's death surprised me. No one seemed to do much or speak much about Jim. There was very little outward display of grief. There seemed to be no need for closure on the relationship between them and Jim. Who he was seemed to fall away and the important matter of money began to surface. The focus of the conversation was on Jim's accounts and who would inherit them. You see Jim was a successful broker. He had a wall of binders with accounts. The brokers in the office began to bicker and fight over these books. I even saw people attempt to sneak into his office to take some of his binders. The branch manager had to confiscate Jim's book and keep them in his office until the distribution of his accounts was settled. The accounts were distributed alphabetically. The office was in bedlam during the process. People were feeling unfairly treated and left out; they were feeling that their worth was based on how many of Jim's accounts they inherited. They were backstabbing each other and outwardly fighting. The place was a mess from my perspective.

You see I had a great seat from which to watch this event play out. I could not have any accounts as I was not licensed. Many of the people in the office were my friends as well as my colleagues. I hung out with these people and I liked them. We went to the South Street Seaport after work and we ate lunch together and laughed about things. They were good people. I knew that most of them had lost perspective about these accounts and about money in general. I also knew that if these people could lose perspective so fast that I would too. I did not know what to do. I did know that I did not want to lose perspective about money. I called a bicycling organization and signed up for a summer bike tour to help me clear my mind. I called a former boss and asked her if I could waitress in her restaurant for a month prior to the bicycling trip and then I gave my two weeks notice and left the firm that I was working for. You see it is so easy to get hooked into the seduction of money, power, fame and pleasure. It can happen to any and all of us unless we remain vigilant to prevent it. I was lucky that I was not a broker at the time of Jim's death. I would have become part of the chaos as I would have been more invested in the outcome. I had the distance to recognize that I would get sucked up into the temptation of money and the power it appears to yield. I am sure that this story is not unusual and I am sure that all of us with any insight will recognize that there have been times when we have lost our of perspective about something in our life that we believed would keep us happy.

### Bargains

So let's say you are pursuing fame. You have an agent and you think that he is great and that he has the kind of connections that will take you far. You make a business bargain. The agent finds you work and he gets a piece of the royalties. Fair, and you both are upfront that you are using each other to get something. This is a symbiotic relationship of true love. It's a win-win situation to start. Time passes and the agent doesn't return your calls that quickly. You wait too long in between jobs. You get annoyed at the agent and you are angry. Your peace is disturbed because you do not feel the business deal was upheld on your agent's end. You bad mouth your agent and look for a new one. So now you have a new agent (who you love) and you begin to do well and get more work then you anticipated. You decide at some point that your agent is not assertive enough for you and you deserve someone with access to more. You begin to feel dissatisfied with what you have. Your previously win-win relationship now leaves you annoyed and wanting. You find yourself looking and hoping for a new agent who can do better by you. You complain and bad mouth this agent and again your happiness is disturbed. You change the rules of the bargain and move on to another agent.

We bargain for employment and the trade off is easy to see. An employer hires you to complete a job and you complete it for some monitory reward. So you are psyched about the great new job you landed. The people you work for initially seem wonderful and you fool yourself into thinking that perhaps this is the place where you could be happy. The place where the nagging discontent and petty office politics won't supercede the love you have of your work. The boss seems professional and fair. You can learn a lot from these folks and it is an upward move. Big raise and that is what you wanted. A couple of months go by and you find that the same pattern of backstabbing occurs at this office as well, the boss expects you to work long hours... this is not the dream job that you envisioned. If only they lived up to their interview personalities you would be happy. There are some good things, but the bad just creeps in. Perhaps you will stay at this job and simply complain about the unfair situation, perhaps you will move on. The happiness that you were seeking evades you once again.

How about that new love of yours? Things are so great, the sex is awesome and he is so thoughtful and kind. He takes you the way you are and you feel like a woman in his company. Does love ever get better than this? You talk for hours. Yep this is the one! The one to take away all your loneliness; truly see you and support all of your endeavors. You know that he will always tell you how he feels. He is open and honest. You are in love. The fairytale ends and reality sets in... like socks on the kitchen table and different expectations and styles of parenting and how about his spending habits. The complete (but momentary) satisfaction of early love eases and the good and the bad of a partner come to light. Then there are the bargains of love; these are manifold and varied. The thought behind them is one of a trade off. I will give you physical comfort but in return I require physical safety. I will give you financial stability and in return I expect a clean home and home cooking. Then the bargains get subtle and unconscious. You will keep me from loneliness and I will give you someone about whom to complain. I will keep you feeling strong and needed and you will indulge my addiction. The list of emotional bargains is endless. The Foundation staff has referred to these bargains as an emotional cannibalism; we take in what we need emotionally from someone outside of ourselves in an attempt to fill ourselves up. Like the food that we ingest, we take what someone has to offer as his love and complain when the whole of our expectations is left unfilled. This is difficult to recognize because we call this love in the world. We get angry with our lovers when they don't meet our needs. We demand that they change and become more like we expect them to be. We complain and blame them for what we lack because we unconsciously believe that they have not held up to their end of the bargain.

If the going gets bad we discard our special love partners and we transfer them over to the special hate section of our thoughts. Like digested food they are discarded as a waste product would be. We are done with them. We took what we needed and left disappointed. An ugly breakup or divorce turns the partner of your life to the enemy you may be repulsed by. If we find that we no longer need someone, like our agent, boss, colleague or partner we can easily turn against him with anger and resentment. We justify our actions telling ourselves how horrible they were, what liars and how they cheated us. We find friends and family to tell our tale of woe to and they heartily agree that we were unfairly treated. We speak of the ones we rejected with venom in our voices, those we used to love and now hate. We rationalize and justify our rage. We hate ourselves for picking such losers to begin with. It is an ugly process and we convince ourselves that our actions are correct because our bargain was not upheld. We did our part and the partner we chose let us down. We have fallen into the trap of being helpless victims once again.

Ken has helped me to see that special love and special hate are not limited to relationships that we have with people. We can have a special relationship with any of the things we believe we can substitute for the Love of God. Drugs, alcohol, food, sex, money, exercise, our pets and our bodies to name just a few of our most favorite special relationships. Addiction of any kind is a special relationship. We feel empty and lonely or we are full of hatred or anger and we want to feel better. We find a substance weather it be alcohol, drugs or food and we take it in thinking that the hole within will be filled by this. Initially, like most but not all special love relationships, we believe we have found the answer to our prayers. We feel better for a time but the hole comes back to haunt us. The pain and suffering have returned and the anxiety about them encourages us to find the substance that kept this pain at bay for a time. The substance causes us to suffer. We continue to use the substance regardless of our suffering for a multitude of reasons. It is often essential to find professional help to deal with addiction. Our bodies become physically addicted. The process of breaking this habit may take professional support and medical intervention.

We leave relationships, jobs and many other life situations thinking on some level that we will get it right next time. The pain, loss and anger we feel will not happen if we could just find the right job or the right partner, the correct way to love and be loved or the right substance. If we had enough money we would no longer have to worry. If people would simply recognize our talent and leadership and provide us with the right expression of this we would be perfectly happy. It rarely occurs to us that all of our endeavors for this elusive happiness are in vain. Happiness is an inside-out process. It can accompany fame, power, money and great love but it is not contingent on them. Inside-out happiness is unconditional. The expectation for something outside of yourself to complete you implies that God created you incomplete. The Almighty does not make such mistakes. Completion lies within you. You can pursue other avenues to attain it, but a feeling of satisfaction will be fleeting without God. The goal of attaining lasting peace and happiness is a mighty goal; the recognition that completion is within is indeed difficult to recognize let alone maintain. To begin to recognize this as the truth is an arduous process for most of us. It requires devotion to accepting help and allowing that help to be your guide. It is a life long process of devotion to the goal of happiness.

The pursuit of goals in life is not a bad thing. Reach for the goals to which you aspire. It is fine if you want to be a millionaire, to fight for the rights of the oppressed, to be a star or to search for your soul mate. I know I keep saying that the world is an illusion, but for most of us this idea is an intellectual construct only. Trying to live as if you have the experience of knowing that this world is an illusion when you do not is not practical. We have to begin where we believe we are. We believe we live in this world and we strive to reach our goals. As you strive keep in mind that nothing in this world will fill you with lasting happiness except the Love of God... and that Love will lead you to a greater experience of this world being an illusion. A practical approach to this practice means that you continue to have the same relationships you always have had, but with a different Teacher. I spoke earlier about my refusal to create abundance in my life partly because I have accepted the incorrect belief that suffering is holy and partly because I was

148

denying the power of my mind. I asked for Spiritual guidance in this area so I could see where I was stuck from the Holy Spirits perspective. I still do things in the world to create abundance but with a different purpose. The goal remains to attain peace and happiness.

Looking at the treachery of specialness is ugly and you might not like what you see. The Holy Spirit explains that you might find the process a bit disconcerting. What you are doing is not because you are an evil, sinful or rotten person, it is simply that you are fearful of the love of God. You insist, like all of us, that you are the individual you see in the mirror each morning (Ken's example). The fear of not knowing who you are and the idea that this individuality is not real causes resistance in all of us. We are not alone in this process. We have replaced the Love that God shares with us with a love of bargains and betrayals. We do not think it unusual for people who love each other to become irate with one another. We call this natural and human. Well in this world it is natural and human; but in the realm of God perhaps that concept is viewed as insane. Love cannot rage. God is not angry. One of the most hopeful ideas that I have learned in my study of the *Course* is that God is not angry. I breathe a sigh of relief and I recognize that the Biblical idea of fearing God is based on a God of vengeance, not a God of Love. It is then that I feel that I can turn to God for help out of this mess. Prior to this I felt that the 'fear of Jesus' was the Judeo-Christian truth. It is not the truth; and the people who teach it are not evil or sinful for their teaching… they are simply afraid, that is all.

I suggest some caution as you examine the ugliness of your specialness. The *Course* does not advocate abandoning all of the relationships in your life because you see the ulterior motives that you use to manipulate and control the people in your life. It does not advocate leaving your job, your family or stopping doing the things that you do in life. It is not suggested that you cancel your insurance or give away your possessions because the world is not real. It also in no way advocates doing whatever it is you please in the world regardless of how unkind it is because the whole thing is make believe anyway. I have often heard Ken explain that the *Course* is a practical guide for average people leading average lives. It encourages us simply to live a normal life doing all the things that we do in life with a different Teacher. That is all. A simple formula, but not an easy undertaking. Perhaps in the process you will make changes in your life… that is fine. Normal people make changes in their lives from time to time. Your life will basically remain the same as you practice; your perspective may change. What you let go, is your investment in pain, suffering, guilt and sacrifice. You stop personalizing people's anger and you see attack as a call for help out of the fear of the ego. You begin to recognize that we are all afraid and in need of compassion and love. This creates a melting away of your defenses... or a removal of the blocks that keep you unaware that you have remained as God created you (Text page 153 T-8.VII.11.1). As you see more of the truth within you, you will experience a happier life regardless of the changes that occur or do not occur in it.

As you continue with the process you begin to grasp on an experiential level, that you can expand your thinking and live this new thought system on a daily practical level. Great spiritual teachers have been able to do this... they walk their talk (or they walk their thoughts) so to speak. Their thinking is expanded. Their relationships and way of relating to others lacks defense. They become the role models that I admire and wish to emulate. I find great comfort in the idea that I have the option to think with defenselessness. How is it possible to begin to walk this talk? I have found that when I look, there are some wonderful role models who teach me, through their example, that living a defenseless thought system is possible, can be practical and it can even be fun!

# Chapter 10:

### Expand Your Thinking (think outside the box)

I spoke earlier in the text about the movie Gandhi and how Gandhi spoke to the English leader and asked that the India people and the English remain friends. Gandhi was clear that the English were expected to leave his country but his anger at the English appeared non-existent to me. I was moved and confused by his request. I do not know how people can have such clarity of purpose and not color it with rage. It is an experience beyond any of my own. During my writing of this book I have been reading His Holiness the Dalai Lama's book *Ethics for the New Millennium.* His Holiness tells a story about his friend and a fellow monk Lopon-la who was imprisoned by the Chinese after the Dalai Lama escaped his country. Lopon-la had been imprisoned for many years and he was forced to renounce his religion and he was tortured. His Holiness explains in his book that when he was united with his friend he was pleased to see that his friend remained serene and peaceful as if his imprisonment had little effect on his peace of mind. The Dalai Lama asks Lopon-la if he was ever afraid during his imprisonment and Lopon-la explains that "there was one thing that scared him: the possibility that he might lose compassion and concern for his jailers." (p102, *Ethics for the new Millennium*) This amazed me... to lose compassion and concern for his jailers is not the thought, let alone the answer, that would have even scratched the surface of how I think. To have compassion and concern for these jailers did not occur to me. To lose it then would be impossible... I would have to have it to begin with. Only if I had compassion for my jailers could the thought of losing it enter my mind. How is it possible that Lopon-la had this compassion to begin with? Maybe Lopon-la does not see specialness as I see it. He appears from His Holiness' explanation to lack any attraction to special hate and special love. I imagine that he saw no difference between himself, his teacher the Dalai Lama and his captors. I am inspired and hopeful that there are some of us humans out there who can do this. This story of Lopon-la has been etched upon my mind since reading it. I still cannot fathom this state of mind so healed that it can love an enemy during an invasion of its right to have basic freedom. I am hopeful that this is possible. It is an ideal that I strive to attain... as a student I am encouraged by the example.

When the Holy Spirit shows you how God observes and interprets specialness you will smile with Joy and perhaps sob with relief at how mistaken we have been. In looking at the concept of specialness the Holy Spirit would see us as small children who have a fantastic belief in magic that an adult would not believe. A child may tell his parent that he will grow wings by morning so that he can fly to a school in a different world where he is king. That would make him more special than all the kids. The parent would not take the fantasy literally. Parents smile at their children's dreams of power and specialness. The child on the other hand may take the idea quiet seriously. He may believe that it is real and play this game for some time. The parent watches. The Holy Spirit knows the truth. We can play with specialness and dream of being individuals with desires for power, fame, money and love. We cannot change Heaven's reality simply because we believe we can (Text page 556 T-26.V.5.3-4) (Text page 402 T-19.II.3.3). The Holy Sprit is smiling at God's children playing a silly game where they have frightened themselves (Text page 623 T-29.IX.6). He is there to ease the fear; we keep refusing the comfort.

The miracle is the comforter. It brings us back to the true power in our mind… to decide against the dream of specialness and for the dream of holiness. The miracle exposes the dream for what it is… an illusion. It is the shift in perspective to truth. In truth we only have two choices, one is to continue to choose the illusion, and the second is to recognize the truth and choose the correction of the Holy Spirit. The Holy Spirit will reinterpret our dreams so that we recognize that we are the dreamers of the dream and not the figures within the dream. The *Course* has very humbly explained that one of our greatest strengths is our capacity to learn and to change our minds. In knowing that you are the dreamer of your dream you recognize that you have thought up imaginary problems and then attempted to fix them with imaginary solutions. That is why we seek happiness but we do not find it. We look in an illusion and solve within the illusion. The Answer lies in recognizing that you are the dreamer (Text page 584 T-27.VII.13) (Text pages 53-54 T-4.I.4). The problem that keeps all of us unhappy is that we believe that we have separated from God and that we cannot find our way home. The hope is that God has provided us with a Teacher who will guide us out of this dream. The mistake was simply that we choose to believe in the dream. Ken has often said that the dream is not even the problem; believing in it and taking it seriously is. I find that I feel incredibly hopeful when I remember that the dream is not sinful… it is a mistake. Mistakes are correctable!

How can we gain perspective on specialness and our desire to bargain and compromise for love? It is helpful to keep in mind that our guilt distorts our perceptions (Text page 523 T-25.III.1). The belief in guilt and the feeling of being guilty are deeply buried within our psyche. It is the law of guilt to project self-guilt from the decision making mind (not the brain) that believes in it into the illusion. Guilt is the mistaken belief that the separation from God actually happened. Ken explains that the mind is terrified by this idea, takes it seriously and in its repulsion projects that thought out and into the world of illusion. We distort the horror of the world through the glasses of guilt. Every time you see that you are motivated by specialness you are attempting to project guilt. Guilt in the eyes of God does not exist so the need to project it is a silly mistake. Assume that until you are consciously aware of being a mind connected to God and not a body that you will project your guilt. Don't be surprised that you do this. When I catch myself, I try to be extremely gentle with myself and I kindly say, "Yep there I go again being an ego. Silly ol' bear that I am". This takes the charge out of the event… No kidding I project. I am not surprised, amazed or impressed. I expect it and I attempt to take it less seriously and ask for help with the reinterpretation. I do not reinterpret… I don't have the Wisdom. I ask for a new interpretation when I catch my projections, my judgments, my hate and anger. I have to see them first, and then I take them to Jesus for correction.

My husband, Matthew, has taught me a great lesson along these lines. He has a gift that I attempt to emulate. Since I have known Matthew I think I can count on one hand how many times I have heard him gossip or speak unkindly about someone. Family, friends, strangers or people on the news it does not matter, he simply does not participate in gossip or negative talk of almost any kind. He has his opinions and he can be strong-willed and stubborn, but he sees no purpose in putting people down so he does not do it. When I first met him this annoyed me to no end. I thought he must have something to say and I would probe and poke him for comments. I thought he was afraid and I wanted him to speak up. He found me somewhat confusing in this area. I asked him to speak up… he had nothing to say. As our friendship grew I recognized that Matthew never talked behind people's backs. I have almost never seen him vacillate from this ethical base upon which he conducts his life. I began to admire and respect his consistency and his lack of judgment. It's not just that Matthew was not gossiping, he was not judging. He accepts people as they are. I might attempt to change them or to change their minds to my point of view. I realized that some of the safety that I felt with Matthew was because I trusted that he would not condemn me or use my vulnerability as a weapon against me. He would not condemn me for being irrational or opinionated. I could be a brat or be afraid and he would not request that I change. I saw in him a gift. He simply watches and observes during conversations that are heated and or unkind. He allows people their opinions and he keeps his; he has no need to push his opinion or judgment onto someone.

I have begun to apply his role modeling to people with whom I get into power struggles. I try to observe their insistence that they are right and I will sometimes keep quiet. I attempt to monitor my judgment and my desire to sway them to my opinion. Often my attempt to do this is filled with disease, but I ask for help in the process. I attempt to look at my judgments and the power struggles with the eye of distance. This distance allows me to let the Holy Spirit lead and teach. So I sit back more and observe. I notice my thoughts. I feel my disease and I know that from a distance I can allow the Holy Spirit to show me what belief I am holding onto that is causing my internal tension without judgment. I can monitor my thoughts a bit more easily. I have found that I have better days with more happiness and fewer struggles with this distance. For me it is surrender of control and of the need to be right. I continue to struggle with this and I cannot say that I have mastered the technique. What I can say is that my days are a bit happier when I am not so invested in my opinion or my ideas being accepted as correct.

Sometimes I gossip. I resist generalizing the process of observing that I know will help me keep my peace. I am amazed that I fight peace with such tenacity. I am a silly ol' bear at times. Other times I feel stuck in a situation that I do not know how to balance. Like when a colleague or a boss is gossiping. I become unclear how to respond. I may recognize within myself that I do not feel at ease commenting or not commenting. I often sit back and I don't comment. I watch and I ask for spiritual help. When I am sitting with someone who I perceive as having some authority over me or the ability to make my life uncomfortable, I fall into the trap of not knowing how to respond. I guess I still hold the belief that power can make me happy. I am not sure. I want to be on the 'winning side' so to speak and I struggle with how to simply watch this process and respond like a normal person. I recognize that it kicks up anxiety and discomfort within me. I am not surprised that this happens. I have come to expect my defensive thinking. The ego is tricky and deeply rooted into our beliefs. It should be no big deal to us that the process of looking at these beliefs can take years to accomplish.

### Two Choices

I have mentioned a number of times that the thought system of defenses and the thought system of defenselessness are mutually exclusive. You are either learning to think with defensiveness or with the Holy Spirit. There are only two teachers or two true choices. This is a teaching of the *Course* (Text page

139 T-8.I.5-6). It implies that the two ways of viewing the world cannot coexist. The two ways of thinking contain within them such polar opposite ideas that a mind cannot have both ideas within it at the same time. The staff at the Foundation for Inner Peace emphasizes this idea in their teaching. The image of this that I see in my head is one of ideas and beliefs being contained in a balloon or a bubble. The bubble is contained and what is within it cannot mix with things that are outside of it. The bubble of defenses contains thoughts of sin, guilt, fear, murder, competition and win or lose. The bubble of defenselessness has ideas and beliefs about love, peace, mutual sharing, giving and receiving. The bubbles or balloons contain your entire thought system at any given time. Now your mind can be in either one bubble or the other bubble but it cannot be in both of these balloons at the same time. The thoughts that your body and personality appear to be thinking are determined by the balloon that your mind is occupying. Your mind can be-bop and bounce around from one bubble to the other whenever it chooses, but under no circumstances can it occupy both balloons at the same instant. Your thoughts are part of the bubble's collective. This is an all or nothing idea. We can move from one collective thought system to the other so fast that we think that perhaps we are taking a middle ground. According the theory of the *Course* this is not possible.

So here is the contrast. Once you know that you have two collective thought systems from which to choose, then the observing of your thoughts can tell you, based on how you are feeling, what thought system bubble you are submerged in. The Holy Spirit is asking that we allow Him to teach us how to become more consciously aware of this choice between collective thought systems. He is basically saying to us that we have been hanging out, for the most part, in a defensive thought system bubble. Once in a while we would jump over to the balloon of defenselessness and consider the experience we had an 'act of God', or an other worldly experience... something psychic or grand that was *done to us* and was not of our choosing. We deny our power by assuming that this experience was not of our choosing. The Holy Spirit is trying to teach us that the choice is always available but it is our mind that has to choose it... the Holy Spirit cannot choose it for us. He asks that we let Him take us to the bubble of His thinking and check it out for a bit. He knows that as we become more comfortable with how He thinks that defensive thinking will become less and less tolerable. Like a child putting down a toy that no longer captures his interest, defensive thinking is slowly and gently put down. No force, no loss- just growing tired of a toy with which it is no longer fun to play. The teaching through contrast is about becoming more adept at be-bopping from the defensive collective thought system to the defenseless collective thought system, and seeing which one I would prefer. The choice is always within our control... that is a fact. The option is always in our control as well.

So in essence we are One Mind connected to God. We believe that we are many. Because we believe that we are many we spend an inordinate amount of time beating the crap out of ourselves (with our thoughts and actions), deeply believing that what we do to others has no effect on our self-concept. Brilliant disguise don't you think? Being One and kicking our self in the face over and over again. If you really knew this to be the truth would you want to keep kicking your own butt? The Wapnicks helped me grasp this concept by teaching a class that looked at large scale worldly events and then contrasted these event by helping students look at their individual lives and how they (we) make the same mistakes on a small scale. To conclude on a hopeful note we looked at how non-defensive thinking might view the same problem. The following chapter examines this idea.

# Chapter 11:

## Teaching Through Contrast

Many of the ideas from this chapter come from a two-week class that I took at he Foundation for *A Course In Miracles*. The class was on the Middle East conflict and how this conflict, although on a global scale, is exactly the same in thought as the conflict that we as individuals have every day. The influence of this chapter is based on how helpful I found that class to be. I have to credit Kenneth and Gloria Wapnick for these ideas. They are not mine, although most of the examples are. This class wowed me. I had heard students of the *Course* say that the war in the world is a microcosm of the war in your living room but I had not put much thought into the concept. I had not really believed that prior to their teaching. The *Course* teaches that there is no order of difficulty in Miracles because one illusion is not harder to overcome than another. Both of them are unreal and therefore the same (Text page 18 T-2.1.5) (Text page 136 T-7.XI.1). The class expanded how I saw the world and all of its problems. I hope that it has a similar impact on the reader of this book.

I want to take the idea of the ego's specialness and help you recognize that we think defensively on a global as well as an individual scale. The entire world... and the universe for that matter are part of two collective thought systems. We are a collective, thinking from one mind, but we have two collective options. This is true on a global and an individual scale. Right now I will compare the ego's thought process and problem solving techniques to the Holy Spirit's thoughts and problem solving skills. When you compare these two ways of thinking on a global scale and then take the ideas down to your life, my hope is that you will begin to see how similar (in thought) the war in your living room is to global discord. Perhaps the idea of the contrast between the two thought systems will allow you to ask the Holy Spirit to let Him show you His thinking.

The places that we as individuals have conflicts are the exact same places that we as communities, states and nations have disagreements, become obsessed and war against each other. This is because the collective thought system is a totality. When you think defensively, you think in a package that includes all of the ugly and unkind thoughts and beliefs. The same is true for non-defensive thinking. The contrast will be in looking at how the Holy Spirit's thinking is the answer to healing your internal war. As each of us on the level of mind takes responsibility for our thinking our dream will reflect our healing. The same exact stuff may be happening in the illusion but our interpretation of it will be part of the Holy Spirit's collective thinking. It is only as individuals accepting responsibility for our thinking that we have any hope of returning to Love.

The world is comprised of individuals. The thought system of the ego which by it's very nature is the result of individuality and defensiveness can be examined closely by looking at how groups of people act and react in the world. Looking at things from a global perspective, for some of us, creates the distance to begin this process of looking within without freaking ourselves out. The thought system of defensiveness is seen in a more extreme light when we view national and global events and how they operate. Initially this can help us make the generalization from how a large group (corporate, government, or masses of people) operates in the world to how I act and function in my life as an individual seem extreme. I am attempting to be extreme here to help drive home the point that defensive thinking leads to suffering, pain, fear and horror. I recognize that as individuals, as nations, as corporations and as communities we can and do choose the thinking of the Holy Spirit. Humans are capable of great acts of kindness. Much of what motivates us to act with kindness and help in the world are based on the thoughts of the Holy Spirit being extended into the world. I am not using the examples of how we can think with Jesus. I know they exist, but the purpose of this is to help us look at when we choose to think and then act with defenses so that we can recognize where we can escape this trap of ego based thinking. We need to see the error in all of its ugliness so that we can bring this mistake to the Holy Spirit and ask for His correction. The contrast of His correction, for me, is the motivating force behind why I continue to look. I wish I could put into words how freeing it is. How grateful I am to know that a collective thought system that is brutal and capable of great horror is not me, and that I have a way out. The liberation of a way out keeps me soaring with hope. And it sounds so crazy to think that you can look at what you most fear and find behind it hope… but it is there I promise.

### Self interest Vs. Shared interest

On a global scale self-interest can be seen in our devotion to nationalism. Most of us hold an allegiance to our nation. As Americans we also may be devoted to the nation of our ancestors. My father is a first generation Italian-American. I grew up believing that I was Italian before I knew I was an American. We identify ourselves with our nation and view being patriotic as a positive attribute. We often accept our nation's political justifications on international policy. We deny that governments have ulterior motives and function from a perspective of keeping themselves in power individually and as a nation. Even if we do agree that governments have ulterior motives and are not always honest about their manipulations, we often do not think that there is any other option or way to change this. In looking back over the history of many nations I feel it is safe to say that most nations in one form or another practiced imperialism. Gloria Wapnick helped me to conceptualize the idea that imperialism is a form of attack. It is the extension of political, economic or psychological power or control from one nation over another nation. It can also be done between corporations. The people in power, whether a government or business have little interest in the people they affect. They create their policy irrespective of whether the extension of this power is beneficent or injurious to whom it is extended. Much of our modern imperialism involves making nations financially dependent on other nations, hostile corporate takeovers, and trying to put a company out of business. The idea of political or corporate self-interest is one of emotional or psychological cannibalism. Your nation or company has something that my nation or company has determined it needs and we will take it from you irrespective of the impact is has on your nation, your employees, the environment, or the people who depend on the service. This selfishness is based on the belief in limited resources, the belief that if I have the power I am entitled to use it and the belief that one of us must lose and only one of us can win. Can you see the similarities to the ideas of specialness on an individual scale? We spoke then of needing something outside of yourself to fill you up. We will bargain and compromise to get these needs met. Nations and corporations do the same thing. They bargain and compromise. When they have more power they simply take and dress up the taking in national or public interest.

Now a government will not come right out and tell you that they are going to enslave a nation, or rape it of it's resources for their gain so they use defense mechanisms just as individuals do. They rationalize and justify their actions so that the people of their nation see the government as helpful and beneficent. Let's look at the example of slavery in this nation. Slave traders manipulated, lied and justified that Africans were less advanced in intelligence and culture, and that they led the lives of savages in need of being civilized. They painted a picture of people that were not really human, less then, and created by God (not a very kind God mind you) to serve their superiors. Slave traders said they were bringing African people to a better place and providing them with a better life. None of this was true, and it certainly did not take a rocket scientist to see the lie. Still the slave traders and the nations that supported and received financial gain from the trade did not care about the truth. They conveniently accepted the lie without question or care for its impact on human suffering. Perhaps as individuals they did care and they did question the ethics of selling people into slavery... I am sure that some people protested and refused to participate. People probably even tried to stop this trade. Keep in mind that if the ethical motivation to stop slavery was full of hate for the traders, it is still then a thought of the ego-collective. For the most part people and governments saw a market and took advantage of the opportunity for their financial gain. They helped their financial lifestyle regardless of the impact that it had on the people who were enslaved and/or the families who were left without their loved ones. This is the idea of imperialism at its most vicious. The absolute disregard for a race of people based on governmental and business self-interest. It is an ugly example and an extreme one. I believe that the racism in this country is based on our not looking at this problem and the feelings of guilt and shame that it causes in people, Black and White. We project that shame and guilt about enslaving and being enslaved out onto others rather then recognizing that ultimately this process of repression and projection keeps us slaves to this guilt and chained into this thought system of defenses.

As nations we disregard how interconnected we are. We focus on the subtle differences such as culture, religion, ethnicity and skin color and we miss the humanity that we share as a species. We place our national interest above the needs of human beings. We care even less about what we call the "lesser species" in the animal and plant kingdoms. We see our nation, our state, our community and our self as the most important and our needs as primary. The wars in Yugoslavia over ethnicity, the war in Ireland between religions, the Arab-Israeli conflict in the middle east, the genocide between the Hutus and the Tutsis in Africa, the colonization of India, the Philippines, Africa, Asia, the current clear cutting of the rain forests and racism in this country, all speak to the idea that as nations we are selfish and care very little for the end result of our actions. We lack prescience as a species. We are driven by self-interest and selfish motives to meet our needs and our desire to win above all else. As you read this and catch yourself thinking, "Yes but what has this to do with me?" and/or, "I would never do that," remember the defense of reaction formation. A strong reaction to any example has to begin in your thoughts and repulsion can be a mask over attraction. This is an ugly part of the ego-collective thought system. I am not trying to make you feel guilty... these examples are simply to help you see that as part of a collective thinking tank these thoughts are part of your ego thinking, my ego thinking and the ego thought system of each and every one of us. There is not one of us who does not contain the whole collective in an individual part (Text page

177 T-9.VII.7.4-10). That *Course* idea is part of the mutually exclusive bubble example. When you are in the bubble you contain all the thoughts of the bubble not just some of them. Keep in mind you are not connected to the bubble except by your choice. You have the key to choose differently. You are not your thoughts. Without keeping these ideas in mind the looking is so ugly and guilt provoking that we would not do it. We cannot take these specialness ideas down to an individual scale alone. This work of looking is not possible without the help of the Holy Spirit.

I want you to keep the important *Course* teaching that "defenses do what they would defend" (Text page 359 T-17.IV.7.1-2) at the forefront of your mind right now. This idea teaches that defenses do the exact opposite of what they are set up to do. This psychological fact works on a national as well as an individual scale. We defend our fears with defense mechanisms that essentially set us up to be fearful, paranoid and vigilant to what we are fearful of. We repress and then project what we fear and are repulsed by about ourselves into the world. We see these qualities in others be they groups of others or one person. We treat them the way we believe someone who has the qualities we hate and are repulsed by should be treated (not very kindly in action or in thought) and in treating them with disregard we feel guilty deep down. The guilt in our mind has just been reinforced. Guilt always demands punishment (Text page 84 T-5.V.3.6)...remember that this is what we do to the guilty. So then believing that punishment is the inevitable outcome of our actions we become afraid and begin to defend against punishment. So the cycle begins yet again. We believe that the oppression that we put upon someone will be put upon us. What goes around comes around. Let's look at the example of slavery again. Many people in this country who owned slaves in the past were fearful of slaves becoming free because they feared the revenge of the people they oppressed. I believe that White people in this country were fearful (and perhaps still are) of Black people gaining power in any way because guilt demands punishment. We all know deep down that nice people don't enslave a race. What White people taught themselves (and perhaps still do) was that they were cruel; cruel people get punished, i.e. when God catches up with me and sees how unkind I was to Blacks He will send me to hell. National (racist) legislation worked hard to prevent Black Americans from having power in this country. Selfish national interest teaches us to make sure that who we have hurt and oppressed cannot do to us what we did to them. This wound continues to run deep in our nation today. I also think that Black people in this country struggle with the same guilt that Whites struggle with but the form is different. Black Americans may struggle with the idea that they were being punished by God (and perhaps still are) because they were guilty. This is part of defensive thinking which is part of the illusion so it is not true, but it may be a deeply rooted belief, i.e. what about our race makes us so weak that we allowed slavery to happen in the first place; and why are we continuing to allow oppression of Black Americans today? Either way Black or White we are stuck... the form may vary but the belief remains the cause... the image in the illusion is the effect of a belief in guilt, suffering, sacrifice, scarcity and punishment.

Selfish acts are always done to get something in return for what you give. They are conditional and usually they are an attempt to attain, fame, and power, money or pleasure. A dear friend of mine recently told me that she has begun to see that giving for the joy of giving is great fun. She had the courage to admit that much of her giving in the past has been to maintain an image of being good, to get ahead of someone socially, to be loved or to feel important. She often had an ulterior motive. She learned that when she gives without any expectation of getting something that she has fun. She was excited by this lesson and thrilled at the joy it is bringing her. To give and to receive from the perspective of the Holy Spirit are the same thing (Text pages 540-541 T-25.IX.10). What you give is what you receive. You see life is a mirror and we reflect back to our self exactly what we believe we have given. If you act out of selfish interest you reinforce selfish motivation in your thinking. This causes you to believe that all people are coming from the perspective of selfishness so you defend against their ulterior motives. Your defenses are built up to protect you from the selfish folks out there. When you give from a position of Love and Joy it is Love and Joy that are reflected back to you. You reinforce Joy so that is what you see. You are a Mind mistakenly believing that you are a body. The thoughts in your mind create the thoughts you believe are in the world. To have and live by the decree of shared interest we must treat people with the respect and understanding that when I give, I give to myself and to you. It will be this thought that will shine from your mind outward so it will be this thought that shines back to you. We are in full command of our state of mind and therefore we are in full command of our peace.

How would the Holy Spirit view national self-interest? He knows not of selfish interest. As God's messenger the Holy Spirit knows that God sees all of His creations as equal. God cannot pick favorites; he does not require suffering, martyrdom or sacrifice for His love. Unconditional as His Love is it is given freely to all. The Holy Spirit knows that to keep love it must be given to all. "To have all, give all to all" (Text page 106 T-6.V.A.6.13). This idea is not about things in the world it is about thoughts and beliefs. For you to have peace it must be peace that you give to everyone. To exclude anyone from the Love of God, changes God by definition. This is not possible as God is eternal and complete. Shared interest where everyone wins is the only option that the Holy Spirit knows. This is inconceivable from the perspective of the world. It is so foreign that it sounds like it is foolish. It is impossible to understand the vision of Christ from the perspective of illusions. I don't pretend to have Christ Vision so I cannot explain it. I believe that I have had glimpses of this truth and I can honestly say those moments were the best moments of my life. Words cannot express a life-changing insight into the vision of Christ. What I can firmly say is that differences and selfish needs disappear in that presence of mind.

## Defense Vs. Defenselessness

We believe that the only option we have to protect ourselves as a nation and as individuals is one of a good defense. There is an underlying defensive belief that we have what we have taken i.e. we stole life from God and He wants it back (Text page 491 T-23.II.9). We have to protect the life that we took. As a nation we act out these beliefs ... as individuals we can examine the beliefs and actively choose a different Teacher to help us understand them. On a national and international level, defense can be seen in the arms race. We have enough explosives in this world to blow the place up numerous times. To protect what we see as ours we will destroy anything that gets in our way. (I am impressed that we have not completed the self-destructive job as yet). We have a strong national defense with advanced technology. Besides our national arsenal we also defend under the guise of making friends and lending money to a nation. Lending huge sums of money to a nation can be a weapon because it breeds dependency. It is easy to manipulate a nation that is dependent on another to feed its people, or for weapons when it is under attack. Defense can be direct or indirect on a national scale.

Let's look at the idea of needing a defense on the level of thought. The need for a defense implies that we believe that attack is inevitable. It also makes the world very real. There is something here and we need to protect it. But thoughts are the cause and the illusion is the effect (Text page 593 T-28.II.5.2-4). So the thought or belief that we are deserving of attack had to precede the defense. The belief that we 'escaped' from Heaven and from the grasp of God is part of the Adam and Eve myth that I discussed earlier. We believe on a deep, unconscious level that God is angry with us for stealing life from Him and becoming individuals. It is important to remember that this is completely unconscious and completely untrue. We have no conscious

163

idea that we are minds or souls; we believe that we are bodies and our conscious awareness begins with being consciously aware of being a body. We have no memory at all to this myth that we stole individuality from God, so we have no conscious connection to the complexity of ideas that motivate us to do most things as a result. This idea that we stole life from God causes us to feel guilty and to believe that we deserve to be punished. We want to avoid punishment because we fear it... (the ego idea that God should be feared is born here). We refuse to take responsibility for the mistaken belief that we stole life from God because we have no intention of giving back what we stole. If we take responsibility for becoming individuals it would mean that we would have to admit that we were mistaken and that this individual self that we created is not the real us. We believe that it would mean that we would be forced to give back what we took. Now on one level, still deeply unconscious, we recognize that we should pay for these individual selves and we pay with our sacrifice and suffering... we do not under any circumstance want to give back our individuality and join the Oneness of Heaven. We feel guilty about this and we fear the punishment that our guilt demands. But until God returns to claim what we stole, we will protect this hidden treasure (our self and our body) with everything we have. Within the dream we defend ourselves from all kinds of things; from disease with vaccinations and antibiotics, from other people with violence, avoidance or isolation; we see the cold and the heat as potential enemies, we need protection from contaminated food, we take vitamins and exercise to ward off illness, we defend ourselves from the sun with sunscreen, we have alarms on our cars and in our houses, we take self-defense and we learn to be assertive in an attempt to defend our self respect, we own weapons and we try to accumulate enough money so that we can keep our bodies safe. If we defend ourselves well we ward off death for a time. (Death of course is God stealing back the life we stole from Him). Psychologically we defend ourselves from guilt with the defenses of repression and projection. We insist that we are not the guilty ones and we put tremendous effort into seeing the bad guy who is, by the way, deserving of punishment as outside of ourselves. We are a bit paranoid as a species but for good reason when you believe that this is reality. The world is a dangerous place for weak and vulnerable bodies.

How would life be different if we all thought with the idea of shared interest and defenselessness? Shared interest makes salvation a collaborative effort. My happiness lies not in pushing you down, but in recognizing that we are part of a larger whole and what I do to and for you, directly impacts upon how I perceive the world I live in. If we knew that we had within our minds the love of the Holy Spirit; if we experienced this Love we would not need to project our fears outward and defend ourselves from seeing them within. We would know that God is not angry that we have mistakenly believed in this illusion. Shared interest means that what you have you give. The Holy Spirit knows that on the level of thought to give and to receive are one and the same in truth (Text pages 540-541 T-25.IX.10). What you give is who you believe you are. If you want to learn that you are an extension of a thought of God you have to give that thought of Love in order to receive it. When we experience the Love of the Holy Spirit He helps us to learn that we are that Love. As part of the Love of God we are complete. God is not our enemy. Fear and the need to project fear disappear when the Holy Spirit is seen as a Friend. An experience of the Truth lets us know that Christ is within each of us and we are all connected together to God as One Son. To attack your neighbor in any way is to attack yourself and reinforce defensive thinking. To give and receive are the same because everything within the illusion is part of the dreaming Mind.

Defenselessness is to recognize that there is no enemy. This illusion has been built around the idea that God is our enemy. If that self-deception is corrected the rest of the defenses are no longer required. They simply disappear because they are illusions and untrue (Text page 487 T-23.I.3). Being built on a lie… and the lie being corrected they are useless. To know this on an experiential level takes a peeling back of layers of defense for most of us. There are some advances souls who know this and can live in the world without defenses. For most of us it is a process that involves deep introspection and recognition that our problem solving skills are severely impaired. We cannot count on the self we believe we are to get us out of this mess. That body that we believe we are is part of the illusion and part of the defense to keep us from our Mind. Our Mind is connected to God. When we look with the Holy Spirit at how insane our defensive system is, and how we continue to make the same mistakes over and over again in millions if not billions of forms, we may decide that perhaps there is another way to look at the world (Text page 628 T-30.I.12.3).

### Face of innocence vs. True Innocence

The Face of Innocence is a *Course* idea that helps us recognize that the face which we project into the world is a mask over some very defensive beliefs that we do not want to see in ourselves. We will portray an image that we want the world, and our self to believe. I am reminded of Bruce Springsteen's song *Brilliant Disguise*. In this song Bruce sings of his relationship to a woman that is strewn with the images that they would prefer to have one another see. Bruce questions if this is the real them they are looking at or if perhaps they have thought up brilliant disguises to mask what they want to hide from each other. This disguise that each and every one of us wears is our attempt at hiding the defensive thought system from ourselves. The disguise is one of self-deception and of course others are deceived along with us. The face of innocence is a mask that is worn unconsciously. We often are clueless about what we are doing. Behind the innocence, once in a blue moon (and for some of us more often then that) we see our ugly, angry, vengeful or violent hidden self and we are repulsed. We don't know where this part of us came from... like a stranger visiting and invading our ideal of how good we are.

So how does one uncover the unconscious face of innocence so that he can look upon it with the Holy Spirit? Recognizing how this face of innocence plays out on a global scale may help you see it within yourself. On a national scale the face of innocence is the justification or rationalization of an action to hide any and all ulterior motives. It is the statement that indicates that "We had to attack and go to war. We were attacked without provocation. It is not our fault. We are only protecting our self". It implies that the only reason that an event occurred was due to self-defense. Gloria Wapnick gave a great example of this in American rhetoric versus American policy prior to our entering World War Two. American national policy was one of political neutrality. While claming to be neutral America had placed an embargo on Japanese assets. We were supporting the British with a lend -lease plan. We lent them our battle ships in return for their leasing bases to us for a period of time. Our government was claiming to be neutral because that's what the people of this country were stating that they wanted. Our government's actions were not neutral. When Pearl Harbor was attacked we were able to say that we were the victims of the aggressive Japanese. As the victims we were justified in entering the war in self-defense; claiming innocence. Our political actions were far from innocent. We were supplying the enemy of the Japanese with the tanks and battle ships that were killing their people. These are not the actions of a neutral country. Whether you agree or disagree with what we did, it was a governmental deception.

WWII is a passionate subject for many of us... any war that effects our sense of right or wrong or one that perhaps directly impacted our family can cause an emotional reaction. I personally am glad that Hitler was stopped. I compare him to the students with whom I work. He was acting out of control and was hurting millions of people. As a world we should attempt to talk someone out of hurting others. There are times when you need to physically stop someone who is very destructive; just as I stop out of control kids. Personally I agree with our entrance into WWII and I am eternally grateful for the people who fought and devoted their time and their lives to stopping Hitler from succeeding in his goals. The point I want to focus on is not about the right or wrong of WWII but the deception of our government to the people. This is a direct lie by the government while claiming innocence. Governments and individuals often use this tactic to manipulate.

I want to take this idea of governmental deception and how governments mislead people to do whatever it is they choose and bring it down to an individual level. Let's start with grass root political movements in this country. When I was in college it was typical for many college woman to take a class called '*Introduction to Feminism*'. Fellow students who had taken the class a semester before often taught this class. This was done because in the political ideal of feminism there is no hierarchy. There was a professor but students often ran the class. I did not take this class myself but I had a number of friends who did. I recall an incident when a dear friend of mine spoke of this class as if it were a war zone. She was learning about the patriarchy and their oppression of women and she was outraged by what she was being taught. She directed her anger at White men, with whom she felt the class was at war, figuratively speaking. She blamed them for the sorry state that women of all races were subject to in this nation and the world at large. My friend who was outraged by men's treatment of women experienced turmoil at how unfairly she felt she was being treated by her female student-teachers. The contradiction was how harsh these young, inexperienced teachers of feminism were on their students. The students in return were often very tough on their teachers. My friend experienced that poor grades were given to students who wrote papers that indicated that they disagreed with the premise that the cause of female oppression was a direct result of the White men abusing power. This felt oppressive to her. Her ability to express herself was limited. A semester later this friend of mine was a teacher in this class. She is Jewish and she incorporated into her lecture the passionate topic of the oppression of her people. She came home very upset and spoke of feeling she was verbally attacked in class for some stereotypes her students believed about Jewish greed and the miserly ways of the Jewish people. She sobbed about this for hours in our apartment. She thought the people in this class were different. She believed that they were pure and without the hate and oppression that she was sure was only in White men. The cold harsh reality that they could dismiss her teaching and oppress her for being Jewish shattered her hope that feminism was a way out of the mess of the world. Now let me clarify that I am sure that these students were not bad or rotten people... they simply were thinking from an ego perspective. They may look ideal and different but if they are thinking with the ego they contain all of its thoughts. Seeing differences is inherent in how the ego thinks (Text page 489 T-23.II.2). Seeing someone else as the cause of your pain and suffering is also to be expected in this mode of thinking. These things are inevitable if you choose defensive thinking as your teacher. The desire of these students was to find a way out of this chaotic mess the world seems to be. The means they chose to escape or fix this problem contain within them the same errors that they were hoping to avoid.

It is true that in this world people with power often abuse that power. It is also true that White men have had much of the power in the world. They may not always use that power in the most benevolent way. I feel it is safe to say that had women had the same power that men have wielded for centuries, the tide would have been turned but the same mistakes would have been made. Women are no more innocent than are men. They are not kinder as part of a species... they too are part of the collective thinking of both the ego and the Holy Spirit. I do not doubt for a second that we as people are capable of great good... women, men of any and all races and ethnicities. And I even question if perhaps the world would have had a few less wars if women were in charge. I don't know this and it may be my ego and the woman in me talking. I am not at all convinced that if women were in charge that the problems of the world would improve greatly. The problems of the world are not about our gender, sex, class, race, religion or political origin. The problem is the thought system that we choose. Everything else is smoke and mirrors. Feminism would not have a corner on kindness. The judgment and fear of oppression in that class was just shifting from one form to the next form. The problem essentially was being ignored. Not because the people wanted to ignore the problem, but because they were looking in the wrong place for the answer. Now, balancing power between all peoples may help us to be more compassionate through a greater understanding of each other. I am not saying that it is not a good idea. It is a good idea; it is not the solution.

Now let's take this face of innocence idea and make it a bit more personal and a bit more individual. Let's say that you have two friends who are going through a divorce that is full of ugly court battles. You have been friends with this couple for years and you don't want to lose either of your friends. You tell them that you are not choosing sides in their dispute, as you love them both dearly. Deep inside you are angry at the pain one of your friends is causing the other. You innocently claim to be neutral but you are not. As the divorce precedes you become angry with one of your friends for cheating and being heartless about the deception. You find that as hard as you try, neutrality is escaping you and you have chosen sides. Outwardly you keep this to yourself, but you let a few secrets 'slip' through to the friend with whom you have sided. You ask that the information stay between you two. You hope that the secrets will help in court. As a friend of both parties you have access to some personal information. You gather this information and disclose it. In court it is obvious that someone has been deceptive and information that was confidential is out in the open. Do you think that if your 'friend' about whom you have been providing information found out that you were the deceiver she would remain your friend? You promised one thing and then for reasons that you believed in you acted in a way that was not in accord with your promise.

This example is obvious. We can be subtler. I was in a staff meeting once when I caught myself setting up a colleague. My colleague is a hard working young teacher who I basically like on a professional level. I was at a meeting with the district social workers when I mentioned something about my colleague that called into question her ethics as a teacher. I implied that she had dangerously poor boundaries with teens in a time of being easily accused of sexual misconduct. Everyone had an opinion about this woman. I watched the chaos for a short time not minding at all. Then I realized what I had just done. I asked Jesus to help me correct this. With a few so-called innocent but very unkind manipulative comments I had brought this woman's professional reputation into question. She, by the way, did not do a thing wrong, but eight people who worked all over a very large district now believed that she had. What I left out of the story was how closely she was being supervised by one of the best principals with whom I have had the privilege to work. I knew the principal was aware of her actions and that as a young, ideal, and maybe naive teacher she still had some things to learn. Her behavior had not been inappropriate but I had implied that it could have been with a few 'innocent' and well-timed comments. I saw what I had done and I attempted to correct the mistake. I spoke of the supervision she received and that she was only in the third year of her career and learning. I spoke of how I was out of line in my comments. I did not feel that the correction I attempted to make was that effective, but the gossip about her stopped. At that point I felt angry and ashamed that I had set up this teacher. I cannot tell you why I did this. I was not consciously aware that I was going to. I was just in a bad mood. Had I noticed that I had chosen the bad mood I would have been able to ask for help earlier. I did not really notice, as my mood was subtle. I was unaware that I was going to set her up until I had made the mistake. The mistake looked innocent but it was full of hate. The fact that I saw the mistake gave me the opportunity to ask for help and correct my error. My defensive thinking is tricky and I am often amazed at how I am enchanted by it. Then if I am lucky enough to see the error I have the opportunity for a new choice. I am not a sinful or evil person, just a human attempting to recognize my defensive thinking and correct it (as innocent as it may appear).

Gloria Wapnick often uses historical examples to show how people continue to make the same mistakes over and over again without recognizing that we are stuck in this thought system. She has said that America as a nation is repeating the history of the demise of the Roman Empire. This face of innocence takes the form of 'progress'. We pursue the money-God with no regard for the impact that it has on the world. We pursue pleasure with the same abandon. We are selfish greedy and demanding of pleasure in an instant. I can see the decay from the inside out. Our selfishness as individuals, our psychological and emotional cannibalism, our constant blame of others for our suffering, our greed and lack of foresight in business, the irresponsible marketing, advertising and television programming and our overall decadent behavior... as a species we are so dumb. As individuals we are overwhelmed about how to stop this runaway train.

I was speaking to a colleague recently about adolescents and how they have lost the art of flirting... they miss out on all the fun and go strait to being sexual as 14 year olds. It is sad but not surprising based on their role models. MTV, Friends, Bay Watch, Melrose Place and 90210 are teaching our youth how to be sexual. My colleague and I both think that this is pathetic and we both recognize that there is big money in selling sex. The cost of that cash flow is flirting, and a slower introduction to sexuality. To those benefiting from that cash flow the cost to our society is irrelevant even if the price is at the expense of our teenagers. Now people in marketing, television, advertising and government may deny, justify and rationalize the impact that they are having on the world, but they do not have a corner on the face of innocence that keeps saying "it's not my fault... I did not do anything". It is the people of this country who are allowing television and advertising to get so out of control who are equally playing innocent. We all justify and rationalize our aggressive selfish behavior. We love to have an enemy and someone to blame. We curse at the person who cuts us off while we are driving, we kick the dog because we had a hard day, and we get drunk because we are stressed. We watch violent shows and we are psyched when things blow up and the guy you want to die gets killed (I am reminded of the Ancient Roman sport of feeding 'criminals' to the lions). Again the form of how we play innocent is not important, and please don't feel guilty if you know that you do this. The ego believes that innocence is purchased at the price of someone being guilty. It is that 'one or the other' idea again. It is based on the thought that we cannot be the same (Text page 467 T-22.in.2). You have to be guilty if I am innocent. Only one of us can be the innocent one. This is part of defensive thinking that is all. We all do this... we all have the same problem and we attempt to solve it with the same defenses. The forms change but the problem remains the same. We are much more alike then we could ever imagine. The Holy Spirit can show you this and can help you stop playing nice and innocent when you are being deceptive. This like every other example is about how we think, not how we live and act in the world. Saying "I am not as nice as I look" and using that as an excuse to be unkind will not help you and most likely will hurt you in the long run.

True innocence is the recognition of how alike we are. We are the Sons of God. One Mind connected to our Father in truth. What we do to others we literally do to our Self. The reason anger is never justified is because it is the projection of guilt. When you accuse someone of being at fault you are accusing yourself. Giving up judgment gives great release because it frees your mind. All of our judgments have at their core the belief that someone else is sinful. This enemy proves my innocence. True innocence is the recognition that it can only be yourself that you condemn. There is no one but you to forgive. And what you ultimately forgive yourself for is for believing in the dream.

Can you imagine how different the world would look if you could look on it with true innocence? How would your life be different if you adopted the thought system of the Holy Spirit and were able to live in the ego-world? How would you view the world if you had no enemies and never took attack personally? If within you there was the experience of an absence of guilt would you recognize yourself? There is no sin. If you knew this as an experience how would you treat those you judge now? I feel the thrill of hope when I ask myself these questions. They expand my mind and fill me with joy.

## Christ's Vision

One of my sisters was functionally blind as a child. She has a disease called amblyopia. People who are functionally blind can still see but their vision is greatly impaired, even with glasses. Jeanine wore both contacts and glasses as a kid. I am not a doctor but I do know that this condition left my sister, Jeanine, with a 'lazy eye'. This means that when Jeanine was the slightest bit tired her eye would wander and although she could see you (as well as someone who is functionally blind can), she would not appear as if she was looking at you. Sometimes she was very crossed eyed from this but for the most part you just could not tell if, or where, she was looking because her eye wandered. Our mother was very determined to find a medical solution to this problem. Our mom refused to give up hope that her daughter would be able to see. She searched for doctors who would help keep her hope alive. She researched new technology and she was always open to trying. Without her help, her patience, her love and determination my sister's vision may not have improved as quickly as it did. When Jeanine was ten she was one of the first people in this country to have laser treatment on her eyes. The treatment was an attempt to correct the shape of her cornea. The shape of Jeanine's cornea left her with no depth perception. Her world was flat. To her everything looked as if she was looking at a photograph. She could not judge depth or distance and she would trip on or into curbs, cars, furniture and things. She also could not place things down without feeling for a surface. She was always thinking that her plate or glass was over the table and dropping them onto the floor. She also lacked peripheral vision on her left side so her visual scope was small (and you could sneak up on her very easily which was great fun as a kid)! The laser treatment met with mild success but her world remained basically flat.

At the age of sixteen Jeanine had surgery. The surgery was to shorten the muscle so that her eye would not wander so. Her vision would improve, but not dramatically. Jeanine's vision at that time was 20/600 in one eye and 20/400 in the other. The average person's vision is 20/20 in both of their eyes. The operation was a success and when Jeanine spoke to you she could now look at you and her eyes would be pointed in the correct direction. Her vision was still very poor.

Contact lenses used to pop out of Jeanine's eyes because of the shape of her cornea. She hated them as they irritated her. By the time she was sixteen contact lens technology had improved. The laser treatment also helped the contacts stay put. My mother encouraged Jeanine to try these contacts. Reluctantly she agreed. The lenses completed the job that the laser treatment had improved and my sister's cornea was correctly shaped for the first time in her life. With these contacts she suddenly had depth perception with 20/30 vision in both of her eyes!

Jeanine and I were always great friends. She is three years older than I am and as a thirteen-year-old I thought the world of her. I remember the summer after she got those contacts with vivid detail. She went from a child who was functionally blind with no depth perception to normal vision with depth perception. She was like a newborn infant with full language. Everything was new to her and it was a blast just to listen to her. She used to stare at our faces, especially our mother's face. Mom would cry every time she caught her doing this. Jeanine was intrigued with things that to me were mundane and so common that I never took the time to see them. I remember how captivated she was with the paneling on the wall of the living room... then she noticed tree bark and the process began anew. She had never seen the contrast of shaded color in brown. Depth was another adventure. My sister's world which had been flat suddenly contained depth... she marveled at how deep houses extended back, that their roofs were angled and the shingles on the roof had obvious separation between them. We spent what felt like and entire afternoon looking into an oil-slicked puddle after a rainstorm watching the rainbow of oily color move around. One day we were lying under a tree and Jeanine was going on about the shades of green in each leaf, how you can distinguish that one leaf is above or below another leaf and the effect of the sun coming through the tree. She was opening a world to me and I was seeing things as if for the first time through her comments. I must have gotten curious about what she used to see so I said that this couldn't be so different she had always seen green and trees. She agreed but explained that she had seen "blobs of green" with no detail. She knew that lawns were green and that blades of grass were single strands because she had touched them but she had never been able to distinguish a blade of grass without touching it. Trees were harder because they were up so high and they too were flat blobs of green. Shading, depth and any distinction escaped my sister's pre-operative and pre-contacted vision. A new world had opened up to her and things that had always been right in front of her face she was suddenly able to see. She shared her vision with me.

The *Course* is a mirror of the story about my sister's newfound vision and depth perception. Within this story are all the symbols of how to practice this thought system. My mother symbolically represents the Holy Spirit. She remained sure in her conviction that my sister had the untapped potential to see clearly. She did not waver in her faith and she found the teachers (doctors) that could guide my sister in the process of seeing. My sister represents each of us. She stumbles and falls a bit. She cannot discern how not to fall because she is not seeing clearly. She relies on our mother, as we need to rely on the Holy Spirit for our help and guidance. I watch the drama unfold. In this story I am the observer. I do nothing. This is exactly what the *Course* suggests we do. That we resign as our teacher and allow the Holy Spirit to work through us. So in this story I play the part of doing nothing and my teacher becomes my sister. She symbolically represents the manifestation of the Holy Spirit. She allowed the vision to be given to her and then she shared it. I watch and listen and without action of any kind I see from her perspective. It is this change of perspective from defensive thinking

173

to the thinking of the Holy Spirit that I want to own. Once I own it then peace from the inside out will be mine. At that point nothing will have the power to take my peace from me.

As I study and practice this thought system a world opens up before me. The world has always been there; right in front of my face but I have not been able to see it. This process and our determination to correct our 'blindness' may take a bit more time than my sister's did, but as your vision improves you will be captivated by what is clearly in your sight. I have come to recognize how natural it is to see; how clearly I have missed the obvious and how simple it can be to have my vision corrected for me. So I ask to wear the Holy Spirit's eyeglasses for a time as I adjust to the change slowly. Eventually as I adjust to the light, the clarity of this new world right under my nose will remain constant.

* * *

To contact Catherine please e-mail her at:
lifeisamirror@lifeisamirror.freeservers.com

Or visit the Life is a Mirror website at:
Lifeisamirror.freeservers.com

To get in touch with the Shenteng Retreat Bed & Breakfast where Catherine runs workshops write to:
128 South Line Rd
Middle Grove, NY 12850
Phone # (518) 882-1853

Visit the Shenteng retreat center's web page at:
www.adkconnection.com/shenteng/
or e-mail the owner of Shenteng, Layla VanHall, at:
Shenteng@aol.com

The Foundation for *"A Course In Miracles"* can be contacted by writing to:

Foundation for *"A Course In Miracles"*
41397 Buecking Dr.
Temecula, CA 92590

# Bibliography *Life is a Mirror*

1. Anonymous, *A Course In Miracles* (California: Foundation For Inner Peace), 1993.

2. Anonymous, *The Song Of Prayer* (California: Foundation For Inner Peace),1992.

3. Frankl, Viktor E. *Man's Search For Meaning* (New York: Simon and Schuster) 1984

4. His Holiness the Dalai Lama, *Ethics For The New Millennium* (New York: Penguin Putnam Inc., 1999)

5. Kilcher, Jewel, *Spirit: Life Uncommon* (California: WB music Corp, 1998)

6. Springsteen, Bruce, *Tunnel of Love, Brilliant Disguise* (New York, Columbia Records, 1987)

7. Teresa, Mother, *No Greater Love* (California, New World Library, 1997)

8. Wapnick, Kenneth, *Separation and Forgiveness The Four Splits and Their Undoing* (New York: Foundation for *A Course in Miracles,* 1999)

9. Wapnick, Kenneth, *Climbing the Ladder Home* (New York: Foundation for *A Course in Miracles,* 1997)

# FOOTNOTES:
## Second Edition of *A Course In Miracles*

| Page #<br>*Life Is A<br>Mirror* | Page #<br>*A Course In Miracles* | Quote Location in<br>*A Course in<br>Miracles* |
|---|---|---|
| 1 | 9 WORKBOOK PAGE 421 | W-252 1-5 |
| 2 | 10 TEXT PAGE 656 | T-31. V.1 |
| 3 | 10 TEXT PAGE 656 | T-31.V.2.1-4 |
| 4 | 11 INTRODUCTION | T-IN.1 |
| 5 | 11 TEXT PAGE 11 | T-IV.2.3.7 |
| 6 | 11 CLARIFICATION OF TERMS<br>PAGE 77 | C-IN.2.5 |
| 7 | 11 TEXT PAGE 153 | T-8.VII.10 |
| 8 | 12 TEXT PAGE 97 | T-6.II.9 |
| 9 | 13 WORKBOOK PAGE 375 | W-196.7(-3) |
| 10 | 14 TEXT PAGES 97-98 | T-6.II.9 |
| 11 | 14 TEXT PAGE 68 | T-4.VI.3 |
| 12 | 15 TEXT PAGE 479 | T-22.V.2.1-5 |
| 13 | 15 TEXT PAGES 97-98 | T-6.II.9 |
| 14 | 16 TEXT PAGES 97-98 | T-6.II.9 |
| 15 | 17 WORKBOOK PAGE 192 | W-107.1 |
| 16 | 18 TEXT PAGE 248 | T-13.V.3.5 |
| 17 | 20 TEXT PAGE 271 | T-14.I.3.3-4 |
| 18 | 22 TEXT PAGE 67 | T-4.V.6.7-10 |
| 19 | 27 TEXT PAGE 281 | T-14.IV.9.5 |
| 20 | 28 TEXT PAGE 359 | T-17.IV.7.1-4 |
| 21 | 29 TEXT PAGE 383 | T-18.V.2.5 |
| 22 | 29 TEXT PAGES 325-326 | T-15.X.6 |
| 23 | 33 TEXT PAGE 420 | T-19.IV.D.3.2-3 |
| 24 | 35 TEXT PAGES 97-98 | T-6.II.9 |
| 25 | 35 TEXT PAGE 445 | T-21.IN.1 |
| 26 | 38 TEXT PAGES 490-491 | T-23.II.7.1-3 |
| 27 | 38 TEXT PAGE 97 | T-II.9.1 |
| 28 | 41 TEXT PAGES 239-240 | T-13.II.1 |
| 29 | 42 TEXT PAGE 359 | T-17.IV.7 |

| | | | |
|---|---|---|---|
| 30 | 49 | TEXT PAGE 97 | T-6.II.9 |
| 31 | 52 | TEXT PAGE 39 | T-3.II.4.5-6 |
| 32 | 53 | TEXT PAGE 623 | T-29.IX.6 |
| 33 | 60 | TEXT PAGES 549-550 | T-26.V.1.7-12 |
| 34 | 61 | WORKBOOK PAGES 192-193 | W-107.5 |
| 35 | 65 | TEXT PAGE 227 | T-12.V.8.3-6 |
| 36 | 65 | TEXT PAGE 31 | T-2.VII.1 |
| 37 | 65 | TEXT PAGE 31 | T-2.VII.1 |
| 38 | 66 | TEXT PAGES 109-110 | T-6.V.C.4 |
| 39 | 74 | WORKBOOK PAGE 29 | W-17.1.3-6 |
| 40 | 74 | WORKBOOK PAGE 30 | W-19.1 |
| 41 | 75 | TEXT PAGE 405 | T-19.III.8 |
| 42 | 76 | WORKBOOK PAGE 419 | W-PII.4.5.2 |
| 43 | 79 | TEXT PAGE 494 | T-23.II.22.6-13 |
| 44 | 79 | TEXT PAGE 626 | T-30.I.3.1-2 |
| 45 | 82 | TEXT PAGE 450 | T-21.II.10 |
| 46 | 85 | WORKBOOK PAGE 23 | W-14.1 |
| 47 | 85 | TEXT PAGE 586 | T-27.VIII.6.2 |
| 48 | 86 | TEXT PAGE 586 | T-27.VIII.6.2 |
| 49 | 86 | MANUAL PAGE 45-46 | M-17.7.11 |
| 50 | 87 | TEXT PAGE 540 | T-25.IX.10 |
| 51 | 93 | TEXT PAGE 217 | T-12.I.8.7-13 |
| 52 | 97 | MANUAL PAGE 45-46 | M-17.7.10 |
| 53 | 103 | TEXT PAGE 402 | T-19.II.1 |
| 54 | 103 | TEXT PAGE 169 | T-9.IV.4-5 |
| 55 | 105 | TEXT PAGE 382 | T-18.IV.7 |
| 56 | 105 | TEXT PAGE 659 | T-31.V.15 |
| 57 | 106 | TEXT PAGE 215 | T-12.I.1 |
| 58 | 106 | TEXT PAGE 563 | T-26.X.4 |
| 59 | 107 | TEXT PAGE 499 | T-24.IN.2 |
| 60 | 107 | WORKBOOK PAGE 69 | W-44.5 |
| 61 | 108 | TEXT PAGE 330 | T-16.I.1 |
| 62 | 110 | WORKBOOK PAGE 141 | W-79.2 |
| 63 | 111 | TEXT PAGE 380 | T-18.IV.2.1-3 |
| 64 | 112 | TEXT PAGE 531 | T-25.VII.3 |
| 65 | 113-114 | TEXT PAGE 110 | T-6.V.C.4.7-10 |
| 66 | 115 | WORKBOOK PAGE 273 | W-RIV.IN.2-3 |
| 67 | 119 | MANUAL PAGE 45-46 | M-17.7 |
| 68 | 121 | TEXT PAGE 11 | T-1.IV.3.1-5 |

| | | | |
|---|---|---|---|
| 69 | 122 | TEXT PAGE 465 | T-21.VIII.1 |
| 70 | 125 | TEXT PAGES 493-494 | T-23.II.19 |
| 71 | 126 | TEXT PAGE 128 | T-7.VII.7.4-8 |
| 72 | 127 | TEXT PAGES 627-628 | T-30.I.12.3 |
| 73 | 127 | TEXT PAGE 128 | T-7.VII.7.4-5 |
| 74 | 127 | TEXT PAGES 129-130 | T-7.VIII.1 |
| 75 | 128 | WORKBOOK PAGE 8 | W-5 |
| 76 | 133 | TEXT PAGE 236 | T-13.IN.3 |
| 77 | 133 | TEXT PAGES 493-494 | T-23.II.19 |
| 78 | 137 | WORKBOOK PAGES 291-293 | W-155.1-14 |
| 79 | 137 | TEXT PAGES 625-629 | T-30.I.1-17 |
| 80 | 140 | TEXT PAGE 58 | T-4.II.7 |
| 81 | 141 | TEXT PAGE 630-631 | T-30.III.2 |
| 82 | 142 | TEXT PAGE 223 | T-12.IV.1 |
| 83 | 143 | TEXT PAGE 500 | T-24.1.3.5 |
| 84 | 143 | TEXT PAGES 112-113 | T-7.I.4 |
| 85 | 143 | TEXT PAGE 451 | T-21.III.1 |
| 86 | 150 | TEXT PAGE 153 | T-8.VII.11.1 |
| 87 | 152 | TEXT PAGE 556 | T-26.V.5.3-4 |
| 88 | 152 | TEXT PAGE 402 | T-19.II.3.3 |
| 89 | 152 | TEXT PAGE 623 | T-29.IX.6 |
| 90 | 152 | TEXT PAGE 584 | T-27.VII.13 |
| 91 | 152 | TEXT PAGES 53-54 | T-4.I.4 |
| 92 | 152 | TEXT PAGE 523 | T-25.III.1 |
| 93 | 154-155 | TEXT PAGE 139 | T-8.I.5-6 |
| 94 | 157 | TEXT PAGE 18 | T-2.1.5 |
| 95 | 157 | TEXT PAGE 136 | T-7-XI.1 |
| 96 | 160-161 | TEXT PAGE 177 | T-9.VII.7.4-10 |
| 97 | 161 | TEXT PAGE 359 | T-17.IV.7.1-2 |
| 98 | 161 | TEXT PAGE 84 | T-5.V.3.6 |
| 99 | 162 | TEXT PAGES 540-541 | T-25.IX.10 |
| 100 | 162 | TEXT PAGE 106 | T-6.V.A.6.13 |
| 101 | 163 | TEXT PAGE 491 | T-23.II.9 |
| 102 | 163 | TEXT PAGE 593 | T-28.II.5.2-4 |
| 103 | 165 | TEXT PAGES 540-541 | T-25.IX.10 |
| 104 | 165 | TEXT PAGE 487 | T-23.I.3 |
| 105 | 165 | TEXT PAGE 628 | T-30.I.12.3 |
| 106 | 168 | TEXT PAGE 489 | T-23.II.2 |
| 107 | 171 | TEXT PAGE 467 | T-22.IN.2 |

Printed in the United States
1417300005B/225